More Praise for

ETHICS IN THE
GLOBAL VILLAGE

"Professor Hill has written a provocative text in which he invites his readers to envision living in the global village in terms of an ethics of re-connection. . . . The text is both a primer in social ethics and a sophisticated ethical reflection upon the meaning of religious and moral life in the 21st century."

> —Marcia Y. Riggs, *J. Erskine Love Professor of Christian Ethics Columbia Theological Seminary*

"All too often Euroamerican ethics is reduced to abstract thoughts. . . . Hill's autobiographical approach guides the reader in new ways of understanding what can be learned from the world's marginalized."

> —Miguel A. De La Torre, *Associate Professor of Social Ethics, Iliff School of Theology*

"Hill reminds us that Jesus is "not one of us," but more importantly is "one of them," the foreigner whose message we need to understand if we are to address the compelling divisions and challenges of our planet."

> —David Pfrimmer, *Principal Dean, Waterloo Lutheran Seminary*

D0391875

ETHICS
IN THE GLOBAL
VILLAGE

ETHICS
IN THE GLOBAL
VILLAGE

MORAL INSIGHTS FOR
THE POST 9-11 USA

Jack A. Hill

POLEBRIDGE PRESS
Santa Rosa, California

Cover and interior design by Robaire Ream

Library of Congress Cataloging-in-Publication Data
Johnson-Hill, Jack A., 1949-
 Ethics in the global village : moral insights for the post 9-11 USA / Jack A. Hill.
     p. cm.
 Includes bibliographical references and index.
 ISBN 1-59815-008-1 (alk. paper)
 1. Social ethics. 2. Moral conditions. 3. United
States--Relations--Foreign countries--Moral and ethical aspects. I. Title.
 HM665.J65 2008
 172.40973--dc22

                                                              2008027320

For Kat

CONTENTS

Preface ix

Acknowledgments xv

Chapter One: The Moral Crises of Our Time 1

Chapter Two: Ethics at the Crossroads 15

Chapter Three: In Search of Our Moral Heritage 29

Chapter Four: Re-connecting with the Earth 49

Chapter Five: Re-connecting with One Another 75

Chapter Six: Re-connecting with the Enemy 99

Chapter Seven: Concluding Remarks 125

Notes 135

Works Consulted 155

Index 169

PREFACE

At the Westar Institute's 2004 Spring Meeting in New York City, Robert Funk delivered what might well be viewed as the last major address of his quite remarkable career.[1] Oddly enough, it was not a treatise in Biblical hermeneutics or New Testament exegesis. Rather, it was a plea for re-envisioning theology in the twenty-first century. In this speech, "An Enlightened Faith for an Enlightened Age," Funk set before us the challenge of re-thinking the insights of the first Axial Age in the light of contemporary circumstances.[2] Drawing on a lifetime of research into traditions related to the words and deeds attributed to Jesus, Funk outlined "ten words" that summed up Jesus' central teachings about the Kingdom of God, or what Funk had begun to call, "the divine domain."[3] As he went on to describe hallmarks of a second Axial Age,[4] from the Copernican revolution to postmodern deconstructionism, I sensed that the root metaphors for the "new enlightenment" he envisioned were epitomized in those "ten words" from Jesus.

Perhaps not surprisingly, the bulk of those words evoked themes that were ethical in character: the visibility and centrality of the poor in the divine domain, love for the enemy, adaptation of a critical standpoint toward primary socialization patterns, forgiving one another, giving to one another, exorcizing the demons within and among us, and appreciating and valuing nature. I say "not surprisingly" because Bob Funk was deeply concerned that the scholarship of the Jesus Seminar reflect an inherent ethical relevance. He bemoaned what he viewed as the death of the "old liberalism," political correctness and postmodern cynicism. He was particularly concerned that we scholars in our academic ivory towers had "lost our public" and he challenged us to "reconnect from the bottom up." More than once he urged me, as an ethicist, to write a book on ethics that would be quality scholarship, but also accessible to non-academics.

This book represents an initial response to Bob's challenge. It is intended to rekindle a wider, non-specialist, public conversation about the divisive issues of our time, and to make connections with those who speak from the margins of the global village. But while I think Bob's "ten words" provide important themes for ethics, I do not share his optimistic appraisal of the second axial period as an "enlightened age." Although I agree that the modern era has given rise to some rather astounding scientific, medical and technological advances, I believe that, to borrow a phrase from Parker Palmer, we increasingly lead "disconnected" lives.[5] We have become more and more "disconnected" or alienated from the natural world, the basic processes of production that support our lavish lifestyles, and political activities that negatively impact millions of persons.[6]

My central contention is that in the second Axial Age, especially during the last century, "Americans"[7] have fallen prey to three "isms": Speciesism, Economism, and Militarism. "Speciesism" refers to an attitude of human "exceptionalism" which assumes "that humans are superior to and more important than other species."[8] It results in discrimination against non-human life forms, and tends ultimately toward the destruction of the earth itself. "Economism" refers to a worldview in which economics becomes, in effect, our religion—our ultimate concern or primary means of transformation.[9] In contemporary American society it is associated with unquestioning support for the growth and expansion of so-called free market capitalism, irrespective of negative consequences for "have-nots" at home and abroad. "Militarism" refers to a predisposition toward vigorous support for a strong military organization.[10] In the current U.S. context, it frequently entails a glorification of a warlike spirit that stands ready to sanction aggressive preparedness for war, regardless of the cost to the environment, the economy, or the political life of human beings.

Taken together, these three "isms" represent a destructive, totalistic worldview. "Speciesism" is contributing to a relentless and even methodical killing of the earth. Although we sometimes put our technology to constructive use to confront environmental devastation, the overall destructive direction is clear and the picture is getting worse by the day.[11] We are progressively and irretrievably cutting ourselves off from our indispensable life-support system. Because of our allegiance to "Economism," those of us who are socially situated among what John Kenneth Galbraith described as "the contented majority,"[12] have tended to isolate ourselves in affluent enclaves, while pursuing decadent lifestyles built on the backs of the world's poor and prostrating ourselves to the consumer goods that have become the religious fetishes of our time. And mesmerized by "Militarism," we Americans have sanctioned the growth of the largest, strongest military machine in human history. The surprise that most Americans show on learning that our Defense Department budget exceeds the combined military expenditures of the next twenty nations of the world suggests how disconnected national policy has become from the body politic.

In this book, therefore, I argue for what I am calling an "ethic of re-connection"—in which we confront Speciesism, Economism and Militarism by reconnecting with the earth, with kindred spirits and with our enemies. But short of some miraculous intervention how is such reconnection to take place? What could possibly ease the near total grip of these "isms" on the psyches of American liberals and conservatives alike? I do not share the hope of many of my colleagues that a simple reformation might yet be possible. Something much more fundamental, more radical, is necessary.

To paraphrase a popular Beatles song, we need "a little help from our friends."[13] Although one of the extraordinary aspects of life today is that we indeed live in a global village, ingrained parochialism, hubris, and other failings make Americans stubbornly resist the idea that we have anything of real significance to learn from those beyond our borders. But having spent nearly half of my career living and teaching in the Two-Thirds World, I know that real alternatives to the "McDonaldization"[14] of culture in post-industrial North America and Western Europe still exist. And the story does not end here. For the more one explores these alternatives and learns about the moral insights they reveal, the more one can appreciate and understand the so-called "hard sayings" of Jesus. Just as these sayings were embedded in oral traditions associated with the early Jesus movement, and that movement was itself a counter-cultural phenomenon, so too are the testimonies of such Two-Thirds World voices as Rastafarians and South African freedom fighters associated with resistance movements. Obviously, great temporal, spatial, and cultural distances separate the Jesus movement and these contemporary initiatives, but fascinating affinities are readily discernable. The most important is that they all represent attempts to reach out to, speak up for, and lift up those who are marginalized and oppressed by dominant political systems. In other words, seeing the world through the eyes of such movements—or through the experiences of those who, like Pacific Islanders, are still not completely alienated from indigenous pre-modern worldviews—enables us to cultivate fresh strategies for seeing the world through the eyes of the historical Jesus.

And this is where the work of the Jesus Seminar and other scholars who have helped us better understand the early Jesus movement becomes especially relevant for ethics. By developing a "database" of apparently authentic primary sayings of and about Jesus of Nazareth, such scholars have provided us with an invaluable repository that can be mined for moral fragments. Despite the element of controversy surrounding the Seminar, its findings can help us envision a sharp, historical-critical, picture of Jesus as an ethical model.[15] Moreover, many of these fragments resonate and even correlate with moral themes and symbols expressed by contemporary indigenous peoples and alternative socio-political movements in the Two-Thirds World today. Because we are closer to the latter in time and space, it makes sense to begin by exploring their moral landscapes, as bizarre and enigmatic as they may first appear. Then, having begun to "mentally migrate" into their landscapes, we will perhaps find it less difficult to make a similar journey into the moral universe delineated by the sayings associated with the early Jesus movement.

I have therefore structured the book with three interrelated themes in mind: the moral and ethical crises in North America today, moral insights from the Two-Thirds World, and core moral sayings of the historical Jesus. In Chapter One, I discuss what I take to be the three most critical moral crises of our time: the war on terror, economic inequity and ecological destruction. In Chapter Two, I introduce the crisis in ethics itself; that is, the problems inherent in living in a late modern world in which we can no longer appeal to universal ethical norms and values. In Chapter Three, I contextualize this crisis by sketching four dominant ethical traditions in the history of the U.S., linking them to contemporary ethical options today. In the process, I suggest how these traditions have compromised themselves and neglected moral insights from alternative ethical voices in the U.S.

The first three chapters thus provide the background for why we need to look beyond our shores for moral inspiration. In Chapter Four I show how Pacific Islanders' views of land, sea, and the animal world represent potential resources for addressing Speciesism. In Chapter Five I describe how Rastafarian notions of self and lifestyle constitute provocative, creative elements for confronting Economism. And in Chapter Six I explore some of the implications of the moral vision of former freedom fighters in South Africa for challenging the ethos of Militarism. In each of these three chapters on moral experience from the margins, I also seek to provide a fresh appreciation of the moral dimension of some of Jesus' sayings by viewing them through the eyes of these "foreigners" from the Two-Thirds World. Finally, in Chapter Seven I sketch out some of the implications of this approach for the crisis in the field of ethics and for the parallel moral crisis in contemporary society.

I have intended this book to be used in small group discussions—whether among informal gatherings of friends, students in university classes, Jesus Seminar Associates, or members of church or sunday school study groups. Therefore, after each chapter I have listed a few "Talking Points" that can be used as written or modified to suit the needs of the group. They might also serve to stimulate private reflections.

In the interests of readability, I have placed most technical references and comments in endnotes after each chapter, so that those who wish to pursue certain topics or issues can profit from the sources I have found useful. In a few cases, I use the endnotes to develop more theoretical aspects of an idea that might be of interest to some readers, but certainly not to all. Readers who are familiar with "social ethics" as an academic exercise and contemporary dilemmas in discourse about ethics may wish to skip over Chapter Two and move quickly to Chapters Three through Six, where I elaborate the major argument of the book. In Chapters Four through Six, I have also tried to blend autobiographical reflections with expository material in an attempt to communicate on a more personal level and to take first-person experiences as points of departure. I am not wholly satisfied with this blending of genres, but if it evokes connections in the experiences of readers, perhaps it will be more helpful than confusing.

Some readers may wonder why I think that I have something significant to say about such a grand topic as "ethics in the global village." What makes me qualified to make judgments about matters that have such broad political, economic, and environmental dimensions? Although I am not a foreign policy expert, I closely follow pertinent debates in the media, and stay current with literature in the field. I am also a trained social ethicist with a broad background in comparative religions and ethics. But perhaps just as important, I have lived and worked for over a decade with social elites as well as marginalized persons on three continents, and have diligently studied the sayings of Jesus with our post 9-11 predicament in mind. I hope and trust, therefore, that the time you spend grappling with the ideas expressed in this book will be worthily spent.

What follows, then, is "an ethics of re-connection" in the global village. If it is persuasive, I hope that it will prompt you and those close to you to think more deeply about how to confront the three-headed specter of Speciesism, Economism and Militarism. Ultimately, I argue, we need to develop a very different consciousness about ourselves, about those who are "other" in the global village, and about how we can live in harmony with those others.[16] In short, we need to develop a new ethic for a new era—a new understanding of what constitutes right social relationships. But let us begin by taking stock of the moral crises of our time, both in terms of the ways we are held captive by the three isms (Chapter 1) and the inability of western ethics—primarily a product of white males—to deal effectively with this bondage (Chapters 2 & 3).

ACKNOWLEDGMENTS

A number of persons have played important roles in the development of this book. While it is impossible to name every person who has contributed to a work in progress over the past three years, and one that draws substantially on research and learning experiences over the past thirty-five, I do wish to pay special tribute to those who have either aided directly in the preparation of the manuscript or who have lent crucial support during the process.

Ron Flowers and Donna Yarri provided detailed editorial and substantive comments on an entire draft of the book. Miguel De La Torre, David Pfrimmer, Larry Rasmussen and Marcia Riggs read an early draft and offered constructive criticisms as well as endorsements. Char Matejovsky at Polebridge Press and Tom Hall have provided skillful editorial assistance. I am especially grateful for Tom's incisive comments and suggestions.

I am also indebted to colleagues at Texas Christian University who have supported and encouraged me throughout the various stages of this project. I am particularly grateful to the entire faculty of the Religion Department. The late Daryl Schmidt and David Grant, my Department Chairs at TCU, both provided collegial and administrative support. Hjamil Martínez-Vázquez and Melanie Harris have been especially important conversation partners. Laurie Loken offered timely technical assistance and Roger Covin helped assemble the bibliography. Manochehr Dorraj and Keith Whitworth offered valuable expertise regarding political and sociological sources. Librarian Diane Boerner, provided reference information. Through its Research and Creative Activities Fund, TCU supported research critical to the book, and Mary Volcansek offered invaluable encouragement.

I am especially grateful for academic mentors. The late Bob Funk inspired me to write this book, and although he would not have entirely agreed with my perspective, he would also have been disappointed if it did not challenge his own views. The late Howard Harrod, my PhD advisor at Vanderbilt University, taught me early on about the necessity of approaching other cultures with rigor, integrity, and empathy. Peter Paris, who served on my dissertation committee, has continued to be a valued intellectual guide. I also wish to honor numerous mentors from "the Two-Thirds world," including my daughter Kelly in New Zealand, brother Glen in Jamaica, Jovili and Lisa Meo from Fiji, and the late Bongani Mazibuko from South Africa—and all the Rastafarians, Pacific Islanders and South Africans who have helped me learn about different strands of ethical wisdom.

Finally, I want to thank my dear wife, Kat, who has played crucial roles in the project. On more than one occasion, her technical savvy and irrepressible exuberance have rescued me from disaster and buoyed my spirits. But most of all she has provided that rarest of treasures in modern life—a place of refuge, care, and acceptance without which the writing of this book would not have been possible. I therefore dedicate this work to her.

This book draws on a number of works that have been previously published but are now either out of print or in publications not easily accessible to the general public. Chapter Six distills information from *Seeds of Transformation: Discerning the Ethics of a New Generation* and draws on sections of an article, "Putting the Township in the University: Moral Resources from Former Freedom Fighters in South Africa," that appeared in *The Journal of Religious Thought*. Chapter Five incorporates brief sections of *I-Sight: The World of Rastafari*. Chapter Four includes a recycling of information about two tales from the South Pacific found in "Doing Ethics in the Pacific Islands: Interpreting the Moral Dimensions of Prose Narrative" that appeared in *Annual of the Society of Christian Ethics* as well as a description of a tale from Vanuatu that appeared in "Global Ethics: What We Can Learn from Christians Overseas," published in *Christian Ethics Today* and was also described in "The Dolphin Christ" in *Horizons*. In Chapter One, I draw on parts of an article published in *The Fourth R*, "Was Jesus Green? Reflection on the Sayings of Jesus from a Cross-Cultural Perspective." In Chapters Two, Three, Five, Six and Seven I greatly expand upon parts of a paper, "The Boy Scout and the Mafia Boss," that I presented at the March 2004 meeting of the Westar Institute in New York City.

CHAPTER 1

THE MORAL CRISES OF OUR TIME

THE WAR ON TERROR

The 9-11 attacks ignited a shock wave felt around the world. At least that was how the attacks were perceived by many Americans, although a minority of us wondered why some such assault had not happened on U.S. soil long before. CNN and the BBC saturated television screens in the earth's remotest regions with apocalyptic images of New York City going up in flames. International phone lines jammed with calls from friends and loved ones in faraway places. Although terrorist bombings had become almost commonplace in many of the world's hot spots, the attacks on the Trade Towers and the Pentagon struck at the very nerve centers of western economic and military might. It was not only that serious damage had been done to infrastructures and that lives had been lost. Core symbols of global capitalism and military muscle had been shown to be highly vulnerable.

Once the significance of the attacks had begun to register in the American psyche, it was not uncommon to hear people say, "Everything has changed!" For conservative evangelicals it was a foretaste of Armageddon—a Big Apple portent of fire and brimstone. Even among more mainline Christians there was a sense that sinister forces had crossed an irreversible line. But rather than turning outward and seeking help from those long experienced with terror around the world, most Americans went into a lockdown, isolationist mode.[1] Like pioneers circling their wagons, Americans rallied around the flag. As had been the case during the so-called "Indian Wars," such random attacks had to be met with even greater force. Although efforts were made to bring on board others—notably the Blair government in the U.K.—to form a

1

"coalition of the willing," the response was from its inception an American-initiated and an American-directed counterattack.

A whole new national focus emerged. In the ensuing months the "war on terror" was declared, America's first Department of Homeland Security was established, and the term "weapons of mass destruction" became a staple on the evening news. On December 13, 2001, President Bush announced that the U.S. would withdraw from the 1972 Anti-Ballistic Missile (ABM) Treaty with the former Soviet Union, despite opposition by leading NATO countries.[2] A classified Pentagon document leaked to the press in early 2002 reported that "The Bush Administration has directed the military to prepare plans to use nuclear weapons against at least seven countries."[3] The newly created Office of Global Communications spread the new ideology of the war on terrorism. The Department of Homeland Security, through its Total Information Awareness Program, began to probe into citizens' private lives in ways that called into question constitutional guarantees of basic civil liberties.[4] American citizens were detained without being informed of the charges against them and without access to legal counsel.[5] Airport security was increased, military guards were posted at check-in counters, and on the basis of what was essentially ethnic profiling, some ticketed passengers were forbidden to board aircraft. In the words of columnist James Carroll, "In half a year [since 9-11], we have reinvented ourselves as the most belligerent people on earth. How did this happen?"[6]

Suddenly, U.S. foreign policy was shifting from the fifty-year old Cold War doctrine of measured détente to an ad hoc strategy of "preemptive" strikes.[7] In December 2002, the Bush Administration unveiled a new anti-proliferation strategy that replaced the 1993 strategy drafted by the Clinton Administration. Prepared jointly by the National Security Council and the White House Office of Homeland Security, the new strategy "codifies a national security evolution that began with the Sept. 11 attacks, and repeats the administration's threat to use pre-emptive and overwhelming force—up to and including nuclear weapons—against what it perceives as an imminent danger of an attack."[8]

Acting on a consensus opinion of intelligence officials, the Administration assigned blame for the 9-11 attacks to the al Qaeda militia and its leader, Osama Bin Laden.[9] Less than a month after 9-11, on the assumption that Bin Laden's network was based in Afghanistan, the U.S. launched a campaign of high-altitude bombing in that country. At the time of this writing, however, the U.S. military had failed to capture or kill Bin Laden.[10]

Simultaneously, the Administration was beginning to charge that Iraq possessed "weapons of mass destruction." It succeeded in getting a resolution passed in the United Nations Security Council authorizing the resumption of onsite inspections of facilities suspected of harboring such weapons. Then, when the U.N. team led by Hans Blix failed to uncover any "smoking gun,"[11] Bush argued that U.S. intelligence reports of such weapons made it necessary to invade Iraq. But by mid-March 2003, on the eve of the invasion, Administration officials were beginning to speak about "rogue regimes which are attempting *to acquire* weapons of mass destruction"[12] (emphasis added) as a justification for invading Iraq. According to some officials, a significant relationship or link existed between Iraq and the al Qaeda terrorist network,[13] and in any event, a "regime change" was necessary because of the evil deeds of Iraq's leader, Saddam Hussein.[14] With support from Tony Blair's Labor government and other allies, the Bush Administration invaded Iraq on March 20, 2003. By late 2006, the ensuing war, dubbed by the White House "Operation Iraqi Freedom" (a nomenclature readily embraced by Fox News and other media outlets), had resulted in tens of thousands of Iraqi and over 3,100 U.S. casualties,[15] the destruction of major elements of Iraq's infrastructure, the occupation of the country by over 135,000 U.S. troops,[16] and the growth of a widespread resistance network of militant sectarians and insurgents.[17] Saddam Hussein and other members of the former regime's leaders were rounded up and a long-term campaign of guerilla warfare ensued. Coalition forces established a provisional regime that was succeeded by an elected but ineffectual government. During the 2004 U.S. elections, the manner of going to war and the conduct of the war were major campaign issues.[18]

These startling geo-political maneuvers notwithstanding, since 9-11 there may be another and more elusive sense in which "everything has changed." In the short term, our basic way of life in the modern west has been jolted. One way to characterize the rise of modernity is to view it as a drive to make the world smooth and continuous.[19] Such technological developments as modern plumbing, privately owned automobiles, low cost air travel, curative and preventive medical care, home entertainment centers, and the information highway have all contributed to what some have termed the "modernist project." This project seeks to create economic and political conditions that promote a relatively steady, predictable, manageable progress for the relatively affluent majority in the wealthier nations and the economic elites in poorer nations. The hallmark of sound technology is that it facilitates an increasing control of our social and material environment—streamlining communications, transportation, work and recreational activities. What is perhaps most exasperating about occasional computer "crashes" is that such malfunctions temporarily interrupt our taken-for-granted expectation of smooth, virtually continuous interactions with others on-line.

This penchant for smoothness and continuity protects a (secular) sacred space that is aptly evoked by the modern phrase, "comfort zone."[20] What 9-11 did was to toss a dart into the heart of America's comfort zone.[21] When people ruefully lament that "everything has changed," they are acknowledging that this comfortableness has been diminished. In particular, the repeated airing of the 9-11 attacks on television thrust the reality of some of the world's violence and suffering into our personal routines and daily lives. Americans could not dismiss 9-11 replays as casually as news reports about bombings in the Middle East or Africa, because they re-presented something that happened too close to home. It happened in America, in one's own city, to one's own friends and relatives—and therefore, by association, to *oneself.*

But in a still deeper sense, 9-11 disrupted our comfortableness because it opened up the possibility that we might have to confront repressed narratives of our past. It prompted searching questions we usually don't ask—and would rather not. The day after the 9-11 attacks, my students at TCU asked in exasperation, "Why would the terrorists attack us?" "What has the U.S. ever done to deserve this?" "How can such seemingly indiscriminate violence happen?" "How can it happen to *us*?" To properly address such questions we would need to conduct deep level inquiries into the past.

In effect, the 9-11 attacks subverted the essentially horizontal, a-historical trajectory of modern consciousness by forcing us to confront once again the discontinuities of history. Seen from a European perspective, the oft-repeated phrase "Americans have short memories" simply underscores the degree to which we Americans seek to protect our comfort zones against the incursion of just such discontinuities. Among other things, expanding our memories would mean examining recent patterns of favoritism lavished on Israeli interests in the Middle East, American complicity in the bombing of Lebanon in 1982 and 2006, and the whole sordid history of Christian crusades against Muslim "infidels." It would also involve beginning a long overdue engagement with the darker sides of U.S. involvements in the trans-Atlantic slave trade, genocide of Native Americans, seizure of Mexican land, the imprisonment of Japanese Americans, and exploitive practices of transnational corporations.[22]

Except in isolated quarters, however, this inquiry has not arisen. True to the modernist concern for smoothness and continuity at all costs, the vaults of historical knowledge were quickly sealed. Take a case in point. The Department of Homeland Security was created ostensibly to reduce the nation's vulnerabilities and thus to protect Americans from further threats, but almost no effort was made to determine why America was the target of these attacks in the first place. The comfort zone could be restored only if Americans and their allies could be seen taking steps to make sure that no likely culprit could ever threaten them again. Launching a war on terrorism and occupying Iraq allowed Americans and their allies to return to the enchantment of their comfortable lives, secure in the knowledge that their nation's leaders were doing their best to take care of the terrorist threat.

Far from closing the case, however, the Bush Administration's response to the 9-11 attacks has opened up a Pandora's Box. The interruption of 9-11, which many in authority had hoped to smooth over by a campaign of overwhelming force, has now mushroomed into a new period of geo-political uncertainty. Questions abound. Did the U.S. and British governments lie about the existence of weapons of mass destruction in Iraq? If not, was their military intelligence severely flawed? And if the latter were the case, how could such intelligence be counted upon in the future? Does the policy of initiating preventive wars in the absence of imminent threat to our own security violate the notion of a just war—let alone basic moral teachings in western civilization? Did the U.S. unilateralist approach undermine the ability of United Nations and NATO efforts to seek multilateral resolutions to regional conflicts?[23] And, given the possibility that the war on terrorism may continue indefinitely in the twenty-first century, should successive U.S. Presidents have continuous authority to suspend civil liberties simply on the basis of perceived threats to national security priorities?

Clearly, this book is not the place to explore all of these questions, and in any case the author does not presume to have the requisite political expertise. Rather, the intent is to sketch some of the moral implications of this multi-faceted crisis that confronts the modern west. It is precisely this moral dimension that is so often neglected in popular talk shows and political commentary about international affairs. Western commentators either presume to be speaking from a moral high ground that is not open for debate, or imagine geo-political strategies to be beyond moral considerations.[24]

What I seek to argue is that the events of 9-11 and its aftermath have not only interrupted our political comfort zone, they have brought to the surface major questions about the moral underpinnings of emerging taken-for-granted political assumptions. Does the U.S. or any sovereign nation have the right to dictate a regime change in another sovereign state? Is it just for one nation to amass most of the weapons of mass destruction for itself? Is it right to permit security to trump such other values as liberty and equity? In Chapter Six, I will argue that we in the United States have something to learn about these matters from investigating the moral outlooks of our overseas neighbors, especially our South

African brothers and sisters. They have not only overthrown perhaps the worst racist regime in history and established a vibrant if fragile democracy; they have also established an extraordinary peace and reconciliation process.

And important as it is to examine the morality of current political developments, we also need to recognize that the moral crisis of our time stretches beyond purely political concerns. For it is not simply with respect to the political status quo that "everything has changed," but the strikingly apocalyptic character of the 9-11 attack prompts deeper fears about threats to our very way of life. We need to address not only the moral foundations of our *political* aspirations, but also the moral crisis implicit in the *economic* underpinnings and larger *ecological* contexts of our comfort zones.

RISING ECONOMIC ANXIETIES

One of the anomalies of contemporary life is that during a period of unprecedented economic prosperity, affluent Americans have become increasingly anxious about personal finances.[25] This is particularly puzzling since practically no one in today's work force has lived in a time of true economic depression. Indeed, according to most economic indicators, life has been good for the majority of Americans during the past half century. The oil crisis of the 1970s and the minor recessions of the 1980s were more like hiccups than dramatic interruptions in the steady onward march of wealth creation. During the 1990s, stock dividends soared, gross incomes increased for all economic groups, and the federal government built a fiscal surplus. Even during the more volatile years between 2000 and 2007, home ownership and overall wages registered steady, if slight, increases.[26]

Still, many Americans were not feeling flush, and consumer confidence has dipped in recent years. Even prior to 9-11, there were forebodings on the horizon. The stock market had begun to experience disturbing fluctuations in response to mixed signals from historically reliable economic indicators. After peaking at a high above 11,000, the Dow Jones Industrial Average plummeted to less than 8,000 several months after 9-11, and although it recovered from that steep decline and roared above 13,000 in 2007, it has ranged up and down below 13,000 in the first quarter of 2008. Between 2001 and 2004, many investors lost considerable sums in the market. Gasoline prices fluctuated in response to uncertainties caused by civil strife in Nigeria, the new aggressive marketing strategies of a Chavez-led Venezuela, and the sabotage of refineries and pipelines in Iraq and other parts of the Middle East. By the summer of 2004, the price of a barrel of crude oil had risen to an all-time high at $55, and at the time of this writing it had hit a new high of $106. By August, 2006, the nationwide average price of gas had topped $3.00 a gallon, and it has returned to that level in 2008. Joblessness has again begun to rise after decades of relatively low unemployment. Following major scandals in large corporations such as Enron, bankruptcies have increased at an alarming rate, spreading to the nation's major airlines and communications industries. Airline employees have been especially hard hit, while throughout the airline industry lay-offs and voluntary pay cuts have become routine. By the fall of 2004, US Airways was announcing that the time was fast approaching when workers might not receive contractually guaranteed pensions.[27]

There is a gnawing sense of agitation in the workplace. Costs of health care, education, utilities, and basic foodstuffs have edged ever higher. The average worker is simultaneously saddled with higher health insurance premiums, higher annual deductibles, and more expensive prescription drugs.[28] Worse yet, at least forty million Americans are without health insurance. Although many medical professionals might argue otherwise, the quality of health care in the U.S. is not demonstrably superior to that in European and other nations where health care is essentially subsidized by government agencies. To compound the problem, the rate of increase of health care costs has outstripped the inflation rate for several years. Even though Social Security payments were scheduled to rise in 2005, higher Medicare premiums absorbed nearly half of a typical beneficiary's increase.[29] A post-secondary education at a private college is fast becoming an elusive option for any not among the upper echelons of society.

The changing economic ethos of the United States during the past fifty years might well persuade the disinterested observer that our quality of life peaked somewhere in the 1960s or early 1970s. In 1970 a student could fly standby half-way across the country for $49, enjoy a multi-course cooked dinner on the flight, and not face the specter of long lines at security check points. Of course in 1970 most Americans had only a few television channels to choose from, but one could watch any of them without paying a cable or satellite fee. Even the commonplace matter of newspaper delivery has changed for the worse. Like many teenagers in 1960, the author had a newspaper route. It was expected that each paper would be delivered to the customer's specification: for Mr. Jones, inside the screen door; for Mrs. Hayes, under the door mat; for Stanley, wedged behind the milk box. Today, papers are flung out of vehicle windows by anonymous delivery persons and may end up on a far corner of the lawn. The money I earned was mostly discretionary income—partly to be saved and partly to be spent on sodas and baseball cards. But the days of the 12 year-old "paperboy" are long gone. Now the delivery person's income may be crucial for survival. Today's "paperboy" is an adult who drives three or four routes in a manic fashion, hoping that car repairs and medical bills do not exceed his or her earnings.

Nostalgia aside, even if most Americans are relatively better off than most of the world's peoples, there is a gathering unease about whether or not we can keep the juggernaut rolling.[30] Baby boomers have always felt that they were entitled to the good life, and many have simply assumed that they would live far better than their parents. But, now they have to work harder, produce more and work longer hours to secure the same "good life" that mom and dad achieved. In many families, both husband and wife must work outside the home in order to pay the bills, and they increasingly worry about how the bills will be paid in retirement. Americans have been advised to supplement their Social Security payments with investments in various pension funds and assorted financial instruments, but several of these funds have registered uneven performances in the stock market. Furthermore, as the federal government's deficits continue to mushroom since the Bush Administration's response to 9-11, many fear that the money set aside for Social Security will be tapped to keep the U.S. government afloat in future decades. Today's younger workers fear that there may not be any Social Security funds for them when they retire.

"Keeping up with the Jones" in these difficult times is an increasingly precarious project. Many Americans not only struggle to make ends meet, but face the fear of poverty; indeed, many families are only 1 or 2 paychecks from serious financial difficulty. Credit card debt has escalated to the degree that between 1989 and 2001, "average credit card debt among all families increased by 53%, from $2,697 to $4,126."[31] And the number of those living in poverty is growing day by day. The familiar cliché is all too true: during the past half-century, the rich *have* grown richer, while the poor *have* grown poorer. The richest 20% of the world's people have increased their share of the world's income from 70% in 1960 to 85% in 1991.[32] Just over two hundred of the world's richest people have a combined wealth almost equal to the annual income of nearly half of the world's people.[33] During this same period, the income share of the poorest 20% of the world's people dropped from 2.3% in 1960 to 1.4% in 1991.[34]

With the increasing use of computer technology and other hi-tech gadgetry in education and the workplace, some commentators speak of a growing "digital divide." The "haves" and the "have-nots" are becoming aligned in accordance with access to and skill in utilizing the latest technologies. The "digitally illiterate" appear to be in danger of constituting a new permanent underclass who will never be able to earn anything approaching the median incomes in their respective societies.[35]

It is also clear that the U.S. political response to 9-11, especially the subsequent war with Iraq, has not only created worldwide geo-political uncertainty, but has also exacerbated economic anxiety. And likely it will have profound economic implications as yet unforeseen. Unlike World War II and the Vietnam War, the war on terrorism appears to have no geographical or temporal limit. And unlike the case in past wars, the support of traditional allies is uncertain. With limited help from England and a handful of less affluent allies, the U.S. may have to shoulder the economic burden of the new conflict.

Indeed, the Bush Administration's war on terrorism is already proving to be very expensive. New fiscal priorities such as hikes in the military budget, seed money for the Department of Homeland Security, and funding for airport security technology—coupled with tax cuts for the wealthy—has resulted in record-breaking budget deficits. And the war on terrorism is only in its infancy. It is unclear how much a prolonged occupation of Iraq, new insurgencies in Afghanistan, and the possible spread of hostilities to other areas might ultimately cost.

On the other hand, Administration spokespersons argue, by weeding out terrorist cells western governments protect vital economic resources. In the case of Iraq, for example, military analysts posit that once the U.S. military has secured Iraqi oil fields, production can exceed previous levels and oil reserves may yet absorb much of the cost of re-building the nation's infrastructure. Hence, western governments will recoup much of the cost of replacing what Coalition bombing and insurgent sabotage has destroyed.

More important, according to this line of thought, increasing the western military presence in the most significant oil-producing region of the world will insure a continuous and economical supply of oil to western consumers. And thus the international patterns of consumption that are both assumed and vital prerequisites of the good life for a majority of Americans and Europeans would not be disturbed. But granting the cogency of this argument suggests that the war on Iraq was not so much about weapons of mass destruction or even regime change as it was a strategy for protecting western economic interests in the Middle East as a whole.

I want to argue that given the demographics of the contemporary global neighborhood, this preoccupation with buttressing one's own economic position represents a serious moral crisis. In view of the global inequities between haves and have-nots, it seems morally outrageous that the most affluent should seek to control their neighbor's resources in order to fuel lifestyles that these neighbors can only dream about. In short, the western response to 9-11 gives the age-old question of economic inequity a new sense of urgency. As one observer asks, "Is it right for 9 or 10% of the world's population to consume nearly half of the world's resources, while nearly one billion people live in absolute poverty?[36] Is it justifiable for individuals to pursue luxurious international patterns of consumption while thousands die of starvation every day?[37] And, given the prospect of rising military budgets, will those at the bottom end of the digital divide have any genuine hope of moving up the ladder?"[38]

These are just some of the basic moral questions that are implicit in the economic dimensions of the western response to 9-11. Before the attacks and the funding of the war on terror, Americans expressed various anxieties about their economic futures, but for the majority the basic hope of attaining the good life remained essentially intact. Now the very expectation of continued economic prosperity has been interrupted. Are we descending into a financial quagmire that will be difficult to exit? Are there alterative ways of organizing our economic life?[39] As bizarre as it might first appear, I want to suggest that we could gain some practical insights from such counter-cultural groups as the Rastafarians of Jamaica. For instance, Rastas do not rely upon the range of technologies that Americans have come to take for granted, yet they distribute scarce resources among themselves in ways that have not only promoted survival, but have also facilitated a certain quality of life. While we must avoid a romanticized view of Rasta lifestyles, it is useful to consider how they represent a practical alternative to our "me-first" consumer-oriented society[40]—and perhaps to recall what Jesus and his prophetic precursors had to say about wealth? I will explore a few of the economic insights of Rastas and Jesus in Chapter Five, but perhaps at this juncture we should take note of an even direr crisis looming on the horizon. Its scope and intensity can be implied in two questions: Can the earth sustain the onslaught of modern technological development? Will there even *be* a healthy environment in which future generations can work and prosper?

EARTH UNDER ASSAULT

It should no longer come as a surprise that we face a major ecological crisis.[41] We are killing our very life support system in a manner unprecedented in human history. And yet, most of us go about our daily lives more or less blissfully indifferent to the devastation. Technically, the word "environment" means simply "that which surrounds us."[42] It ordinarily denotes what is in the background, distant and outside of ourselves. But it also has more technical connotations. For example, in behavioral genetics, it refers to everything that lies outside the scope of genetic encoding.[43] We don't usually connect to this issue personally, as we do to more immediate "life and death" or "bread and butter" concerns like terrorist threats or job losses. Because the ecological crisis does not appear on most people's radars as a "hot" topic, and because we have become aware of it only gradually and in subtle ways, it may be helpful to consider an autobiographical example.

In the late 1950s, when I was a youth growing up in the Midwest, my family vacationed in Manitou Springs, Colorado nearly every summer. My grandfather had a house at the foot of Pike's Peak and my father, older brother and I would spend days hiking deep into the Rocky Mountain wilderness. I remember incredibly blue skies, lush green forests and deep, icy cold mountain streams. I especially remember *drinking* out of those streams. In fact, after we returned from several days of backpacking, we would routinely fill up jugs of mineral water from a stream in downtown Manitou Springs for making lemonade. When I returned to the area four years ago, it was unsafe to even consider drinking water from the town stream and mountain climbers had to treat any water collected from higher elevations.

The pollution of mountain streams is just the tip of the iceberg. Taking a global view since the beginning of this century, we see that fresh water use is exceeding aquifer replenishment,[44] soil erosion has begun to exceed soil formation, species extinction has begun to exceed species evolution, fish catches are exceeding fish reproduction, forest destruction is exceeding forest regeneration, and carbon emissions are exceeding carbon fixation.[45] The rapid evolution of the problem becomes particularly apparent when one realizes that the pace of this change is simply unprecedented in human history. In the past century we have also developed such new environmental problems as a sharp spike in global warming;[46] the production, storage, transport and disposal of nuclear materials; and a steadily increasing rate of the depletion of fossil fuels.

Because of the sheer magnitude of the ecological crisis, any scholar who even begins to unpack it risks being labeled a "doomsayer." A certain amount of pollution, for example, is an inevitable by-product of human activity. Any production process entails waste, and therefore "we can no more 'stop polluting' than we can halt our natural body functions."[47] For most of us in the affluent nations, twentieth-century technology has wrought wonders in the forms of agricultural production, the delivery of goods and services, lifestyle comforts, medical remedies, electronic and communications innovations, and the doubling of life expectancies. Very few of us seriously want to return to a pre-1900's existence.

But the "good life through modern technology" comes with a hefty price tag. It is a cost that must be borne in one fashion or another. Consider the pollution of our mountain stream as a case in point. A business firm or a local government that discharges waste that eventually contaminates the stream either pays the cost of rectifying the situation or shifts the cost to others. If the latter, then individuals, other firms, or government entities must pay the "cost" by cleaning up the waste and/or by losing the use of the river for recreational, aesthetic, or water supply purposes.

Viewing aspects of the ecological crisis in terms of such a "cost-benefits" analysis is a practical, constructive way of temporarily addressing isolated parts of the crisis at particular times in specific locales. It is an important part of public policy advocacy and needs to be accelerated on a number of fronts. But such a piecemeal approach does not begin to address either the root causes or the global reach of the crisis. While most affluent Americans can still live their lives without significant "environmental interruptions," the time is fast approaching when oil and water shortages will have a dramatic impact on daily routines in certain regions of the country.

Furthermore, to frame problems such as global warming or toxic waste disposal simply as evidences of bad management is to be trapped within the modernist paradigm of control and technological manipulation.[48] This paradigm presupposes that technological progress is normative and therefore that technologically generated problems (like nuclear waste disposal!) can be successfully handled by new and better applications of technology. It may be, however, that such a re-doubling of efforts is not sufficient, and in some cases it may even exacerbate ecological problems. While we may no longer be able to return to a subsistence lifestyle, we can still re-think our relationship to the ecosystem.

Although the ecological crisis has been emerging for decades, like the economic crisis its onset has been accelerated by the war on terror. The ecological effects of America's invasion of Iraq have yet to be determined, but the relentless bombing campaigns have no doubt damaged Iraq's ecosystem, especially its water supply routes. During the initial months of bombing, infants were dying of dehydration, water was scarce in major urban centers, electricity was in short supply, and widespread pollution of agricultural areas was reported.

In order to put the 9-11 attacks in ecological perspective, it is interesting to note that they occurred in the larger context of the U.S.'s refusal to sign the Kyoto Treaty—a major international effort to reduce global warming.[49] While the specific planning and execution of the attacks were no doubt unrelated to this country's rejection of the treaty, the point is that they came on the heels of years of resentment of America's unilateral approach to international initiatives, including global ecological issues.

Although such macro-effects of modern warfare as alterations in atmospheric conditions have yet to be examined in depth, the environmental ravages of war in Iraq prompt fundamental ethical questions. What does it mean to be good stewards of the earth while pursuing military actions?[50] How do western lifestyles contribute to eco-destructive practices?[51] How can the world's affluent nations play greater roles in reducing pollution?[52] How can people of the western world develop more intimate relationships to other species? In Chapter Four, I will attempt to show how the interactions of Pacific Islanders with land and sea can provide a fresh, eco-friendly outlook for contemporary Americans.

In sum, this book assumes that genuine, constructive responses to the moral crises of our times—to the interrelated problems of violence across cultures, economic injustice and ecological destruction—require thinking "outside the box"—beyond the boundaries of business as usual.[53] But in order to do this we need to go to the very roots of the problem. We need to take a fresh look at how we think *inside* our boxes. In what respects have we lost our moral moorings? What has happened to undermine our capacity to think in social ethical terms? In the following chapter, I will discuss the nature of ethics and explore the crisis in the field. In particular I hope to show why we can no longer appeal to universal ethical principles or standards of moral value.

TALKING POINTS

For personal soul searching, one-on-one conversation, or small group discussion

THE WAR ON TERROR

- When and where did you first hear about the 9-11 attacks? How did you respond? Why do you think America was the target of these attacks?
- Brainstorm on the word "terrorist." How would you define it? Why do people become terrorists? Who stands to benefit from the existence of terrorists?
- Think about times you have heard people use the word, "safe." When do you feel safe? What do you need to be safe? How do you think Jesus might have answered this question?
- How do you imagine people overseas view America? Is America an *empire*? Why or why not?

RISING ECONOMIC ANXIETIES

- Would you consider yourself "affluent"? How so, or why not?
- What material things do people really *need* to live a good life? List 9 or 10 items. Are any of these things scarce commodities? Could *everyone* have them?

- What is the role of markets in making choices? Should there be limits to the market? Give two examples of *good* capitalism and two examples of *bad* capitalism.
- Search the latest newspaper for economic news. Discuss whose views are being heard. Who is not being heard? What perspectives are missing? Describe them.

EARTH UNDER ASSAULT

- What aspect of your immediate environment is most important to you? In what ways are you connected to it? What might enhance that connection? What would imperil it?
- Think back to your early childhood and remember the first time you became aware that not everything was right with the environment. What was it that worried you? Does it still concern you today? In what ways?
- Read aloud *The Lorax*, by Dr. Seuss. Then do a "who, what, when, where and how" analysis of the destruction of the Truffula trees. How might this analysis be applied to a contemporary issue in your vicinity?
- How are "humans" different from non-human animal species? In general, why do non-vegetarians eat cows and chickens, but not dogs or horses?

CHAPTER 2

ETHICS AT THE CROSSROADS

WHAT IS ETHICS?
WHAT IS SOCIAL ETHICS?

Traditionally, ethics has been understood as rigorous reflection on moral experience.[1] Moral experience, in turn, refers to complex webs of values, norms, worldviews, language, perceptions of "the facts," principles, attitudes, predispositions, actions, states or qualities of being, notions of the self, the community, and the good, as well as criteria for decision making. We enter into the realm of moral experience every time we have a gut feeling or intuition that we *ought* to perform (or refrain from performing) this or that possible course of action. To a certain extent, moral experience pertains to just this sort of consciousness—to an awareness, in various times and places, of feeling some *pressure of* obligation.

The central question of ethics is therefore, "What *should* I (or we) do or be?"[2] It concerns both an awareness of obligation and of our behavior in response to that awareness. It assumes several things. First and foremost, it is an exercise geared toward doing (or not doing) and being (or not being). I call this the *practical* dimension of ethical reflection. In Aristotle's classic statement in the *Nichomachean Ethics*, the focus of ethical reflection is eminently practical and experiential.[3] It is assumed that the ethical question is worth asking; namely, that it is a meaningful question and that, practically speaking, it is at least possible to arrive at satisfactory answers. And the very asking of the question presupposes that our choice of action is limited—that moral behavior entails constraints.

Second, the question of ethics assumes an understanding of the *subject* who acts. I call this the *self* dimension of ethical thought.[4] It both presupposes that "I" *can* ask the question, that I have a certain amount of

15

freedom and autonomy, that I (or "you" or "we") may answer the question in different ways, and that the answer itself is not self-evident or completely obvious—hence the question. Until recently, it has also assumed that there is an integrated or centered self who asks the question.

Third, ethics focuses attention on what I (or you or we) *ought* to do in a *context of relationships*. It presupposes that we do *not* exist as islands unto ourselves, but that our actions (or inactions) are performed or lived out in relation to some "otherness" that is not ourselves. I call this the *other* dimension of ethics. There is an "other-regarding" tenor to all ethical discourse.[5] Even the ethical egoist thinks that acting in his or her own self-interest is good precisely because if all people acted in their own true self-interest, the result would serve *everyone's* best interest!

When we begin to focus the lens of our ethical questioning on the "other," we are moving in the direction of social ethics. "Social ethics" pertains to thinking about right or good social relationships. It asks questions such as, "How should we treat one another?" "What are fair or equitable public policies?" "When does social, economic or political transformation become a moral imperative?" Social ethics is increasingly problematical today not only because we face rapid social changes, but because we are increasingly living in a global village—where we confront a multiplicity of ethical perspectives. While most of us are sometimes unsure about how to act ethically as individuals within our own moral traditions, we are really at a loss when it comes to knowing how to act in today's pluralistic, global neighborhood. And this neighborhood continues to change and grow at a maddening rate. As we seek to come to grips with the ethics of those whom we may perceive as very different from ourselves—whether Muslim jihadists, Christian fundamentalists, Marxist revolutionaries, or advocates of indigenous rights—we confront a complex matrix of values, norms and worldviews. In order to find our bearings at such a crossroads, it will be helpful to describe some of the main aspects of what some commentators are calling our "late-modern" age.[6]

MORAL "DIS-EASE" IN OUR LATE-MODERN LIMBO

In the words of the pastoral counselor Howard Clinebell, our age is marked by "an epidemic of moral confusion and value distortion."[7] We live in an increasingly pluralistic society, yet at the same time yearn for some unifying moral authority. We want to affirm everyone's rights to their own moral beliefs, but we also desperately want some shared moral compass. We are like children torn by a divorce, trying to decide which parent to live with—the relativist or the dogmatist. If the former, then everyone is entitled to his or her own moral preferences and no one's values are any better then anyone else's. That is, making valid ethical judgments is ultimately impossible and therefore to try is a waste of time. But if the latter, then those who differ with us are wrong, so we are likely to end up shouting our opinions and dismissing each other as crazy, stupid, or morally depraved. That is, discussing ethical questions is a waste of time because the correct answers are self-evident to any right-minded person!

But to frame our moral epidemic in this polar fashion is to ignore broad spectrums of actual moral experience. In fact, certain things strike virtually all of as morally abhorrent, including sexual abuse, interrogating a criminal by putting a gun to the head of his daughter, or genocide. We may not be able to articulate this very well, but most Americans seem to share a common moral sensibility. For instance, for most of us, things such as torture or terrorism are not simply matters of bad taste. On the other hand, none of us has a corner on all moral truth. Each of us has some idea of the right and the good, but none of us sees the whole picture. In this respect, our predicament is reminiscent of the ancient Buddhist story of the blind men who are asked to describe an elephant.[8]

> The one who feels the trunk says the elephant is like a tree branch. The one grasping a leg argues that an elephant is like a pillar. The one feeling the ear asserts that an elephant is like a fan. The one grasping the tail insists that an elephant is like a rope. And the one who encounters the side of the elephant argues that the others are all wrong; an elephant is like a wall.[9]

While the story teaches a lesson about the relativity of our individual vantage points, it is important to stress that each person *does* have a partial grasp of something. That is, based on their respective experiences of the elephant, they each form understandings that are true to their experiences. Albeit in very limited ways, elephants *do* resemble ropes, branches, fans, etc.

Taking the analogy one step further, we could imagine that after arguing vociferously, the blind man who touched the tail takes the blind man who touched the ear over to the tail and places his hand on the tail. "See," he might say, "the elephant is like a rope after all!" We could also imagine the surprised comrade taking his self-assured colleague over to the ear, placing his hand on the ear, and replying, "Yes, but the elephant is *also* like a fan!" We could then imagine the development of intense debate about whether "tailness" or "earness" is really the defining characteristic of "elephantness," with each side arguing that the object of the other's point of reference was essentially an appendage.

This scenario strikes me as analogous to the predicament of morality in America today. The nation's moral ethos is, like the elephant, an amalgam of different textures, shapes and sizes.[10] Like the blind men catching hold of different parts of the beast, each of us adopts certain portions of the ethos, and we assemble what become conventional understandings based on our perception of these elements. To the extent that we *consciously* build up our storehouses of moral conventions, we give "consent" to some conventions and reject others. In this sense, we can be said to be participating in what Richard Holloway describes as "our new lightweight moral traditions."[11] We may even be challenged to experience a different moral perspective, but we inevitably do so from the vantage point of our own. Try as we may, we seem irretrievably captive to the perspectives embedded in our worlds of experience. Even the postmodernist contention that it is naive to posit any underlying ethical unity appears in the light of the elephant parable to be simply another view of the problem.

Given this predicament, we need to acknowledge the ambiguity of the American moral landscape. We have no one authoritative moral tradition. While there are traditions, such as absolutist ethics,[12] which claim to have access to absolute moral truths, they would not claim that all or even most Americans concur in that claim. But given this moral pluralism, it is important to grant the reality and preliminary legitimacy of each ongoing strand of the ethical landscape. To the extent that any particular moral tradition operates to provide adherents with a sense of immediate identity, a vision of where they are going, and rules of thumb about how to live, it should at least be taken seriously, if only in a provisional way. As we will see below, moral traditions are frequently used for purposes of self-delusion. They can also become major weapons in cultural struggles.

Indeed, given the increasingly mean-spirited, divisive and rancorous climate in the U.S. media, Congress and academia, the contemporary emphasis in America on values, moral education, and ethical leadership is ironic. Since the 1960s, many Americans have taken up sides in what has become known as the "culture wars" between "leftists" and "right-wingers." In his recent book, *The Great Divide*, John Sperling re-frames this cultural divide as one between "retros" and "metros." Retros listen to country music, love the NRA, and take the Bible literally. Metros listen to NPR, watch *Queer Eye for the Straight Guy* and interpret the Bible figuratively. And the two sides are equally adamant about what is right and wrong. But for a good number of Americans in "the middle," what constitutes core ethical values, moral rules or good leadership is not so "black and white." And in any event, even when the true believer thinks she or he knows what *ought* to be done, doing it is often another matter altogether.

It is not surprising, then, that faced with an increasingly contentious world and a proliferation of moral choices, we experience a kind of moral "dis-ease." The sad, sometimes unwitting, emergence of this moral malaise—with its symptoms of division, perplexity, vacuity or paralysis—is poignantly illustrated by the following story.

On a rocky seacoast where shipwrecks often occur there was once a crude little lifesaving station. The building was just a hut, and there was only one boat, but the few devoted members kept a constant watch over the sea, and with no thought of themselves, went out day and night tirelessly searching for the lost. The members knew each other very well. Having risked their lives in dangerous seas on numerous occasions, they formed extraordinary bonds that went very deep. They looked out for each other and would do virtually anything to help a brother in distress. They viewed their friendships as sacred trusts.

Many lives were saved because of this wonderful little station, so that it became famous. Some of those who were saved, and various others in the surrounding area, became associated with the station and gave of their time, money and effort for the support of its work. New boats were bought and new crews trained. The little lifesaving station grew.

But some of the members were unhappy that the building was so crude and poorly equipped. They felt that the first refuge of those saved from the sea should be a more comfortable place. So they enlarged the building, replaced the emergency cots with beds, and bought better furniture. And, since some of the members had become more prosperous and adopted more sedentary lifestyles, they built a physical fitness center with the latest technological equipment and hired a personal trainer. They also began to sponsor workshops on wholeness and healing, such as forums on coping with stress and depression, since some of the younger members had never encountered death and dying first-hand.

Now the lifesaving station became a popular gathering place for its members, and they decorated it beautifully and furnished it exquisitely. It became a sort of club. Fewer members were now interested in going out to sea on lifesaving missions, so they hired lifeboat crews to do this work. The lifesaving motif still prevailed in this club's decoration, and a symbolic lifeboat stood in the room where the club initiations were held.

About this time a large ship was wrecked off the coast, and the hired crews brought in boatloads of cold, wet, and half-drowned people. They were dirty and sick, and some of them had black skin and some had yellow skin. The beautiful new club was in chaos. The property committee immediately had a shower house built outside the club where victims of shipwreck could be cleaned up before coming inside.

At the next meeting, a split developed in the club membership. Most of the members wanted to end the club's lifesaving activities, which had become an unpleasant hindrance to the normal social life of the club. Some members insisted upon retaining lifesaving as their primary purpose and pointed out that they were still called a lifesaving station. These were finally voted down and told that if they wanted to save the lives of all the various

kinds of people who were shipwrecked in those waters, they could begin
their own lifesaving station down the coast. They did.

As the years went by, the new station experienced the same changes that
had occurred in the old. It evolved into a club, and yet another lifesaving
station was founded. History continued to repeat itself, and if you visit that
seacoast today, you will find a number of exclusive clubs along that shore.
Shipwrecks are still frequent in those waters, but now most of the victims
drown.[13]

In its original state, we could say, the lifesaving station embodied
four exemplary strands of moral tradition in American life: a profound
sense of community (we're all in this together); a commitment to mission
(we're for others, especially those in distress); a practical, commonsense
approach to growth and change (we strive to make the world a better
place); and a vision of personal fulfillment (we want to be all that we can
be).[14] In the next section, I will explicate the historical contours of each
of these themes which, taken together, constitute the brighter sides of our
American moral narrative. In the process, I will also describe both the
darker sides of this narrative and allude to subversive, alternative narratives that call us back to, and deepen, the brighter sides. Indeed, for many
of us, the best of these traditions have died serial deaths of attrition—in
ways analogous to the sorry history of the succession of lifesaving stations in the story. The original visions have been severely romanticized
and compromised. Things appear to have gone terribly wrong. How has
this happened? Why have we ended up in such a moral abyss? Although
there are no simple answers to these questions, it will be useful at least to
highlight a few of the contributing factors.

In the West, moral education has traditionally been the task of familial,
ecclesial and educational authorities. But today all of these authorities are
being challenged in fundamental ways. The two-parent family—in which
dad is head of the household and mom raises the kids at home—is no
longer normative. The authority of churches has receded in importance
not only in Europe, where only small minorities attend religious services
regularly, but for many cosmopolitan Americans as well. Forty years ago,
sociologists observed that western religious institutions had begun to pass
from an "extremely significant position, socio-politically speaking—to
a position that is rather secondary, with a competitive structure similar
to that of the contemporary commercial market."[15] The liberal arts, bas-
tions of ethical reflection in higher education, now have to justify their
existence in a market-driven, consumerist society. In America a pervasive cynicism discredits the significance and/or ethical competence of
academics, who are often viewed as ineffectual, ivory tower "egg heads."
The nation is littered with Departments of Religion and Philosophy that

appear to manifest what the sociologist Max Weber feared most—the coming of an age of "specialists without spirit, sensualists without heart."[16] In actual practice, many Americans tend to collapse ethics into private, individual preferences, and ethical decision-making tends to give way to instantaneous, impulsive behavior.

Perhaps one way to grasp the situation is to view ourselves as living in between a modern and a late-modern existence. In fact, contemporary life is already "late-modern" in several senses.[17] The last half of the twentieth century saw a movement from the industrial age to the information age. The digital revolution is in full swing. Technology has spawned hundreds of television channels and e-mail is rapidly replacing "snail" mail. Paper airline tickets are going the way of the dinosaurs. The modern welfare state has evolved into the late-modern security state[18] that defends markets for transnational conglomerates in far-flung corners of the globe.[19] The post WWII East-West bi-polarization of power has given way to a monolithic geo-political order that is dominated by the United States.[20] Nuclear weapons have spread well beyond stockpiles in the U.S. and the former Soviet Union. And the mid-1970s witnessed a major economic shift: for the first time in history, the majority of the world's populace no longer lived by growing food and herding animals.[21]

In philosophy, the supremacy of human reason epitomized by modern science has become increasingly suspect. Legions of scholars have begun to doubt the modernist view that precise and definitive knowledge of the world is theoretically possible. Wittgenstein's transformative insight about language—that it does not simply mirror some independent reality out there, but rather is expressive of the meaning-worlds we inhabit,[22] has undermined commonsense notions of external or objective truth.[23] Indeed, some scholars are now viewing scientific truth as little more than narrative practice, a part of the language games played by specialized communities of practitioners.[24] And to further complicate matters, the movement away from timeless, universal truths has made us aware that we are socially situated within certain narrative traditions that may well be incommensurable.[25]

But strangely enough, religion is alive and well in the postmodern era. The secularization thesis—that religion would die out as persons "came of age" in the twentieth century—has lost much of its currency. The modernist view of religion as a childlike, immature hangover from a pre-modern worldview—is now open to reconsideration. Although many mainline Protestant denominations have seen a decline in attendance since the 1960s, evangelical and fundamentalist Christianity has flourished worldwide. In the west, the mega-church phenomenon is part of a new para-church, non-denominational religious development that threatens to eclipse the mainline, denominational movements. Increasing numbers of religious adherents espouse complex, diffuse faith orientations that often combine elements of various traditions—New Age, Buddhist, and Secularist—in unique syncretistic forms of "spirituality."[26] At the same time, the primary locus of Christianity has shifted from North America and Europe to Latin America and Africa. There are now more Christians in Africa than in all of Europe and North America combined. And in North America, Islam has eclipsed Judaism as the second largest non-Christian faith tradition. Thus, in the midst of the pluralism and relativity of late-modern existence, religious practice and alternative spiritualities not only persist, but have evolved in new directions.

THE DE-CENTERED SELF
& MODES OF ETHICAL REASONING

At the same time, at least in the western world, our late-modern predicament is marked by a de-centering of the self. The modernist idea of a rational, integrated ego in control of individual consciousness has been challenged by late-modern portrayals of a fragmented, multi-dimensional self. Social scientist Diane Margolis delineates three images of self that she correlates with three ideal-typical moral orientations in American life, any one of which a single individual may bring to the surface to suit varying circumstances.[27] The dominant image in North America today is the self-interested rational self—the *exchanger*. This aspect of self strives for emotional control by "perpetually balancing the quid pro quos of life."[28] The exchanger acts as if free from enduring social entanglements, and therefore can make and break commitments at will.

A much older and more traditional image of personhood is the *obligated* self, which is devoted to serving and nurturing others rather than to self-interest.[29] It is acutely conscious of operating within a network of obligations and managing the affective aspects of social relationships. Finally, the *cosmic* image of self stresses a continuity "with spiritual existence and is incorporated into an organic universe."[30] This self has no boundaries, and sees life as "a never-ending search for oneness with the universe."[31] Although most of us will tend to favor one of these three models of self in day-to-day life, at any given moment, we may shift from one to another.[32]

With its repudiation of universalism and the de-centering of the self, the late-modern ethos entails a double challenge, for it suggests that every individual is composed of competing selves interfacing with competing truths. And this appears to be an apt description of precisely what we find when we think critically about the landscape of ethics in the modern period. For example, these competing notions of self can be correlated with the three dominant approaches to ethical decision-making—or at least the three approaches most emphasized by mainstream Enlightenment ethicists: deontological, teleological, and relational methods of ethics. In order to see how this is the case, let us briefly review these approaches

In the **deontological** approach, we decide about the moral status of an activity by asking questions such as, "Who is the supreme authority?" or, "What is the right principle, rule or command to follow?" This approach is called "the ethics of the right" and emphasizes obedience and obligation. In the American context, deontologists may appeal to authorities such as God, the President or the Supreme Court; or ground their decisions on rules and commands from Scripture, the American Constitution, legal statutes, or professional codes of conduct. In deontological ethics, important rules (such as the Ten Commandments) can have the status of ironclad laws that rarely or never admit of exceptions. In this approach there is also a tendency to view certain activities themselves as inherently right or wrong. For instance, one might argue that lying is always wrong, even if by telling the truth you might cause someone serious harm. The deontological approach resonates in some ways with the obligated self's focus on acting with reference to a series of obligations and serving those perceived to be in authority to oneself.

In the **teleological** approach, on the other hand, we decide what to do by asking about the goal or end of human life. The Greek word for "end" or "aim" is *telos*; hence, "teleological" refers to thinking about ends or goals. Since the end is associated with what the teleologist thinks is good or worthy of being attained, this method is called "the ethics of the good." Also, since appeals to what we expect will result in good outcomes entail estimations of the future consequences of actions, the teleological approach is sometimes referred to as consequentialist ethics. Moreover, because the teleologist is often focused on utility—or concerned with ascertaining the means that are most useful in achieving the desired end—it is frequently called utilitarian ethics.

Whether resorting to hunches about what is likely to happen or relying on scientific projections of likely outcomes, the teleologist chooses among and prioritizes values. This is clearly different from being guided by the pre-established laws, rules, or norms of the deontologist. In America, for instance, a teleologist might decide to abort a fetus diagnosed with down's syndrome after weighing such possible outcomes and relevant values as the anticipated quality of life of the child, the impact of a down's syndrome baby on the quality of life of other siblings, the extraordinary financial burden, and risks to the mother's physical, psychological, or spiritual well-being. The teleologist has affinities with Margolis' *exchanger* self, who calculates the *quid pro quos* of life, and acts as if free from involuntary social commitments.

Strictly applied, each of the two above approaches has major limitations. By minimizing the importance of an act's consequences, the deontological method may well ignore morally relevant factors in a decision. Similarly, by presuming that one can know what the future holds, the teleological approach can degenerate into an abstract calculus of "the greatest good for the greatest number" that runs roughshod over the interests of minorities and individuals. To a certain extent, the idea that we must always choose between the two involves a false dichotomy.

In the modern history of ethics, a number of attempts have been made to refine these approaches, and to meld dimensions of both methods into new alternatives. For instance, H. Richard Niebuhr argued for a **relational** approach that asks not, "What is the rule or supreme authority?" nor "What is the greatest good to be realized?" but rather, "What is the most fitting action in this particular context?"[33] A relationalist might well incorporate both deontological and teleological methods in discerning what to do. Because a relational ethic stresses the moral agent's capacity to respond to what is happening to her or him in a context of relationships, it is called the "ethics of response" or, in some cases, "contextual ethics."

For example, a relationalist might decide that smoking marijuana for medicinal purposes is ethically justifiable not because the Bible fails to forbid it or because it would likely lead to better health, but because it provides the most fitting response to the situation of someone dying from cancer. This approach has affinities with the *cosmic* self's focus on transcending ordinary boundaries and searching for unity and oneness in the wider world. Like the other methods, the relational approach has noteworthy limitations. In particular, it tends to broaden the contours of what constitute morally relevant factors to such an extent that in practice it is often difficult to arrive at a definitive decision, let alone decide what values, principles, or norms may or may not be relevant in a particular circumstance.

In fact, none of these three modes of decision-making goes far enough in providing definitive guidance in most situations. The problem is not so much whether one appeals to rules or ends, authorities or good consequences, but what is the *nature* of the rules, *which* authorities are to be invoked, *what* ends are deemed praiseworthy, and *which* consequences are desired?[34] Moreover, if we view ourselves as living in a truly global context of relationships, how do we make decisions that do justice to that wider context? How are a plethora of relationships to be prioritized, and how can I anticipate responses to my responses so as to accurately discern the "fitting response"? And who is the "I" who discerns all of this? In actual practice, most of us rarely act purely as either an *exchanger, obligated* or *cosmic* self, but rather as some eclectic mixture of all three.

Understandably, American ethicists have responded to this predicament in different ways. Today, the unified ethos evoked in the story of the lifesaving station above has been fragmented into four "mainstream" schools of ethical thought—what I call communalism, neo-conservatism, liberalism, and postmodernism.[35] In addition, a number of alternative, "marginal" traditions have developed in the Americas, including feminist, womanist, gay and lesbian, African American, Latin American, Native American, and Asian American perspectives.[36] Although many of these perspectives overlap and intersect with mainline streams in certain respects, what distinguishes them from the latter is a shared concern for liberation from a hegemonic discourse, primarily one carried on by relatively affluent, white Anglo-Saxon males. Nevertheless, while all of these perspectives articulate important themes, we always come back to the postmodern conundrum: competing selves and competing truths.

And thus we come full circle to what amounts to a crisis in ethics in our late-modern world. The traditional appeal to so-called universal values or principles—for example in the work of such modernist thinkers as the social ethicist John Rawls[37]—was once assumed to be essential to ethical reasoning. Indeed, some have argued for what might be termed a "post-liberal" perspective[38] in which grounds for universality can still be recovered by focusing on such human experiences as emotions,[39] existential forebodings of death,[40] or structures of consciousness,[41] all of which appear to be universal in character. But if all value preferences are simply expressions of context-dependent narrative traditions, then how can one meaningfully speak of universal human attributes or experiences, let alone universal rights and obligations? And if there is no single, autonomous center of agency in the self, then how is coherent moral reasoning possible? Indeed, the postmodern turn has been viewed as dangerous precisely because it can be construed as leading toward a nihilistic rejection of even the possibility of normative ethics.

However, I want to argue that the way forward does not necessitate clinging to modernist claims about universal values or human experiences. Nor do I think that it is particularly helpful to latch on to any one of the competing ethical options, draw lines in the sand around that school's positions, and then take up arms against the other options. On a practical level, most Americans probably embrace aspects of each of the mainstream options. And each of these options, in turn, is rooted in broader currents of life and thought in American history. What we need to do is to view today's mainstream ethical options in historical context in order to begin to recover a sense of the breadth and scope of this hegemonic heritage, as well as to become critically aware of its limitations.

While the late-modern ethos makes it no longer possible to ascribe "universal truth" to any of these historical traditions, it is also disingenuous to proceed as if no positive moral themes were latent in our ethical heritage. In the next chapter, therefore, I will outline the contours of four overarching, mainstream stories or "cultural narratives" in American history: the Biblical covenant, the mission of America, the Enlightenment vision of progress and the baby boomer quest for personal well-being.[42] In the process, I will describe how each of today's mainstream ethical options represents an outgrowth of these larger moral traditions. I will also note how each of these options emphasizes at least one of the positive themes evoked in the parable of the lifesaving station—a profound sense of community, a commitment to mission, a rational approach to change, and a vision of personal fulfillment. Then, in subsequent chapters, I will explore strategies by which these themes can be revitalized and deepened by re-connecting with "the other" in the global neighborhood. But that is getting ahead of ourselves. What we need to do first is become re-acquainted with the mainstream moral traditions that have shaped the moral life of a majority of Ameicans, and to those I now turn.

TALKING POINTS

WHAT IS ETHICS? WHAT IS SOCIAL ETHICS?

- Try to remember doing something that you later regretted. What was it that you *knew better* than to do, but did anyway? What didn't you do at the time? Reflect on that particular case of *knowing better*. What values or principles were implied? What got in the way or prevented you from doing what you *knew was better?*
- Think about a "hot button" moral issue that really gets under your skin. To what extent, if any, would you say that this is a "social" issue? Why or why not?
- What do you personally think is "the highest good"? Why do you think this? Would everyone in your family agree with you, or would some of your relatives think in terms of other "highest goods"? Discuss.
- Think about an ethical decision you've made in the past month or so. How did you decide what to do? Did your decision presuppose any religious values or teachings? If so, what were they? If not, how would you justify your decision?

MORAL "DIS-EASE" IN OUR LATE-MODERN LIMBO

- Do you think there are *universal* moral values or rules (that is, values or rules that are true for everyone in all times and places)? If so, what are they and how do we know they are true? If not, how do you tell right from wrong?
- Take your moral blood pressure. Reflecting on how you treat people, what are your strengths and weaknesses? Are you fulfilling your ethical obligations? What are two things you could change about you to be a more responsible self?
- Does the parable of the lifesaving station remind you of your own place of worship? If so, how? If not, how has it avoided these pitfalls? How would you characterize the mission or purpose of the community you most identify with?
- Without looking in the footnotes, can you name authors or advocates associated with the "marginal" ethical perspectives alluded to in the chapter? Who are they? What do you know about them? If you have trouble naming any of them, why do you think you are not familiar with them?

CHAPTER 3

IN SEARCH OF OUR MORAL HERITAGE

DRINKING FROM OLD WINESKINS[1]

THE BIBLICAL COVENANT & CONTEMPORARY COMMUNALISTS

The Pilgrims who landed in New England in the 1600s intended to build what H. Richard Niebuhr has called "the Kingdom of God in America."[2] Although the majority of early American settlers did not have such aspirations, there is no doubt that the Pilgrims viewed themselves as obedient servants in a covenant relationship with God. From their vantage point, God gave them a promised land and the assurance of future prosperity on this land, in exchange for their undying trust and loyalty. While the Pilgrims were thus subservient to God, they were also, like their Israelite counterparts, the elect or chosen among all peoples. In covenant relation with God, they saw themselves as stewards, not owners, of God's creation.

Pilgrims were obliged to love both God and neighbor, and this entailed practicing a kinship *shalom* (or brotherly well-being) which in turn generated an ethos of voluntary self-sacrifice.[3] This ethos extended to warfare, for according to the Biblical story, God gives the gift of land to Israel, in part at least, to punish the present inhabitants of the land.[4] At the same time, just as Abigail appealed to David's better instincts, the Pilgrims were to preserve life in acts of peacemaking.[5] Cognizant of the need for social justice as espoused by Old Testament prophets, they were also to obey all of God's laws, including that of having no other gods but "him," Sabbath-keeping, treating workers fairly, and caring for orphans, the poor, strangers, and widows.[6]

As Christians, the Pilgrims developed the Biblical story further by adducing the life and teachings of Jesus. Jesus proclaims the reign of God by teaching in aphorisms and parables that often suggest such reversals of ordinary expectations as the rejection of the rich and the exaltation of the lowly.[7] And since Jesus' life was typified by self-denial, so you and I are likewise called to give sacrificially of ourselves. Indeed, in the Biblical covenant narrative, the primary view of Jesus is that of the sacrificial Christ of faith. He is the Son of God who is sent into the world to reconcile it with God. He is God's gift freely given to us, and thus the one to whom we must respond in discipleship.

To a certain extent, contemporary communalists have notable affinities with the Pilgrim covenanters. The communalist, typified by the 20th century philosopher Alasdair MacIntyre,[8] stresses an existential commitment to the beliefs, institutions, and practices of his or her particular community. Communities are believed to be essential for sustaining moral beliefs. Traditional values and mores are disclosed in certain texts and voices, which have a special authority. Over time, new interpretations of the moral life can and do emerge, but they are constrained by the parameters of the community ethos disclosed in what are considered to be the authoritative texts and debates or, in MacIntyre's phraseology, the "tradition-constitutive enquiries," within the tradition. The many varieties of communalists range from the conservative evangelical followers of Lewis Smedes,[9] to those of the anti-enlightenment pacifist, Stanley Hauerwas.[10] They can be found in both "red" and "blue" America. They represent a wide range of perspectives on issues such as the relationship of church and state, although they are generally suspicious of schools of thought and institutions beyond their sectarian perimeters.

One of the central elements in both Biblical Covenant and sectarian communalist moral visions is a profound sense of community. In a sermon aboard the *Arbella*, John Winthrop exhorted the colonists who would establish the Massachusetts Bay Colony in 1630 in these words:

> We must entertain each other in brotherly affection; we must be willing to abridge ourselves of our superfluities for the supply of others' necessities. . . . We must delight in each other, make others' conditions our own, rejoice together, mourn together, labor and suffer together. . . .[11]

For the Pilgrims, the quality of community experience was linked to their response to God's gifts—it was a manifestation of both love of God and the love of neighbor that the love of God entailed.[12]

Within this ethical tradition, things begin to go awry when adherents forget that the community owes its very existence to a being, power, or "tradition-constituted" heritage that not only brought it into being, but still nurtures it and sustains it. Losing sight of its "foundation myth" renders the community vulnerable to the self-deception of reducing the covenantal relationship to a formulaic simplicity.[13] Rather than existing in a free, open-ended relationship of trust in which God may respond to our responses in unpredictable ways, we begin to think that if *I* trust and obey, then *I* will necessarily prosper; or, if *I* suffer disaster, then it has to be because *I* have sinned. In the American context, we who are healthy and wealthy delude ourselves into thinking that it must be due to our righteousness; it naturally follows that those who are poor—whether here or in the Two-Thirds world—must be so because they are less righteous or somehow less deserving. The prophet's call for social justice is drowned out in easy condemnations of those who are simply not favored by God.[14] By contrast, liberation theologies argue that God is working in history to liberate all of creation, and is partial to the poor, who occupy a special place in God's plan of salvation. In this connection, some womanist theologians have begun to argue for cross-cultural and non-sectarian approaches to ethics that reach across traditions.[15]

A concomitant problem is that covenanters and communitarians tend to view their own sectarian belief systems and practices as inherently superior to those of outsiders. After all, either God elects them, or they have had the peculiar good fortune to be born into what they deem the best tradition in the world. Therefore, while cultivating extraordinary bonds of community among themselves, and even while debating or practicing mutual criticism within their own enclaves, they tend not to see a need for critical assessment of their own communities in the light of outside perspectives. Why reach across ethical divides if all the answers you need are provided in your own tradition?

Thus, the common good begins to be seen as the common good *of the members of the covenantal community.* And one of the strengths of the covenantal position—that it resists attempts to justify action in terms of personal or group self-interest[16]—becomes compromised when the interest of one's tribe or nation becomes the locus of the moral life. Reflecting back on our lifesaving station parable, the station loses its moral vision—and begins to loose its profound sense of community—as soon as it perceives those dirty, divergent people as negatively affecting their club's social life. What should be a series of interactions recalling the very *raison d'être* of the station—that is, reaching out in compassion to aid the strange newcomers—becomes instead a motive for circling the wagons and excluding anyone foreign to the community. By not embracing the other who is really "other," they subvert their own community. And yet, at its best, the covenantal tradition evokes a sense of order in which we can depend upon God's gifts of land and community, and freely respond as gift-givers, with special regard for the poor and the oppressed.

THE MISSION OF AMERICA AND TODAY'S "NEOCONS"

In the American colonies, the story of the Biblical covenant quickly became intertwined with the story of the mission of America when the Pilgrims joined hands with—and sometimes morphed into—the patriots of an emerging world power.[17] This mission of America story was two-fold. First, Americans began to view themselves as having a special worldwide destiny to be an example of God's plan for a free and democratic nation. Second, they had a responsibility to encourage the spread of these values, by force if necessary, to all people everywhere, "leading them toward a future world state of . . . liberty yet unknown."[18] Like the Israelites of old, Americans had experienced an exodus—fleeing Europe and traversing the Atlantic—and had been given a new land. And this was just the beginning. The first Great Awakening (1730–60) and the American Revolution (1776) were viewed as harbingers of a coming millennial age.[19] The former united the many different denominations on the frontier by enabling individual Americans to see themselves as part of a corporate nation state on a mission. The Revolution gave birth to a nation of free people with supposedly unalienable rights under a government opposed in principle to treating people unjustly. America would become the prototypical nation of the millennial age.

Furthermore, the Biblical story's image of the faithful self soon merged with the "mission of America" image of the faithful nation.[20] The second Great Awakening (1800–1830) gave rise to a host of schools, religious education programs, associations, and movements for temperance and world peace—all calling on America to be an example to the world.[21] In addition, Americans began to believe that America had its own unique Manifest Destiny. Herman Melville spoke of the political Messiah as having "come to *us* [Americans]."[22] Josiah Strong stretched manifest destiny into a global racial doctrine when he argued that, "God was training the Anglo-Saxon race in America for a mission to the whole world."[23]

Although the "mission of America" story has since undergone reformulations—as anti-communist crusade in the Cold War and Vietnam eras and more recently as the worldwide anti-terrorist campaign since 9-11—it is still alive and well in the American moral landscape. The recent ascendancy of the so-called "neoconservative" or "neocon" movement represents a particularly high profile incarnation of the story. Neocons are associated with the political ideologies of a host of thinkers, including the philosopher Leo Strauss[24] and the authors Alan Bloom[25] and Irving Kristol.[26] They are also affiliated with policy think tanks such as the American Enterprise Institute, the Heritage Foundation and the Project for the New American Century.

While the term "neocon" is somewhat controversial—detractors of neocons often use it in a pejorative sense, and some neocons are averse to being so labeled—it does reference a distinctive set of political goals and ideologies.[27] Neocons espouse an aggressive, militant approach to a foreign policy that champions the universality of democracy, "regime changes" for "rogue" nations to make them more reflective of U.S. values, "moral clarity" in military incursions, free trade, and when necessary, military unilateralism. Since many of the prominent figures labeled as neocons are actually registered Democrats (Irving Kristol once described a neocon as a "liberal mugged by reality"), the term is non-partisan, though Strauss and others have no doubt influenced prominent neocon ideologues in the second Bush Administration, including Vice-President Dick Cheney, former Defense Secretary Donald Rumsfeld and Deputy Defense Secretary Paul Wolfowitz.

In their unbridled commitment to patriotism and nationalism, their zeal to use military power to spread democracy worldwide, and their determination to maintain and expand America's military strength lest any nation eclipse American military might, today's neocons represent a continuation of the "mission of America" legacy. In his recent book, *The Pentagon's New Map,* the neocon Thomas Barnett stresses the need to defend America's nexus of power and influence (the "core") against encroachments by the poor countries of the Two-Thirds world (the "gap").[28] Clearly, this defensive concern to protect America's interests is in tension with the altruistic goal of spreading American values—while not necessarily spreading the economic benefits of the American way of life!

The trouble with the mission of America story, and especially its recent neocon edition, is not simply that it tends to bifurcate the world into "us" and "them," the "good guys" and "bad guys," the "liberators" and the "terrorists," or the "free world" and the "socialists." A greater danger is that it can lead to a Machiavellian view of both domestic and international politics. Acting on such slogans as Barry Goldwater's "America: Right or Wrong" would undermine the very values of freedom and democracy that are supposedly sacred to neocons. The recent war in Iraq—frequently viewed as a neocon foreign policy coup—has been waged on the pretext of freeing Iraqi citizens from tyranny, but it has also been charged with compromising the government's honesty as well as the human rights of both Americans and foreigners. Indeed, neocons like Jeanne Kirkpatrick have long been willing to support what she termed "moderately repressive regimes" on the grounds of realpolitik.

In terms of the moral ethos of the lifesaving station, the "mission" of helping those in distress gets lost in the rush to build and expand an empire. Like the builders of successive stations in the parable, today's neocons appear to be extending America's military dominance abroad in the service of protecting America's comfort zone at home, while the world's poor, hungry, and diseased are dying outside the door. This parochial patriotism has lost touch with the Biblical story's emphasis on peace and justice for all. When the mission becomes reinforcing a pattern of consumption, how far behind are cynicism, deceit and corruption? To be sure, the neo-cons' missionary commitment is to make the world a better place that resonates with the altruistic ends of the first lifesavers in our parable, and most have not lost this sense of mission, but the mission has tended to serve as a cover story for the building of an empire that both at home and abroad benefits only a few. One clear indicator of this is that Hispanic theologians who have grown up in or near the U.S. have been particularly outspoken critics of the imperialistic nature of neocon policies.[29]

ENLIGHTENMENT LIBERALISM AND TODAY'S "LIBERALS"

During the first century of the American experiment, a public or civil religion emerged alongside the Biblical covenant and mission of America narratives. For men like Benjamin Franklin and Thomas Jefferson, Enlightenment notions of reason, progress and natural law began to supplant Biblical notions of grace, faith and covenant.[30] God was still involved with the world as creator and judge, but for persons of the Enlightenment, the moral life increasingly became a thing of one's own creation. Jefferson's universal gospel, *The Life and Morals of Jesus of Nazareth*, consists of excerpts from the canonical gospels that contain non-miraculous events and teachings that appeal to reason. The "self-made" man of Franklin's *Autobiography* develops his moral character not by surrendering himself in obedience to God, but by following a program of practical moral wisdom that enhances personal success. His "project of arriving at moral perfection" focuses on such clear, practical virtues as "resolution," "industry," "justice," and "moderation"—which combined to promote material well-being and social acceptance. Indeed, financial success and public renown were evidence of good character. In a rational, cause-and-effect world, hard work, thrift, self-discipline and sincerity not only led to wealth and fame, but also became the preeminent marks of high moral stature.

In the emerging civil religion of worldly success, public virtue mattered more than private salvation. Both Franklin and Jefferson stressed the need for a common morality based on reason and a rational apprehension of the fundamental laws of the universe.[31] The Declaration of Independence articulated a public religion—sometimes called "the democratic faith"—in terms of what were invoked as universal and self-evident moral values:

equality, life, liberty, happiness and unalienable individual rights. The United States Constitution represented a fusing of biblical and natural law to form a moral law that was viewed as having God's stamp of approval. To be a responsible citizen in the New Republic meant that one took charge of one's life, exercising power responsibly according to the moral law. This meant living out one's calling, which was to pursue personal goals that simultaneously benefited the community. The highest good was to succeed in one's calling.

During the Industrial Revolution of the late 1800s, this sense of a socially responsible "calling" as an element of the pursuit of individual success becomes wedded to evolutionary notions of progress and to what the philosopher Herbert Spencer described as "the survival of the fittest."[32] The righteous individual who works hard, invests capital wisely, and competes effectively in the marketplace will not only survive, but becomes an architect of his own future, reaping huge profits.[33] This "gospel of wealth" valued individualism, private property, accumulation of wealth, and competition.[34] The individual's quest for unlimited economic success now becomes a single vision of life in which the best and the brightest lead the rest of us toward unparalleled progress. While those at the lower end of the economy may suffer, the championing of this scenario ensures the survival of the fittest—who are, of course, enjoined to be generous toward the less fortunate. Since economic growth is viewed as potentially unlimited, and jobs at the upper echelons are always being created, anyone with intelligence, ambition, and self-discipline should be able to rise from rags to riches.

Today's liberals, the latest successors of the Enlightenment narrative, have become a weary, embattled minority in American culture. Indeed, the term "liberal" is increasingly used in even more pejorative ways than is the case with the term "neocon." Our colloquial uses of the term often obscure its original denotations, which date from the Enlightenment and are associated with the "modernist" perspective. Within this broader historical context, many of us are still essentially "liberals," whether we recognize it or not. Notable liberal authors include John Kenneth Galbraith, Michael Walzer,[35] and Michael Lind.[36]

Contemporary liberals, following in the footsteps of the 18th century philosopher Immanuel Kant,[37] use reason to claim that they can discover the good apart from any particular social allegiance or loyalty. Liberals conceive of the individual and individual human rights, as having ultimate moral value. They also emphasize the idea of universal human progress, the empirical search for truth, the scientific method and the examination of traditional values and mores under the penetrating light of reason. In the context of the culture wars, such questioning can reach a fever pitch. In *Reasonable Creatures*, for example, the feminist Katha Pollitt has entitled one of her chapters, "Why I Hate Family Values."[38] Other liberals are associated with a wide range of ethical positions, from the objectivism of Ayn Rand[39] to the secular humanism of Paul Kurtz.[40]

Anyone who combines a distrust of traditionalist approaches to problem-solving ("But we've always done it this way") with a reliance on reason and a concern for progress will understand the lifesaver's initial interest in enhancing and updating their station. But the Enlightenment liberal's glorification of self-control and mastery results in a singular vision of one's own competency that disavows the Bible's insistence that life, land, and fortune are gifts. The myth of the uninterrupted march of progress tends to deny the contingencies and mysteries of human life.

Another problem is that by exalting the individual and the individual's autonomous capacity for reasoning, the liberal often distrusts institutional authorities. Liberalism can degenerate into a programmatic attack on the status quo when it repudiates conventional values and celebrates change for change's sake. In the contemporary American context, liberals sometimes appear "anti-American" because they revel in critiques of patriotic displays and appeal to broader humanistic values.[41] Finally, because they put such a premium on our capacity to guide our lives by reason, they often overlook the degree to which social position constrains and constricts the very nature of rationality. In short, from the perspective of the oppressed, liberals often appear to pontificate about freedom and social justice while blissfully living the comfortable middle-class lives of what Galbraith calls "the contented majority."[42] Unaware of how their own social situation influences their thinking, they loftily assume that they know everything they need to know about how "the-other-half" lives. Still, even though various liberation theologies—African American, Native American, Latin American and Asian American—have correctly exposed the moral shallowness that too often afflicts liberalism, its advocacy for rational discourse, individual freedoms, and constructive social change is important for the moral life.

BABY BOOMERS AND POSTMODERNISTS

In post-World War II America, the Enlightenment liberal's gospel of hard work and economic success began to be overshadowed by a widespread concern for personal self-esteem and well-being. As the face-to-face familiarity of rural America gave way to the faceless anonymity of urban life, individuals turned inward for a sense of value, meaning, and purpose. As women entered the workforce in record numbers and middle-class youth were afforded unprecedented educational opportunities, the Baby Boomer generation achieved relative affluence in an ever-expanding economy. Freed from fears of scarcity (which their parents had experienced in the Depression years) but culturally adrift in a rapidly changing, pluralistic society, many boomers found themselves in a moral and spiritual vacuum. Lacking the anchor of a biblical covenant, cynical about the mission of America, and more or less successful in professional careers, many boomers sought meaning and purpose by taking up social causes and by adopting therapeutic or techno-consumerist visions of the good life.[43]

The union, women's suffrage, civil rights, anti-war, farm worker, feminist, environmental and gay rights movements of the twentieth century all represented moral crusades for social reform. Each provided opportunities to become involved in a cause greater than oneself. As part of such a movement, one could re-capture a sense of social connectedness and moral purpose in what might seem an otherwise alien, anomic, or even immoral society. But, unlike the Pilgrims and many of today's super patriots, war resisters and feminists seldom acted in response to a biblical covenant or a notion of manifest destiny. Rather, they advocated for peace and women's full humanity out of largely individualistic convictions about justice and human rights. While their detractors frequently appealed to biblical or patriotic worldviews, these "leftists" appealed to such humanistic (i.e., Enlightenment) concepts as equality, distributive justice, mutuality and sustainability. By identifying with a social cause, the activist created a purpose in life.

Once the sixties generation began to settle into America's suburban enclaves, however, many turned to therapeutic models of the good life. Although the majority may not have sought psychological counseling, they nonetheless found meaning and direction in life by developing quality interpersonal relationships.[44] Magazines entitled *Self* and *Psychology Today* reflected the new emphasis on personality, shared feelings, authenticity ("being real") and integrity ("being whole"). "Pulling yourself together," letting go of "hang-ups," and having "meaningful relationships" with "significant others" typified the spirit of this search.[45] A critical element in this story is that the relationship in question is evaluated in terms of its potential to enable each person to "do his or her own thing." The movie, *Looking for Mr. Goodbar*—in which a woman leads a double life as a conventional teacher by day and as a seductive siren by night—epitomized the shadowy side of an ethos in which making fleeting romantic connections can become one's *raison d'etre*.

Finally, extraordinary technological innovations have combined with a growth economy to create the techno-consumerist story of well-being. In this narrative, the good life is achieved through increasing use of, and engagement with, the latest technological gadget or system. It is a story of the computer geek, the perpetual tourist, and the inveterate shopper. It is achieving well-being through "international patterns of consumption"—purchasing the products of transnational corporations sold by means of mass advertising. It frequently entails a submersion in mass entertainment.

Such mass communication media as the cinema, television with its hundreds of cable and satellite channels, and recently the internet, have enticed Americans to spend more and more time gratifying their desire to be entertained. For fanatical sports fans, bored housewives and under-employed senior citizens, watching television has become a way of entering another life of sports heroes, sit-coms, and game shows. For those of generations X and Y, surfing, chatting, gambling and purchasing on the Internet have become major elements of the contemporary lifestyle. Unlike the Pilgrims, today's consumerist sees well-being as dependent not on obedience to a covenant with God, but on owning or at least enjoying the latest entertainment system or computer technology. While the story of the mission of America evokes a heritage of military and political heroism with strong links to natural and international communities, the consumerist myth celebrates the individual's own private quest for happiness in the pursuit of purely personal interests and relationships. And, in contradistinction to the enlightenment story of success earned by self-denial and hard work, the story of personal well-being through technology is a narrative of self-gratification and pleasure. Although it usually entails holding down a job (rather than contributing to community life by pursuing one's "calling"), it is primarily a "living for the now" centered on the leisure activities made possible by the job's income.

To a certain extent, today's postmodernists are the intellectual cousins of the baby boomers, particularly regarding the latter's preoccupation with personal well-being. As noted in the previous section, the postmodernism exemplified by philosopher Jacques Derrida[46] calls into question the universality of reason presupposed by the Enlightenment liberal. "Postmodernism" as a broad interdisciplinary constellation of thought defies any attempt at definition beyond listing family resemblances and, as noted earlier, should be distinguished from the term "postmodern," which refers simply to our social location in the "postmodern" world. Postmodernism is usually described in terms of what it rejects with respect to modernity, although it includes both deconstructive and reconstructive trajectories.[47] Indeed, it is important to be aware that the "post" of "postmodern" suggests a linkage with the "modern" which follows it. "Constructive" postmodernists, such as Jurgen Habermas[48] and David Tracy,[49] seek to extend and complete the modern project by building on the intellectual categories and social practices of the modern world.

"Deconstructive" postmodernists, such as Michael Foucault[50] and Mark C. Taylor,[51] reject the modernist project altogether by attacking all apparent necessities and absolutes.

The baby boomers and their postmodern counterparts articulate values that resonate with the later cadre of "life-savers" in our parable. Those who built the physical fitness center, hired the personal trainer, sponsored wellness workshops, and paid underlings to perform the actual work of rescuing of the shipwrecked have affinities with boomers who strive for their own personal sense of the good life. This has both altruistic and non-altruistic vectors. For example, while some or those fictitious members resisted ending the club's lifesaving activities, they eventually capitulated to more selfish preoccupations and formed exclusivist groups that allocated funds to decorations and liturgical paraphernalia. Their initial interest in the social cause of rescuing those lost at sea all too soon evaporated.

And this is precisely the problem with the boomer and postmodern focus on well-being through participation in a social cause. An intellectual and/or emotional attraction to helping others or promoting justice, unless rooted in either a long-standing tradition of social action or in solidarity with a community of suffering, is likely to dissipate when it encounters difficulties. Moreover, the pursuit of one's own physical and emotional well-being doesn't allow for repeated interruptions of one's routine or for invasions of one's personal space. Hence, as in the parable, the club eventually has to abandon all lifesaving activities in order to protect the exclusivity of the club's turf. This contrasts with the plea of the Latin American liberation theologian Gustavo Gutierrez, who argues that we must intentionally interrupt our normal routines in search of the other who is in dire need.[52]

Furthermore, like the liberal and the neocon, the postmodernist is frequently the prisoner of a self-created and peculiarly affluent-western subjectivity. For instance, academic life in North America is constitutive of a myriad of small life-worlds, each with its own operative values, norms, and taken-for-granted assumptions about the nature of reality, practices, and institutional affiliations. Viewed from an anthropological perspective, each academic institution becomes a tribal enclave of its own making.[53] Finally, because the postmodernist eschews any substantive moral foundations, she not only loses the neocon's sense of mission and purpose, but she cannot persuasively appeal to the liberal's moral ideals to counter those who attack such ideals. She is the consummate solipsist because she thinks that she cannot be aware of anything beyond her own experiences. In the American context, this orientation is characterized by a kind of moral atrophy, expressed in such phrases as: "Different strokes for different folks," "If it feels good, do it," and "To each his own."

The postmodernist lives in a sort of amoral abyss—simply leaping ahead by impulse, "going for it" on a hunch, impulse or whim. This essentially amoral posture stands in stark contrast to the morally pregnant disposition of Native American ethicists who ground moral action in harmonious relationships with nature and the human community.[54]

However, to the credit of boomers and postmodernists alike, we can no longer impose a single authorized version of moral or political truth on the rest of the world.[55] By insisting that moral knowledge is the creation of a particular community in a particular place at a particular time, postmodernists bring us down to earth and force us to recognize the degree to which we all really are socially situated within certain narrative traditions. Postmodernists may fail to appreciate that this is as true for them as for anyone else, yet ironically their concern for "otherness" is crucial for ethics. Indeed, as I will next propose, it is by migrating from our own multi-faceted moral heritage into the world of the "other" that we recognize anew and begin to transform that very heritage.[56]

IN SEARCH OF NEW WINESKINS

The old wineskins of our American moral heritage—the Biblical covenant, the mission of America, the Enlightenment, and the Baby Boomer moral narratives together with their contemporary successors—have bequeathed us a vintage wine. It is a blend of four core moral orientations: the covenanter's profound sense of community, the neocon's commitment to mission, the liberal's celebration of change and progress, and the boomer's quest for self-realization. These wineskins hail from an earlier era and have served their purpose. The fact that they are leaking badly should not be cause for despair, nor should their present inadequacy deter us from savoring and salvaging the wine they contained.

Indeed, each of the core moral orientations has something valuable to contribute to our moral life today. Further, the postmodern insight that all knowledge is context-specific does not therefore necessarily imply that the values associated with these orientations cannot be shared within or across cultures. In the United States, for example, we have all participated in and inherited a single, albeit diverse, moral tapestry that is still being woven today. The problem is largely our failure to see the tapestry as a whole; we tend to operate in our own patch of cloth, to overlook the limitations of that patch, and to derogate other patches. Like competing weavers who are jealous of each other's fabrics, we get bogged down by in-fighting. What we need to do, in short, is to see ourselves from the perspective of someone beyond the loom.

Since we find ourselves in the early stages of a new axial age, I propose that two compelling factors can provide that vision. First, while the postmodern predicament may initially seem to present an alarming prospect of incompleteness and relativism, it can also serve as an open-ended invitation to new ethical insights. What appeared fixed and immovable is now seen as potentially fluid and changeable. The postmodern turn prompts an unhinging of our attachment to existing ethical assumptions and an openness to traditions very different from our own, especially non-western traditions. Second, the globalization process is generating a phenomenon unprecedented in human history: the "global village." We drive cars from Japan, buy furniture assembled in China, eat bananas from Columbia, drink wine from Chile, vacation in the Caribbean, and hang Christmas ornaments made in India. Most of the garments in most of our closets are made outside of North America. The prospect of engaging and even embracing our global neighbors holds out new possibilities of seeing ourselves as others see us and being exposed to novel moral ideals and lifestyles that have elsewhere stood the test of time.

In this regard, the existence of vital, practical, innovative moral traditions in far corners of the globe represents an extraordinary resource for ethics. If only as a practical matter, we need to take these traditions seriously because our post-modern predicament admits of no other choice. The old wineskins have dried and split, and new wineskins have yet to be fashioned. Trying to return to our old, culturally specific wineskins would be equivalent to trying to return to a pre-modern past with pre-modern technology. In any event, without learning about the perspectives of these "others," it is not possible to do justice to the radical pluralism of the global village,[57] nor adequately address the crisis of ethics in the small life-worlds of our postmodern age. I will conclude this chapter by describing three personal experiences that have shed light on the process of how new wineskins might be created: conversations with Indian scholars, coming to understand the value of social movements (including the Jesus movement), and gaining a renewed appreciation of remote societies.

While traveling through India in the summer of 2003, I was invited to speak about global ethics at the University of Madras.[58] I stressed the importance of local contexts, critiqued the notion of a monolithic ethic, and argued for a multilateral sharing of value traditions. Although appreciative of my concern for context, the Indian theologian Felix Wilfred[59] responded, "We need to be pulled by what others challenge us to be." Wilfred asserted that it was not enough to simply draw on the best ethical reflection in one's own tradition and then argue a particular context-laden position in relation to others. That is, ethics is more than merely espousing the values particular to our own moral heritage. It involves a dynamic encounter with moral traditions different from our own. In fact, for Wilfred, ethical contemplation really begins when our moral contexts collide with the moral contexts of others, pulling us in new directions. It implies a continual stretching beyond parochial political, economic, and cultural loyalties.

But this conception of ethics begs a prior question, namely, "How do our encounters with others result in our being pulled in new directions?" Surely not everyone who simply encounters people of other cultures is seriously affected or changed by such experiences. What about all the academics, diplomats, military personnel or missionaries who interact with foreigners only to retire at the end of the day even more convinced of the essential rightness of their own convictions? Indeed, a great deal depends on the quality, nature, and scope of encounters with our global neighbors—and on the predispositions, agendas and flexibility of those who embark on cross-cultural ventures.

For one thing, we must in the first place acknowledge a need to be pulled. Following H. R. Niebuhr, we should resolve not to pursue a course of action with the idea that all righteousness is on our side.[60] Second, we have to recognize that undergoing the experience of being pulled is integral to our own moral development. It is not merely a question of being humble about one's own degree of righteousness, but of realizing the need to encounter a position other than one's own in order to experience moral growth. As the Peruvian theologian Gustavo Gutierrez insists, it is crucial that we enter an "altogether unfamiliar world" by going out of our way to encounter the "dominated and the oppressed."[61] Third, our own perspective needs to change. In my case, such change has been rooted in a series of existential experiences of solidarity, suffering, and acknowledgment of self-deception, happenings that I will describe in the ensuing chapters.[62]

But not all changes are *good* changes. If we cast about for moral anchors, how will we know that we're not being duped? No one is completely neutral. Whom can we trust to guide us in the search for new wineskins? Given a readiness to be pulled by the other who is "other," Wilfred suggests that we focus on social movements rather than on more established cultural or religious institutions. Let us reflect on a couple of definitions in this connection. A "movement" is a "change of place, position or posture" that entails "a connected and long continued series of acts and events tending toward some . . . end."[63] "Social movements" are defined as "diffusely organized or heterogeneous groups of people . . . tending toward . . . a generalized common goal."[64] Hence, we could characterize social movements as heterogeneous collectivities of persons concerned about social change who are working together toward a shared end or *telos*. The concerns for "changing places" and acting "toward some end" imply a moral critique, however subtle, regarding the prevailing status quo.

In India, for example, the movement for independence from colonial rule constituted a powerful wave of moral experience. By bringing together a wide array of groups, it cut across caste, racial, and ethnic lines, representing a dynamic mix of religious traditions. Mahatma Gandhi's ethical orientation combined elements of Hindu and Christian moral teachings. Because social movements bring together *heterogeneous* persons and groups, they represent potential laboratories for being "pulled by" others. Because they coalesce around common goals or aims, they also constitute enclaves of *shared* moral experience. That is, genuine encounters with otherness occur alongside of discrete moments of consensus building around issues of moral significance. Consequently, a strong and enduring social movement can develop authoritative moral perspectives in a pluralistic context.

The problem of course, is that not all social movements are *good* social movements. The Nazi movement and today's neo-Nazi clones are clearly grim reminders of the demonic side of movements. But others are less clear-cut. For example, former Disciples of Christ pastor Jim Jones formed a church that initially stressed interracial equality and ministry to the poor, but what began as an outreach movement quickly turned inward, vilifying those outside the movement and dehumanizing those within. Such apparently "good" movements can turn sour when they lose or suppress what Mathies refers to as "dissenting strands within a tradition."[65]

To summarize the above argument, I contend that a "good" social movement is one that is *both* "other-regarding" rather than self-serving, *and* one that maintains its heterogeneous character so that dissenting strands of opinion are acknowledged and even nurtured. Such a movement treats its neighbors, near and far, especially those outside the group, with compassion and dignity. It will resist developing a personality cult around the leader such that her or his views attain the status of unquestioned doctrine. But above all, to be transformative of the status quo a movement must embody both heterogeneity of peoples and ideas and a shared *telos* regarding the need for change.

This argument applies to the moral narratives of social movements as well. Just as it is difficult to identify dissenting strands within Nazi nationalism, so the work of a Christian communitarian such as Stanley Hauerwas is vulnerable to the critique that it is really not open to serious engagement with such radically different, cross-cultural narratives as those associated with a Buddhist or a Taoist tradition. What is needed rather, is what Douglas Hicks has termed "respectful pluralism"—creating a culture of mutual respect.[66] Such pluralism resists exclusivist beliefs and honors cultural diversity. Indeed, the very Enlightenment ethics rejected by Hauerwas honors—at least in theory—such values as tolerance, pluralism and dialogue. The most fundamental problem with Enlightenment ethics is its Eurocentric bias, for while it may extol the *telos* of justice and human rights, it lacks the thoroughgoing heterogeneous vision of justice required for living in today's global village. Movements such as the Rastafarians of Jamaica and the South African freedom fighters (featured in Chapters Five and Six respectively) represent significant moral resources in this regard.

And this is where Jesus becomes particularly relevant. While we westerners may see Jesus as some kind of individualistic savior, itinerant cynic philosopher, superhuman guardian spirit, shaman, prophet, or moral hero, it is important to recognize him as part of a movement—one which, like that of the Buddha, eventually took on his name.[67] And what makes the Jesus movement so ethically significant is that it ultimately derived from the First Axial Age. This was a time with many parallels to our postmodern situation, one in which long-accepted patterns of authority were being challenged, a traditional metaphysic was under attack, the old religions were not working as well as they used to, and common certainties and assumptions were being widely questioned.[68] The original Jesus movement discerned by the Jesus Seminar championed a God who shocked people, showed little interest in an afterlife, countenanced acts of disobedience, and modeled degrees of selflessness and suffering that went against the grain of established authority. It also emerged in a Jewish world where competing schools of thought—including Sadducees, Pharisees, Essenes and Zealots—were all seeking adherents. This is not the place to develop such a line of research, but it would be fascinating to compare and contrast these schools with the four American moral options outlined above. Would today's neocons have some affinities with the Zealots of Jesus' time? Would not our liberals share family resemblances with the Pharisees?

In any event, it appears that the historical Jesus, whether we consider the individual or the movement, never identified completely with any of the competing options of his time, although his followers probably included representatives of many factions. I contend that the movement's heterogeneity and singular commitment to a vision of the divine domain mark it as a crucial ethical resource for our dawning axial age. In each of the chapters that follow, therefore, we shall discuss the potential relevance of Jesus as another "foreigner" who can provide us with a fresh look at ourselves. The irony is that in the United States, where Christianity has been the dominant religious tradition almost from the inception of the Republic, institutional Christianity has rarely encountered Jesus as foreigner. While the American image of Jesus has assumed many forms in the past three hundred years—from a muscular fighter to a mild-mannered healer and miracle worker—many contemporary Christians· imagine that if alive today, Jesus would be the nation's number one cheerleader, extolling democracy and championing private enterprise.[69] But if we are serious about successfully navigating the paradigm shift in values that is emerging in the present age, we need to get to know the Jesus who galvanized the counter-cultural movement that produced what New Testament scholar Wayne Meeks has described as a "tectonic shift of cultural values."[70]

Finally, we can also learn something in our postmodern world by spending time with contemporaries from remote, partially pre-modern regions of the world, especially islanders in the South Pacific. We can learn at least three valuable lessons from them. First, by focusing on how persons treat one another and the earth in the microcosm of an "island village," we can re-envision social and ecological ethics in the "global village." Islanders offer us moral insights for survival in this new world, because for centuries they have survived and coexisted in fragile habitats. And except for the most daring among them, like us today who inhabit a vulnerable and precarious planet, they had nowhere else to go.

Second, Pacific Islanders love to tell stories, and their legends are repositories of moral wisdom. And given the essentially oral nature of island cultures, their moral traditions are rooted in everyday experience, not the abstractions of our highly literate late-modern world.[71] That is, they convey an *existential authenticity* that is frequently lacking in our own stories today. Even though the art of storytelling is rapidly dying out across the Pacific, one can still find remnants of narrative traditions in the remote Polynesian islands, and anthropologists have carefully preserved many tales that predate these remnants.

Third, though social change has had a disruptive effect on traditional family structures in the islands, many islanders still have a profoundly corporate, communal understanding of themselves. In the words of Tongan theologian Keiti Ann Kanongata'a, Pacific Islanders are "people-oriented" persons.[72] Their close identification with ethnic group and family is very different from our western celebration of individuality and self-differentiation.[73] In Chapter Four, then, I will begin our search for new moral wineskins by exploring the astonishing moral awareness of self, other, and creation that is disclosed in tales from the South Pacific.

To sum up, we can no longer assume the existence of a universal master narrative or one overarching moral order, and therefore a comprehensive and context-sensitive approach to ethics demands that we become open to ethical traditions that are different from our own. Further, our social and cultural disconnection in the late-modern limbo is so radical that we have no alternative but to encounter persons in other worlds who reflect forms of solidarity, suffering, and spirituality that are alien to the very existence of what Galbraith called the "contented majority." The ensuing investigations of the moral teachings of remote islanders and cutting edge social movements will provide fresh resources with which to address the weaknesses we have identified in our moral heritage. It will also help us to take seriously concerns about liberation voiced in alternative traditions in the U.S.

Such a pragmatic, cross-cultural ethics—one of being ready to be "pulled-by-others"—can enable us to transcend the nostalgic penchant for retreat of the communalist, the self-absorption of the neocon, the bourgeois rationalism of the Enlightenment liberal, and the solipsism of the postmodernist. By seriously engaging alternative movements and the narratives of indigenous peoples, we can begin to envision ethics in the global village and initiate a moral program that will champion ecological awareness, economic justice and peace-making.

TALKING POINTS
DRINKING FROM OLD WINESKINS

- Are you "proud to be an American" (or a Canadian or of some other nationality)? Or, are you a bit put off by this question? Why? Why not? When you see the American (Canadian) flag, what images, feelings and beliefs come to mind? Are any of these worth dying for? Why or why not?
- Recall a time when you disagreed about a moral issue with someone you really admired—a teacher, parent, neighbor, or celebrity. Discuss the disagreement and why you felt the way you did.
- If you had to choose, would you consider yourself more of a communalist, neocon, liberal or postmodernist? In your family, are you in the majority or the minority? Either way, how do you handle this? Which of these four ethical options do you find most offensive? Why?
- Imagine your "ideal neighborhood." Illustrate it with crayons. Who would be in it? What things would they share? What activities would be pursued? How would you like to be known to those outside of the neighborhood?

IN SEARCH OF NEW WINESKINS

- Have you ever had the experience of changing your mind about a moral question? Where? When? How did the change occur? What brought it about?
- Think of a moral position that you feel is completely irrational. Then put yourself in the shoes of people who hold that position and imagine

what *they* think. Conjure up three reasons *they* might give to support what you consider to be that crazy position. Do any of those reasons now begin to seem sensible?

- Have you ever been a part of a social movement? If so, describe why you joined and what you did. If not, why do you think you never did this? What has prevented you from joining a social movement? Would you have been attracted to the Jesus movement? Why or why not?
- Have you ever visited, seen or read about folks who live in rural, remote or isolated places? What values and lifestyles seem to be important to them? Can you see yourself changing your ethical perspective in the light of any of these values or lifestyles? How so?

CHAPTER 4

RE-CONNECTING WITH THE EARTH

ADVENTURES IN THE SOUTH SEAS

During the summer of 2002 I spent three days aboard a small ship, the *M. V. Tokelau*, traveling over rough seas en route to the Tokelau Islands; three tiny South Pacific atolls located about 300 miles north of Samoa. The second day at sea, I was struck by the moral outrage Tokelauans expressed when two fellow travelers tossed coconuts overboard without first breaking them open. On inquiring why this was offensive, I was informed that the malefactors were stealing from the fish. They were satisfying their thirst by enjoying these "drinking nuts" (green coconuts that retain an abundance of water), but neglecting their responsibility toward the fish in the sea. As the islanders explained, even the greenest of drinking coconuts has a layer of "white meat" inside the outer shell, and therefore to throw a coconut into the sea without cracking it open is to deprive fish of a valuable source of food.

This story illustrates several core ethical orientations. First, it entails a notion of the sea as a part of our moral universe, its inhabitants as moral agents, and its entirety as an "other" in relation to which we have responsibilities. It is neither a dumping ground for debris nor an alien and therefore amoral presence. Second, the incident invites us into a distinct world of moral practice in which, for example, the way we consume food is replete with moral implications and enshrouded in taboos, and in which we have not only a right but also an obligation to hold our neighbors accountable for their patterns of consumption. It challenges us to reevaluate a world in which eating is seldom a moral matter, and in which we are loath to infringe on another individual's "right" to consume and discard food at will. Third, it presupposes a strikingly fluid notion of group identity in which we are all bound together—journeying on the same frail vessel, intimately affected by each other's actions, and quick to feel hurt when someone aboard our liner is seen injuring an "other." Such an identity concept views the human self as kin to the fish of the sea and the birds of the air; it rejects our atomistic Western notion of the self as a detached, independent monad, largely separate from others and essentially distinct from the natural world over which we humans rightfully reign.

These core ethical elements represent *de facto* existential notions of "the other," moral action, and social identity. When interrelated, they constitute a way of thinking about how to live a moral life, a specific ethical perspective. While we may be quite familiar with our own personal ethics, we often fail to concern ourselves with the ethics of our neighbors, a problem that grows exponentially in the case of people from other cultures or religious traditions, especially those on the fringes of the modern world. In fact, the history of anthropological research, missionary endeavors, and failed diplomacy testify to the tendency of westerners to view non-westerners as morally suspect, inferior, or even demonic. While it is true that the latter often view westerners in a similar light, life in the emerging global village will require us to rise above our arrogance, suspicion, and fear. And the first step involves getting to know some of these "foreign" neighbors. In this chapter I will begin by focusing on people from one of the remotest parts of our global village, the islanders of the South Pacific. As my anecdote from the *M. V. Tokelau* suggests, islanders have a highly developed moral sensitivity, particularly concerning fish, the sea, and the natural world as a whole.

The South Pacific, which spans nearly one-quarter of the earth's surface, contains the broad culture regions of Polynesia, Melanesia and Micronesia. Geographically speaking, Polynesia includes islands within a triangle ranging from New Zealand eastward to Easter Island, and north to the Hawaii group, including such island groups as Tonga, Samoa, Tahiti, Tokelau and the Cook Islands. Melanesia refers to the islands roughly west of Polynesia, including Fiji, Kanaky (formerly, New Caledonia), Vanuatu, the Solomon Islands and Papua New Guinea. Micronesia encompasses the smaller islands north and generally west of Melanesia, including Kiribati, the Federated States of Micronesia, the Marshall Islands, the Marianas and Guam. To be sure, this traditional division is somewhat arbitrary, since Fiji represents a blend of Polynesian cultural traditions and Melanesian ethnic characteristics. The eastern Fijian islands, for example, lie close to the Tongan group and share the hierarchical social system typical of Polynesian cultures.

One of the ways we can get to know Pacific Islanders and explore their ethical traditions is by getting acquainted with their stories. Despite rapid social changes stemming in large part from modern technologies, islanders still enjoy telling stories. While teaching at Pacific Theological College in Fiji,[1] I heard countless stories, tales, and legends told by students from over thirty different island nations throughout the Pacific. These stories were usually told in connection with rituals of farewell, welcome, mourning, reconciliation, twenty-first birthdays and any number of ethnic celebrations. I taught classes in religion and contextual ethics, in the course of which island students wrote down and interpreted stories they had learned growing up in their various cultures.[2] I also spent parts of two summers in New Zealand, reading transcripts of stories told by Tokelau Islanders, and visited with Tokelauans, both in Tokelau and in New Zealand.

Stories are powerfully related to ethics.[3] With every telling, they "re-present" moral insights that have stood the test of time. Preserved and handed on in narrative form, these insights become embedded in the consciousness of each generation. Consider the case of Americans, who at an early age imbibe the myth of Santa Claus, the benign father figure who brings presents to children who have been "good"—or the many "rags to riches" stories: Ben Franklin whose hard work and parsimony made him a wealthy entrepreneur, or Dale Carnegie, the penniless immigrant who amassed a fortune.

But it is not immediately clear why we should concern ourselves with stories from South Pacific Islanders. In western literature, these "natives" are still commonly portrayed as either carefree children in paradise or savage cannibals with no identifiable or coherent moral traditions.[4] On the whole, one searches in vain for substantive treatments of the ethics of Pacific Islanders. And yet, as we noted earlier, their primarily oral cultures impart a compelling sense of reality to their stories.[5] That is, where storytelling still represents a primary mode of communication, knowledge dissemination, and recreation; the stories told in such places can mediate moral values in ways that are not unduly abstracted from the cultural context in question. And finally, after centuries of cross-cultural fertilization in the Pacific, many of these stories have come to express moral orientations shared by islanders throughout the region.[6]

In this chapter, then, I will focus on four stories that come from different parts of the Pacific: a legend of conflict between father and daughter in Fiji, a narrative of a marital dispute in the Cook Islands, the tale of the killing of a bird in Tokelau, and the account of an extraordinary rescue by dolphins in Vanuatu. In each case, I will try to show how the ethical elements of the "other," moral action, and social identity expressed in the respective stories shed light on present-day ecological concerns. Obviously, such an undertaking calls for a familiarity with the conventions of oral narrative associated with each story, the relevant cultural contexts, the intentions of the storytellers (and in the case of a written transcript, the transcriber and translator), the dynamics of oral performance, and last but not least our own predispositions to "hear" what we wish and expect to hear. In other words, following the path of narrative to an understanding of these islanders' moral experience involves a complex task of interpretation. And because of their obvious entertainment value, one must take great care not to "read" them as if their sole intent was to reveal moral insights—let alone those we find familiar and comfortable.

On the other hand, a narrative need not have a moral intent in order to disclose moral values and ideas. Often the genius of a bawdy tale is that it communicates on several different levels simultaneously: at the same time we're laughing, we're being nudged toward a moral orientation that while not articulated is nonetheless implicit in what was said—or in how something was said. We can all recall tales we grew up with—the Adventures of Robin Hood or the Lone Ranger—that show how seemingly simple adventure stories can have subterranean levels of moral meaning. The reader may be dubious about some of my interpretations, but I hope that my awareness of the cultural context and familiarity with narrative interpretation will minimize errors in discerning the moral themes evoked by the stories. Let us now turn to the first of our four narratives—a romantic tale from one of the most beautiful of the Fiji Islands.

PACIFIC TALES

THE LEGEND OF *TAGIMOUCIA* ("TEARS OF DESPAIR")

I first heard the story of *Tagimoucia* in 1998 from Marama Savaki, a Fijian student at the Pacific Theological College and a native of Taveuni.[7] Often referred to as the "Garden Island" because of its extraordinary beauty, Taveuni is one of the more than three hundred Fiji islands. The "*tagimoucia*"—a delicate, bright red flower, with multiple petals and white centers—is one of the world's rarest wild flowers. It thrives only at high elevations and grows wild on Taveuni, which rises abruptly from sea level to over four thousand feet. Paraphrasing from Savaki's telling, but also drawing heavily on the version printed in Amadio's *Pacifica*, I offer the following rendition of this ancient legend.

Once, long long ago in a village on the Fiji Island of Taveuni, *Adi*[8] (the high ranking) Perena, the beautiful young daughter of a chief, was enjoying the delights of falling in love. Her eyes sparkled and her face glowed with happiness as she went about her life in the village. Her friends soon noticed the glances she gave to the handsome young man of her choice. If he was sitting near the *kava* bowl,[9] she would go out of her way to walk close to him, leaning close to touch the bowl.[10] The young man, Taitusi, was poor—not a suitable match for the daughter of a chief—but they could not deny the attraction they felt for one another.

A traditional game of flirtation played in the village was called the lemon game (*vakagigi moli*). On sunlit afternoons young people would play, rolling lemons along the ground towards each other. It was recognized as a public declaration of affection if a boy bowled a lemon at his sweetheart. It was no secret how Perena and Taitusi felt about each other. One day, while the young people played this game, Perena's father called her to his hut. Happy in her games of love with Taitusi, Perena did not suspect the pain awaiting her. She looked around the hut and saw an old man sitting across the room in a position of honor. She knelt obediently in front of her father.

"I have good news," her father told her. "I have chosen your husband." He pointed to the old man. "It is my royal command that you marry Tuki Kuto and strengthen the ties between us!"[11] Perena could not believe this dreadful news. In horror she looked around and saw her mother sitting silently watching. Perena pleaded with her eyes. Her mother saw her misery but was not able to interfere. Perena walked down to the beach and sat alone, watching the waves breaking on the sand. She was desperately sad. She realized how deeply she cared for Taitusi. In the shadows of the trees watching her stood the anguished Taitusi. She could not bring herself to break her promise of love to him and marry the old man, so in torment she decided to run away.

Before dawn the next morning, Perena set out. Through the forests and parklands, through the slopes and valleys of her abundant homeland she ran. She took no notice of the natural gardens of her island, but started climbing, and at last she came to a high lake and a waterfall. Exhausted and desperate, Perena collapsed. She felt her heart breaking. As she wept, the tears fell on the earth beside her. As they fell, her tears became flowers—the blood red flowers of despair, *tagimoucia*—meaning "tears of despair."

Her father, alarmed by her disappearance, set out with his men to search for her. They searched every part of the island and found her at last by a waterfall. Perena's father, who loved his daughter, was deeply moved by her suffering. He was a chief, and he knew the truth of things when he saw them. He held up the red flowers she had wept and saw in the color and shape of her flowers of tears how deeply she loved Taitusi. He now resolved that his daughter should marry the man she loved. The couple proudly walked side by side, radiant in their traditional wedding costumes. Perena wore the prestigious sash of brown *masi*,[12] and the ceremony was celebrated with full honor.

In view of the intensely hierarchical social system of the eastern Fijian islands, the legend depicts at least three surprising developments.[13] First, it would not be appropriate for the daughter of a chief to express romantic sentiments for a commoner. And yet we are told that Perena does not hide her feelings, but "glances" at Taitusi in public, goes "near" him while he is drinking *kava* (a ceremonial herbal drink) with the men, and plays the traditional *vakagigi moli* (lemon game) of flirtation. She has promised her love to Taitusi, and their feelings for each other were common knowledge in the village.

Second, a chief's daughter would normally be obliged to obey her father's wishes regarding a suitable marriage partner. His authority was virtually absolute. But again we see that Perena resists. We are told that she pleads to her mother with her eyes and that her mother sees her misery, but does not interfere. Perena broods at the beach and then decides to run away before dawn the next morning, rather than marry the old man. Third, a chief would almost never reverse a decision, especially when he had made his will known in a public setting. That would be especially true in this case, for Fijian marriages have traditionally entailed unions between large extended families, and when they united the families of chiefs, could involve hundreds of relatives in festivities with major economic and political consequences. We are not told the extent of the marriage arrangements which the chief had undertaken, but he stood to lose considerable face and perhaps economic and political leverage by changing his mind. In addition, when he allowed Perena to marry Taitusi, he superseded the primacy of rank by deferring to his daughter's wishes.

Let us examine these surprises in turn. Perena's strikingly overt displays of affection suggest a degree of self-regard we might miss if we interpret her flirtatious behavior as merely willful disobedience. After all, as the daughter of a chief she enjoys an elevated status. Her love for Taitusi is no doubt passionate, and perhaps deep—we are told that her eyes "sparkled" and that her face "glowed" with happiness. In following her heart, she exhibits both a basic need for intimacy and the seriousness of the promise she has made to Taitusi.

At the same time, she honors the traditional Fijian values of order and security by not causing a scene in front of her father. She pleads with her eyes to her mother, but does not verbalize her disappointment or otherwise manifest her protest.[14] Rather than show her feelings, Perena retreats to the beach as Taitusi watches from afar. The fact that Taitusi keeps his distance is likely a carefully considered decision; after all, who is he, a lowly commoner, to participate in Perena's act of rebellion? Lacking encouragement from Perena, he may well be timid and submissive in the face of her father's decision. Finally, Perena makes a clandestine departure from the village; rather than overtly challenge her father she resists him by escaping his control.

In retrospect, Perena's course of action suggests a moral tension between self-regard and obedience to the *vakaturaga* (meaning, "chiefly way").[15] Indeed, it implies that in the Fijian moral universe, there is space for individual self-assertion over against the collectivity of the group epitomized in the *vakaturaga*. Thus her self-assertion takes the form of claiming a need for intimacy—to be known by another person and to be affirmed and accepted for who she is. That means that honoring of the hierarchical system of authority does not necessarily entail the suppression of individual preference.[16] Perena's love for a commoner and her open flirting with him imply a flexibility in attitudes toward the social structure that is not usually reflected in structural analyses of Polynesian cultures.[17]

But I would like to argue that the legend has additional moral significance, and this is where the environment becomes a key factor. Perena's flight suggests that, in situations of conflict, it is crucial to find creative ways to demonstrate one's opposition. Perena could have run off with Taitusi, perhaps to another island (though such an "elopement" would have been highly unlikely because of the close interrelationship between Fijians' personal and social identities). Or she could have publicly protested. Or she might even have "gone through the motions" by marrying the old man and then shown by a pattern of grudging compliance her unhappiness with her father's decision. But instead she retreats to the beach, forest, mountains, and lake, and thus creates a liminal[18] space apart from the ordinary, everyday context of village life.

As liminal arenas, the beach, forest, mountains, and lake become contexts of moral agency in the story. First, by taking refuge in the natural world, Perena gives her father and the larger family an opportunity both to recognize the depths and ponder the roots of her opposition. Second, her disappearance gains her time and avoids a tragic outcome resulting from a hasty decision. Third, and perhaps most significant, it reaffirms the sense in which our relationship to the land can be a resource for liberation. The Fijian word for land, *vanua*, denotes sea and air as well. Furthermore, *vanua* includes all the persons and ancestors associated with the geographical area, all the natural and humanly constructed artifacts rooted in the land, and all the traditions and rituals that give expression to the basic value of the land.[19]

From the standpoint of our relationship with the land in this larger sense, Perena's seeking refuge in nature not only suggests the therapeutic value of re-connecting with the eco-system, but also the transformative power latent in such reconnection. Here the earth becomes a saving agent. It is from the womb of the earth that new life in the form of the flower springs forth in response to Perena's yearning. When the land transforms her tears into the delicately shaped white and red *tagimoucia*, it creates a multi-faceted symbol of love, despair, passion, beauty and reconciliation.

Furthermore, the land is a source of liberation not only for Perena, but for her father as well. When he sees Perena's tears in the shape and color of the *tagimoucia* plant, he has a change of heart. He realizes how dearly Perena loves Taitusi. The narrative informs us that, because he is a chief, he "knew the truth of things when he saw them." He becomes reconciled with his daughter and also agrees to embrace the commoner, Taitusi, as his future son-in-law. The climax of the plot points to the profound significance of reconciliation as a forgiveness of willful acts of separation from community life. In this case, the father's reconciliatory action attests to a range of give and take in interpersonal relations and dramatizes a willingness to set aside conventional cultural norms in the interest of a fuller and deeper sense of what constitutes right social relationships.

In terms of classical understandings of ethics, we might also argue that since "the face of nature" is reflected in the flowering of the *tagimoucia* and the flower in turn mirrors the moral imperatives of compassion, forgiveness, and reconciliation; then the legend evokes a "natural law" moral orientation. That is, we discover who we are, where we are headed, and what we are to do by discerning or "reading" what is disclosed in nature. Such revelations find further expression in a myth from the Cook Islands involving marital discord.

THE LEGEND OF *TE ANA TAKITAKI* ("THE CAVE TO WHICH ONE IS LED")

I first heard the narrative of *Te Ana Takitaki* in 1999 from the late Tua Tome Tapurau, a Cook Island student at the Pacific Theological College.[20] It is a Polynesian story from the island of Atiu, north of Rarotonga in the Cook Islands.[21] Atiu, also known as *"Tauranga"* and *"Enuamara,"* is known as a locus of sacred power. Cook Island creation myths speak of the first inhabitants of Atiu as having originated from the ancestor *Atiu-Mua*, whose father was the supreme divinity *Tangaroa*. All people on Atiu claim relationship to one another as descendants of *Tangaroa*. The title of the legend, *"Te Ana Takitaki,"* which can best be rendered "the cave to which one is led," points to both the cave and being led by a spirit as key symbols in the narrative. The protagonists in the legend are Inutoto and Pararo, a young married couple. The story begins at a time of heightened ritual activity. A special dance, the Moonlight Dance, is being held on a night of the full moon.[22]

Inutoto is described as a beautiful, graceful woman who loves dancing and looks forward to this special occasion. The plot arises from a command by Pararo forbidding her to attend the dance. Pararo, who then leaves to go fishing, is surprised at his failure to catch anything and wonders why the sea seems empty of fish. He hears the distant sound of the drumming at the dance, feels uneasy, even senses that the gods are against him—but continues to fish. Inutoto eventually gives in to her desire to go dancing, puts a red hibiscus flower in her hair, and swaying seductively, joins the dancers. When Pararo returns home and discovers his wife missing, he concludes she has gone to the dance, and on finding her there, forcibly drags her away and curses her for disobeying him.

That night in their hut, Inutoto lies awake feeling hurt by what she perceives as the injustice of Pararo's anger and the humiliation of being manhandled and reviled in front of her friends. While Pararo is sleeping, she slips out of bed and runs away. Initially, Pararo discounts her absence because she has run away before but always returned after a cooling off period at the home of her brother, Ngarue. But on discovering that she hasn't gone to Ngarue's home, he becomes alarmed and the two of them set out to find her. After several days of unsuccessful searching, Pararo becomes desperate and prays to the gods for help. At that moment, a kingfisher bird appears and leads Pararo into the secret recesses of a mysterious cave. When he calls to Inutoto, she comes to him out of the darkness of the depths of the caverns. They embrace and forgive each other, and Pararo leads her out of the cave.

From the vantage point of a western culture dedicated to human rights and sympathetic to feminist thought, Inutoto is the victim of an authoritarian husband and is justified in fleeing a demeaning conflict situation. It seems outrageous that Pararo "forbids" her to go to a communal ceremony and subsequently insults her and compels her to return home. It is at least disturbing that the legend concludes by stating that they "forgave each other"—as if Inutoto had personally wronged Pararo, or as if her wrongdoing was equivalent to his.

But such a reading not only ignores the cultural context of the story, it also obfuscates several of the central moral features evoked in the narrative. First of all, the dance itself represents a communal celebration with links to the regenerative power of *Atiu-Mua* (ancestor being) and *Tangaroa* (supreme divinity), and as such it constitutes a significant context for enacting and expressing right social relationships. Indeed, community dances were traditionally an important component of Cook Island village activities, and represented a pervasive orientation toward physical, interpersonal contact in the culture.[23] What made Inutoto's attendance at the dance problematic was not the erotic nature of the dance, but disobedience to her husband. In disobeying his express command, Inutoto not only wounds her spouse, but undermines the larger patrilineal social fabric in which wives are expected to obey husbands.[24] In this traditional island context, Pararo has every reason to be furious at her behavior.

At the same time, Pararo is hardly free from blame. One of the anomalies of the legend is Pararo's insistence on going fishing on the night of a full moon. It is widely believed in the islands that fish don't bite during the full moon.[25] Either Pararo is acting irrationally, or he is being intentionally irreverent, or he is enticing his wife to disobey him. In any event, we are told that while fishing he heard the drums and felt uneasy. He was surprised that the sea seemed "empty of fish" and felt that the gods were "against him." It was as if he had been driven by some unnatural desire to push against and defy the taboos of the cosmic order. Yet he continued to paddle across the sea in a futile effort to obtain a catch.

In the context of everyday life in the islands, it is also surprising that Pararo would go fishing alone. Traditionally, fishing is a group activity. The image of Pararo drifting alone in his canoe while a large group of relatives are celebrating within earshot suggests that he has isolated himself from community life. A number of islanders I know have attested that he ought to have accompanied his wife to the dance—in all likelihood an event involving the entire community. One cannot help but wonder why Pararo did not join them.

A contextual reading of the narrative thus points to a husband who disregards the relational character of the cosmic and communal order. Pararo acts as if he is so dismissive of the gods that, full moon or not, he can catch fish anyway. Inutoto's willful disobedience is thus matched by Pararo's willful self-assertion in his rejection of communal expectations and the wishes of the gods. Moreover, although Pararo would have been expected to assert his familial authority—and custom allowed a husband to beat his wife, especially for disobedience[26]—his aggressive and public display of anger may well have crossed the line. It would certainly have highlighted the fact that he had not accompanied his wife in the first place, and by introducing violent discord into a festive occasion, it would have disturbed the cosmic harmony symbolized by the unity of drum, dance, and moon.

It is instructive to note that like Perena, Inutoto flees rather than self-destructs, and seeks refuge in nature. According to Cook Islanders, it was not uncommon for women either to accord grudging submission to their husbands or, in cases of extreme abuse, to commit suicide. Further, her entry into the cave symbolizes a journey back into the depths of creation, and her emergence evokes not only reconciliation and reunion, but a sense of rebirth as well. It is as if Inutoto intuits at some deep level that Pararo would never have found her without a change of heart that entailed reestablishing links with the gods. And this happens, of course, through encounters with natural phenomena. As soon as Pararo reached out by seeking his wife, the kingfisher bird came to his aid. Having been humbled, Pararo may now be more likely to enter into community. Perhaps Inutoto will develop a deeper regard for Pararo's newfound integrity; their embrace on leaving the cave and reentering daily life seems to suggest so. At the very least, the story leaves open the possibility of interpersonal transformation within the norms of the traditional social and religious context.

The story dramatizes one other important element of Pacific island ethics: morality is inseparable from a religious apperception of the ecosystem. Right social relationships in the human community are grounded in proper relationships with the spirit world, which in turn is directly encountered through such natural phenomena as the sea and the kingfisher. Further, the title of the legend, "The cave to which one is led," suggests the importance of responding to the inherent directionality of this nature-spirit world. That Pararo is led to the cave raises an additional point. A key feature of his moral experience is his ordeal of suffering. The unabridged version of the story tells that as he is being led to the cave, he "stumbles down" into a depression, climbs over "sharp coral" and enters "great gloomy chambers." Rather than leading, he has to follow, and all the while he follows this perilous path, he fears that he will not find Inutoto. Indeed, he almost doesn't find her; she answers only when he asks "one last time."

In addition to the interrelatedness of morality, the ecosystem, and the element of suffering, the legend highlights the centrality of forgiveness. Just as Perena's father readily forgives her disobedience when he "sees the truth of things," so the gods forgive and assist Pararo when he prays to them. Inutoto forgives Pararo for humiliating her at the dance, and Pararo forgives Inutoto for disobeying his command. In both narratives the plot climax involves reciprocal acts of forgiveness.

An understanding of such acts is crucial if we are to move beyond the two common stereotypes—the primeval paradise and the land of fearful savages—that are perpetrated in the bulk of expatriate literature about the South Pacific. The legend of *Te Ana Takitaki* in particular suggests that the roots of moral discord or rupture may lie in a profound alienation from our inner selves, the promptings of the spirits manifest in nature, and the social fabric as a whole. Both legends argue that moral experience involves distinctive cultural responses to deep-seated conflicts; both also stress our oneness with the environment and its potentially transformative role. Interwoven with this eco-consciousness are participation in community rituals and what we might call an interpersonal flexibility.[27] These themes are particularly evident in a tale of love and death from the Tokelau Islands.

THE TALE OF THE *TAVAKE* (TROPICAL BIRD)

The Tale of the *Tavake* is an indigenous Tokelauan *kakai*, or "story of tales,"[28] that recounts a child's interactions with a tropical bird called

Tavake.[29] It was told to the anthropologist Judith Huntsman by Manuele Palehau, a well-known Tokelauan storyteller and the long-time *pulenuku* (mayor) of Nukunonu,[30] at a semi-formal gathering on March 28, 1968. Palehau was enrolled in a Catholic Mission school in Samoa until he was fourteen, when after his father's death he returned to Nukunonu to assume family responsibilities. He received his knowledge of *kakai* from both his mother's father and from relations on his father's side. Huntsman relates that Palehau was able to amass an unusually rich and broad knowledge of tales because, "unlike his contemporaries, he had no father to teach him, so that all of the elders, out of sympathy and concern for the orphaned child, took it upon themselves to teach him what they knew."[31] The following is a brief synopsis of the "Tale of the *Tavake*" as told before a live audience nearly thirty-nine years ago on the remote island of Nukunonu.[32]

> There is a rock situated at the canoe pass called the Rock of the *Tavake*. An hour comes when that standing place of the *Tavake* is visible to you. As for Hina and her parents. The house of Hina's parents (I do not really know [the names of] Hina's parents, I have simply forgotten, but Hina is their child). There is a raised pavement built at the front of the house, that house of Hina's parents, as a place for Hina to play upon in the mornings and the afternoons.
>
> Well. In the mornings then Hina goes and sits on that raised pavement and gazes at the flight of birds going at dawn to fish beyond the outer reefs. Well, Hina thinks: the birds are going at dawn again to fish. Well, those kind thoughts of hers are directed to birds. Well, when evening comes, Hina goes sitting on top of that raised pavement. The birds again are flocking back from the sea, she thinks too. Hina says to herself as before: The birds are flocking back from the sea, going again to their nesting places.
>
> Well, the birds are also aware of Hina's presence. It keeps on like that. . . .

This prologue is repeated in a slightly different form, and then the storyteller prepares the listeners for the first of two dramatic developments by noting simply that while Hina sat there, the birds began to bring "proposals" to her because they were "attracted" to her. The introduction to the story thus consists of Hina's sitting, gazing and thinking. She ponders about the birds, their flight patterns, their comings and goings, and their quests for food. In fact the "action" in the story to this point has essentially to do with Hina and the birds becoming increasingly aware of one another's existence.[33] Of particular significance is their mutual compassion. We are told that Hina has "kind thoughts"[34] directed at birds. The birds in turn are "attracted" to Hina's presence. The listener or reader is immediately drawn into an inter-subjective awareness between Hina and the birds that is characterized by mutual concern.

From the standpoint of ethics, the story suggests that an intentional, compassionate attitude toward non-human animal species may be crucial to a right relationship with our environment. Unless we are actively directing our attention toward animal life, we may alienate ourselves from the ecosystems we inhabit. And without acknowledging our attraction for non-human species, we may be living affectively impoverished lives—unnecessarily isolating ourselves in the narrow confines of life-worlds that attribute altruistic subjectivity only to human beings.[35] Since this compassionate thinking sets the stage for the subsequent dramatic action in the tale, it represents a moral foreground.

The next part of the story tells of various proposals from four different birds, all of whom are attracted to Hina and want her to come and live with them. They all send a smaller bird of a similar color as a messenger with the same initial petition. In each case, Hina consults her parents, who respond by telling her to ask the birds where they will sleep. Since the first two birds (the Frigate-bird and the Red-footed Booby) say that they will reside in the crown of a tree, their offers are rejected, because it would be difficult for Hina to climb the tree and she would not have enough space to do her plaiting.[36] She would also face harm from the elements and the danger of falling. The third bird, the Curlew, says that they will sleep "in the hole in the shore reef," but this is rejected also, because Hina and her plaiting would be drenched at high tide.

But when the *Tavake* proposes that they sleep in a hole in a *puka* tree,[37] Hina's parents accept, noting that Hina's plaiting will be sheltered. The White tern who conveyed the *Tavake's* proposal now summons a flock of terns, and they lift Hina along with her plaiting paraphernalia to the hole in the *puka* where Hina and the *Tavake* will reside. After Hina has been there a long time, she gets a craving for fish, suggesting that she has become pregnant.[38] The *Tavake* then tells her to stay put while he goes to the rock beyond the canoe pass to catch fish. "He stands there, he searches for a delicacy for them."

At this point, the narrative abruptly shifts to a meeting called by the fish, the understood purpose of which is to discuss how to kill the *Tavake*. The shark opens the meeting, feigns a desire to consult the will of the group, and then tells how he would do the killing. However, the fish quickly reject his plan because he would be seen by the *Tavake* and fail in his mission. They also reject a similar plan by the Trevally fish for the same reason. At this juncture, they seem to be unclear about what to do "so they sit there." Then the *Gagale* (Camouflaged Parrot-fish), who is described as "sitting right there near those fish who are not likely to be considered," whispers "I can do it." This declaration is conveyed by these lesser fish to the elders, who ask him how he will do it. The *Gagale* says that he will float along just like a leaf, camouflaging himself in such a way that he can get close to the rock where the *Tavake* is, and at the right moment, grab him when he isn't looking. The elders give their consent.

The *Gagale* drifts to where the tail end of the *Tavake* is turned and suddenly grabs it. The *Tavake*, startled, stabs furiously at the *Gagale*, but the *Gagale*, encouraged by the shouts of his supporting fish, holds on tenaciously. Two small fish (the Flute-mouth and the Butterfly-fish) manage to slip through the narrow reef shallows and pluck tail feathers from the *Tavake*, who dies. The *Gagale* now "stands there on high" distributing the *Tavake's* feathers to various fish. Finally, the eel comes by, and the *Gagale* says all the flesh has already been eaten, but that he may eat the bones of the *Tavake*. The narrator ends the tale by noting that the eel's late arrival is why he had to eat the bones and that this in turn is why the eel is bony.

As our earlier comments on the introduction of the story would suggest, beyond these simple, amusing points about the eel, the tale evokes a world in which human and animal species are radically interrelated. The impregnation of Hina by a bird will result, metaphorically, in the birth of a hybrid, part human and part bird but not entirely either. In other Tokelau tales, Hina herself is portrayed as the offspring of human and non-human parents. In the Tale of the *Fahua* (clam),[39] for example, Hina undertakes a quest to discover the identity of her father. Directed by her mother, who is a clam, she goes to the *pou* (post) and asks the *fua-aitu* (the fruit-seeding spirit that is protector of the post) whether it is her father. Then she goes to the *fatutaolalaga* (the stone used for holding plaiting in place) and asks its spirit protector whether it is her father. Finally, she discovers that the legendary male figure, *Tinilau*, is her father, but only after having addressed spirits of the cosmos, whom she is led to believe could have been her father. Thus in this tale Hina's identity quest is associated with animal, plant, inorganic, and spiritual elements in the wider cosmos.

In addition to stressing the practice of empathetic thinking and the self's existential interrelatedness with non-human animal species, Tokelau oral narratives portray the "other" we ought to be in terms of complex renderings of violence and justice, aggression and humility, marginality and leadership. In the Tale of the *Tavake*, fish and birds feed upon one another, just as humans feed upon fish, other creatures of the sea, and birds. It is not a romanticized view of nature. Rather, it reflects a very commonsense orientation to the world of nature, in which humans, animals and plants are intertwined in a complex process of birth, growth, decay and death. In this regard it is interesting to note that in virtually all of the tales Palehau performed in the spring of 1968 that Huntsman recorded, we find such violent episodes as the theft of a life-soul, the systematic murder of innocent women, the killing of a thief, several abductions, and the slaying of an abductor.[40]

But in each case there is clear provocation for the violent displays. Though often evoking a sense of the tragic, such displays restore balance and harmony to community life. Note that a number of reasons might be advanced to explain the plot of the fish to murder the *Tavake*, even if the storyteller was apparently unconcerned about the moral justifiability of the homicide. After all, the *Tavake* had in effect abducted Hina. Tokelauans might have viewed Hina as some kind of metaphorical hybrid self (perhaps part clam and part human), and therefore when she is abducted by a bird of the air, the fish of the sea take offense that one of their own marine creatures has been kidnapped and raped. Or it could be that by re-locating and confining her to his tree, the *Tavake* has effectively terminated Hina's heretofore compassionate activity of thinking about the birds. These are only a few of the possible reasons why the fish murdered the Tavake, not to mention that fish and birds may simply dislike each other, or that the fish may envy the *Tavake's* feathers! But in each of these scenarios, an attack on the harmony of the cosmos is checked and countered in such a way that the aggressor is justly punished. Moreover, humility is highlighted in various ways; even the aggressive "other" must not be immodest in the tale. The Shark's self-promotion is quickly rejected by the group; the *Gagale's* proposal is spoken in a quiet voice and relayed to the elders by fish who sit at the margins. Rather than boasting about overpowering the bird or attacking him head-on, the *Gagale* employs a subtle strategy for getting near to the *Tavake;* he camouflages himself. He also uses his diminutive size to swim through narrow passageways in the reef when the tide is out, and the two fish who join in the attack are likewise able to navigate these tiny passageways.

This emphasis on the value of humility is underscored in ethnographic descriptions of Tokelauan cultural life. In public meetings of the council (*fono*), speakers customarily express divergent viewpoints in a humble manner. Standard oratorical techniques include the use of the first person pronoun (*kita*), which literally translates "my insignificant self," and prefacing one's comments with an expression such as *he manatu tauanoa*— "an insignificant thought."[41] These represent but one moral nuance of the Tokelauan proverb, *Uluki loco o te fata*: "enter into the rock"—a saying that refers to Tokelau's coral boulders, which are riddled with holes and crannies in which small fish can safely hide from predators.[42] Moreover, the *Gagale*, by camouflaging himself such that he appears to be a floating leaf, blends into his natural surroundings. From an ethical standpoint, all this may imply that in the Tokelauan worldview, right relationships in the larger biosphere entail thinking and acting in ways that allow one to live unobtrusively in the nooks and crannies of a complex, ecological web that also entails violence and aggression.

The non-pacifist, humble aggressor is also a marginal fish who becomes the heroic "can-do" special operations agent. He is not an elder and is depicted as "sitting right there near those fish who are not likely to be considered." Indeed, his proposal is relayed to the elders by other lesser fish. Yet this marginal member of the group becomes a key leader when he is selected to lead the attack on behalf of the entire fish community, and is assisted in his deed by two other smaller fish. After the *Tavake* is killed, he assumes an important leadership role by distributing the spoils of war. His "distribution" of the *Tavake's* flesh, feathers, and bones could even be construed as a transformative act in which the fish, by receiving these elements of the bird's body, intensify their kinship with other species in the ecosystem.

In sum, Tokelau Islanders understand that a normative relation to the natural world involves above all else being existentially present in it. It requires that one *actively attend to nature with an empathetic consciousness*—that is, practice the art of "kind thinking" in relation to nature. It is to discern a biological kinship with other species, to view all species as fundamentally related to one another, and to acknowledge personal relationships with spirit-filled animate and inanimate objects in the environment. Moreover, the small, humble *marginal agent facilitates right relationships* in the larger ecosystem. We need to be alert for the voice from the margins and the latent power of those perceived to be relatively powerless in the ecosystem as a whole. Might does not make right.[43]

Finally, although the ecological movement is focused on how humans need to preserve natural habitats, we also need to appreciate the degree to which non-human species support and preserve human life. This is strikingly illustrated in our fourth and final narrative from the Pacific Islands, a story of rescue at sea by dolphins.

THE STORY OF THE DOLPHIN CHRIST

Sitting around the *kava* bowl one night in Fiji, I heard a fascinating story told by a seminary student from Vanuatu.[44] Willi had been traveling with his family on a small inter-island ferry that was struck at nightfall by a powerful storm. When the churning seas capsized the ferry, Willi and his two daughters leaped overboard and managed to cling to a piece of wood in the open sea. Willi's youngest daughter, not quite two years old, quickly weakened, and soon disappeared under a huge wave. Willi dove and retrieved her, but after supporting the limp body for several hours, he too was losing strength. In desperation his ten-year old daughter, Vivian, pleaded with her father, "Let her go, Daddy." In the middle of that vast ocean, Willi improvised a funeral service for his little girl and let her go home to the depths of the sea.

Drifting for the rest of the night, and growing weaker by the hour, they cried out to God in desperation. When dawn broke, Willi suddenly remembered an ancient song his father had taught him to "call the dolphins." Willi sang this song, and after a short while a dolphin appeared with a coconut in its mouth and plopped it down near him. Willi cracked a hole in the hard shell with his teeth, breaking two in the process. But drinking the lifesaving coconut juice and eating the nourishing white meat within the husk reinvigorated him and Vivian. And for the next thirty-six hours, when a passing boat finally rescued them, a school of dolphins continued to swim in a protective circle around them.

After their rescue, Willi learned from a young woman named Roslyn how the dolphins had also befriended her. After the boat sank, he reported, Roslyn found herself in the stormy sea with nothing to hold onto. When she called for help, two dolphins appeared carrying in their mouths *bele* (a nourishing leafy vegetable), which they gave to Roslyn. Then the dolphins swam to either side of her, each gently nudging a fin beneath her arms, and in this way they supported her for many hours, swimming away only when rescuers pulled her aboard their boat.

Although both episodes sound so miraculous that they strain credibility, I have every reason to believe that they are "true" episodes in the sense that they refer to events that actually happened.[45] Willi, then training to enter the Anglican priesthood, spoke with an authority and seriousness that could not be lightly dismissed. But there was also "truth" in another sense. To a community of Christian theological students in the Pacific Islands, these stories evoked a profound understanding of salvation. To Willi and the other islanders, the dolphins represented not only part of the interconnected web of life, but salvific figures as well. Reflecting theologically on his experience, Willi spoke of the dolphin who brought the coconut as "the Dolphin Christ." Such a Christ reflects a belief in the radical immanence of God in the animal kingdom. When Willi calls out to the Dolphin, it responds with Christ-like compassion, presenting the lifesaving coconut.

ISLANDERS, JESUS, AND SPECIESISM

When I first told the story of Willi and the dolphin to students at Texas Christian University, they reacted with incredulity. "You've got to be kidding, right?" "People can't talk to dolphins." While many of these same students have no problem interpreting Scripture literally—they might readily argue that Jonah survived in the belly of a whale for three days—they have difficulty accepting the possibility of such seemingly miraculous human-

animal interactions in today's world. And yet, as they hear other stories
from the South Pacific, their incredulity slowly turns to puzzlement, wonder, and awe. In some cases, they become frustrated and angry, for Willi's
account of his experience and the chief's epiphany at the sight of the *tagimoucia* flower show that we in the West have lost contact with something
very basic. We think of dolphins as objects of study or exotic creatures
to preserve and gawk at in "sea worlds," but not as ecological partners,
let alone rescuers. We view flowers as ornamental extras to place on a
windowsill or admire by the roadside, and animal flesh as something we
consume with no thought of honoring the life force within.

What has gone wrong? How have we reached the stage where a simple
act such as conversing with birds seems ludicrous and absurd? How
have we become so alienated from a vital relatedness to non-human life?
Clearly, our sense of interdependence with the natural world began to fade
long before the advent of the cultural narratives outlined in the previous
chapter. The alienation no doubt has its origin in the dawn of civilization
some six to eight thousand years ago, and may be related to the advent
of writing, metallurgy and urbanization.[46] Although this is not the place
to explore the primordial origins of this predicament, it seems clear that
the empirical mindset of the Enlightenment has contributed to a further
distancing of ourselves from other life forms in the world.

More and more, we have tended to objectify ourselves in terms of
mechanistic models and to view ourselves in terms of systems of psycho-
social functions that are pre-programmed to move through predictable
stages of development. Our bodies have become complexes of chemi-
cal and neurological circuits, and computer analogies have reduced our
thought processes to cellular networks. In these and other ways, we
compromise and chip away at our identity as natural, organic "species
beings."[47]

Consequently, we find ourselves tragically alone in the universe. This
profound aloneness is a defining characteristic of "Speciesism"—an ideology of human exceptionalism that sees humans as exceptions within (or
even supernatural agents inserted into) the earth's biosphere. The eco-
philosopher Anne Primavesi offers a compelling account of how Christian
theologians have used the Genesis creation story to claim that human
beings are not part of the natural evolutionary cycle.[48] From this it would
follow that human salvation could come *only* from a supernatural intervention involving an incarnation of being from beyond nature. But such
a "salvation history" has the effect of abstracting human being from the
process of the earth's evolutionary history. In fact, I would contend that
the proponents of "creationism" are not merely objecting to evolutionary

science as such, but more fundamentally, to the fear that humans are *not* exceptional, penultimate beings in the first place.

Nevertheless, Speciesism is not confined to pockets of fundamentalism. It is rampant throughout society in the late-modern world. It has resulted in a "not knowing" other life forms in the earth, just as we do not really "know" our neighbors in far reaches of the global village. Since we no longer know how to depend upon other life forms, we fear for our own survival. Consequently, we try to ensure massive energy supplies, but we are fast draining the earth of its mineral resources. The question before us then must be, "How should we respond to Speciesism?" To be more specific, we might put the question thus: "What have stories from far away places like the South Seas or ancient Palestine got to do with us? How can they help us come to grips with our own deep-seated captivity to Speciesism?" This is obviously a difficult and multi-faceted challenge. It will not be solved overnight even though many minds are addressing it on many different levels. But by attending to the stories of Islanders, we can envision at least two "reconnection projects."

First, by seeking to enter the imaginative universe evoked by tales from the South Pacific, we can initiate a "re-situating" of ourselves in the world. Second, as we thus become re-oriented within our own worlds, we can better "mentally migrate" into the world evoked by parallel stories in the Jesus tradition, and gain a new appreciation of their ecological significance.[49] I will conclude this chapter by commenting on these two projects in turn.

What do these tales from the South Seas suggest about re-situating ourselves in the world? First, a basic concern with *physical place* is indispensable. In the legends of *Tagimoucia* and *Te Ana Takitaki*, the land functions as refuge, source of renewal, and context for interpersonal transformation. By observing the blood red *tagimoucia* high up in the mountains, Perena's father is moved to change his mind and forgive his daughter. By first noting and then following the kingfisher bird into the depths of the cave, Pararo finds and reconciles with Inutoto. And Hina goes out to the Rock of the *Tavake*, where she meditates on the goings and comings of birds out to sea.

The word "environment" literally means, "that which surrounds us." And these stories evoke a world in which persons are intimately invested in their surroundings. By analogy, they pose a question for us: What are the mountains, lakes, deep caverns, and gateway rocks in our daily experience? Even densely populated urban habitats have great heights and depths and places of refuge that can provide a portal or crossroads to serve as a nexus for our personal journeys. We need to recapture a sense of embodying or "living-in" the covert, yet powerful places of our lives. We need to pay attention to the physicality of where we are and to rediscover nature as a powerful resource for re-charging our lives, providing contexts for conflict-resolution, and empowering transformation.

Just as Perena, Inutoto and Hina seek out the mountain lake, cave, and rock by the sea, so we must search out equivalent places. Such questing for special locales will further necessitate deviating from our daily routines, extracting ourselves from our usual mazes, and sometimes risking travels into unknown territories. It should also be noted that both Perena and Intuoto experienced periods of *solitude*. An ironic aspect of our disconnection in modernity is that we need to find spaces and places of genuine solitude before we can re-establish vital connections. We will have to re-think "business as usual," take leisure and vacation time more seriously, and become more conscious of how we can preserve the wilderness areas that in the past have provided places of refuge and renewal.

Second, these stories highlight a need to *attend to other species* in our environment. In the *Te Ana Takitaki* legend, Pararo finds Inutoto only *because* he sees and then follows the kingfisher bird. In the Dolphin Christ narrative, Willi survives only *because* he remembers how to call the dolphins. In the *Tagimoucia* story, Perena's father reverses his decision only *because* he sees Perena's love-agony-yearning-desperation-anger-bewilderment in the blood red flower. And perhaps most strikingly, in the Tale of the *Tavake*, we are told that Hina spends a great deal of time simply "having kind thoughts" for the birds, and that they in turn "are attracted" to her. I am not suggesting that we should drop everything and follow a bird to find our long lost love, or try to call on marine mammals to come to our aid—even if we could still learn the requisite visual and communications skills; but surely we would do well to attend much more closely to non-human life forms around us. This might entail being a bit less focused on work and a bit more contemplative as we commute. Perhaps we will need to open our car windows, or better yet, get out and bicycle or walk. What might we begin to notice about the birds, insects, and plants around us if we spent sixty minutes a day looking for them as we walked to our workplaces? And what if we started trying to send "kind thoughts" in their direction? What if hundreds or thousands of us began doing this? What might happen?

At the very least, we would *notice* changes in the seasonal flights of birds. We would *notice* if the mosquito population doubled or tripled. We would *notice* if more and more trees had dead limbs. Instead of reading about the effects of global warming, we would *notice* them in our daily experience! But unless we re-situate ourselves by becoming more aware of the world around us, we will remain oblivious even to striking climatic changes. Comfortably cocooned in our narcissistic climate-controlled homes, vehicles and workplaces, we will continue to ignore, as well as isolate ourselves from, the reality that surrounds us.

Finally, a careful reading of tales from the South Pacific can prompt us to *re-imagine nature as an interconnected whole*. In Willi's story the dolphins are more than simply non-alien creatures; they are neighbors in a time of need. In the Tale of the *Tavake*, Hina's future is intertwined with that of the birds and the fish. In the Legend of *Tagimoucia*, humans, flowers, kava bowls, mountains, masi cloths and lemons are all interrelated and overlapping core symbols in a narrative of communal reconciliation. Rather than thinking in terms of polarities—of animate vs. inanimate, of spiritual vs. material—we need to re-envision the world as an organic whole. We may think of fish and dolphins as exploitable organic matter and water as an inanimate commodity, but our global neighbors ought to remind us that we are dealing with agential forces and spiritual beings—with the wise but humble *Gagale* or the Dolphin Christ.

In short, we need to begin thinking in more holistic terms. Parker Palmer, a noted educator, suggests spending time in "solitude and silence, meditative readings and walking in the woods, keeping a journal, finding a friend who will listen . . . . (and learning) as many ways as we can of 'talking to ourselves.'"[50] If we undertake this process in earnest, we will invariably discover that we have several internal conversation partners. Recall our references in Chapter Two to the notion of a "de-centered self," and to Margolis' description of three aspects or dimensions of self. In the Dolphin story, Willi's actions certainly evoke a cosmic self, though they are not alien to the obligated self of a parent trying to save his daughters' lives. Perhaps viewing our moral life in relation to Willi's experience, or imagining the various actors in the Tale of the *Tavake* as different aspects of a single self will help us appreciate how self-interested and one-dimensional we have become. In ethical decision-making, for instance, our appeals to categorical or utilitarian criteria often take on the appearance of egoistic rationalizations of fractured exchanger selves. How can such selves reconnect to the earth, let alone presume to instruct our neighbors in the Two-Thirds world about "right social relationships" or "how to live well"?

On the other hand, if these island traditions help us re-situate ourselves in the world; if we can embody the space around us so as to find special places of refuge and renewal; if we can begin to attend to non-human species and send "warm thoughts" in their direction; and if we can re-imagine the world as an interconnected whole; then we may also be able to see the Jesus tradition afresh. Indeed, we may be better prepared to appreciate parallel themes or resources in the sayings attributed to Jesus.

But the Jesus tradition poses a major hermeneutical problem that we do not encounter in the South Pacific tales. The Jesus tradition we know is primarily disclosed in the canonical gospels (Matthew, Mark, Luke & John) and in fragments of other gospels that originated in the first two centuries of the Common Era.[51] We do not therefore have a living oral tradition like that of contemporary Pacific Island story tellers. That is to say, we do not have the direct words of Jesus of Nazareth—the historical figure who was called Jesus—a Galilean Jew who was executed in the first century by the Romans. What we do have comes almost exclusively from traditions that the gospel writers adapted to suit their own particular circumstances and the ongoing experience of their faith communities.

To be sure, a number of Biblical scholars think that it is possible to distinguish between at least two layers of material in these gospel accounts.[52] While a large part is the product of the early Christian movement's ideas about Jesus (what Marcus Borg called the "post-Easter Jesus"),[53] an earlier oral tradition can be attributed with varying degrees of probability to Borg's "pre-Easter Jesus"—the one considered to have a degree of historical authenticity. In short, there are at least two voices being "sounded" in the gospels—the voice of the pre-Easter, "historical" Jesus and the voice of the community in the post-Easter milieu.

The signal contribution of the Jesus Seminar has been its effort to separate these two layers. From 1985 to 1997 well over a hundred biblical scholars strove to isolate the sayings and deeds of what they understood to be the historical Jesus from the rest of the gospel accounts. Drawing on a variety of sophisticated hermeneutical methods, these scholars sought to work their way through the post-Easter accretions in order to isolate what they now deem to be the actual voice of the teacher from Galilee.[54] Although their approach to Biblical interpretation and reliance on voting to determine levels of agreement were roundly criticized by other biblical scholars,[55] they did arrive at something close to consensus about specific passages of Scripture. What emerges from the "red" passages in *The Five Gospels* (those texts that the Seminar scholars considered highly accurate representations of Jesus' sayings) is a coherent, morally compelling "voice."[56] When I refer to "the Jesus tradition," it is primarily these "red sayings" that I have in mind. Of course, future groups of scholars may revisit the whole question of how the gospel texts are to be interpreted. For instance, it may be that non-historical, more phenomenological approaches to Scripture and other materials of faith experience might well yield a more nuanced, multi-faceted "voice" of Jesus that would be even more useful for ethics than what the Jesus Seminar produced. After all, the search for the historical Jesus has been going on for some time.[57] But for our exploratory purposes in this book, the voice of the "Jesus-Seminar Jesus" is certainly a worthy basis for ethical reflection.

Regarding the unity of the ecosystem, for example, Jesus shows awareness of and concern for non-human life forms.[58] In his parables, he speaks of sparrows, and lilies, and the tiniest of seeds that becomes a bush and provides a "shelter for birds" (Thom 20:2–4).[59] He notes that God watches over sparrows and feeds them (Luke 12:6), even though they neither sow nor harvest (Matt 6:26); and says that God lets none fall without his consent (Matt 10:29).

Such sayings reflect a consciousness of the love of God for all life forms. While God apparently values the human world above the natural, Jesus' observation that a wild lily outshines King Solomon's finest raiment (Matt 6:28–29) could be seen to suggest aesthetic appreciation of nature for its own sake. Sheep, wolves, snakes, and doves (Matt 10:16), and especially foxes and birds (Thom 86), can be interpreted allegorically to illustrate human interaction and morality. In the Thomas passage Jesus implies that foxes and birds have an existential affinity with "this mother's son." Animals not only share situational predicaments with Jesus and all humans, but display such human traits as guile and innocence.

Although Jesus clearly sees humans as distinct from animals, and probably never imagined a category including both flora and fauna, the life-world of God's domain is one shot through with love. According to Matt 5:48, Jesus said, "You are to be as liberal in your love as your heavenly father is." Luke records a similar injunction: "Be as compassionate as God is" (Luke 6:36). Borg explains that in both Hebrew and Aramaic, the quality of love that is usually rendered by the word "compassion" was associated with the womb, and "located in a certain part of the body—namely in the loins."[60] If compassion is then a "womb-like" feeling, and Jesus witnesses to God's compassion for all living things, then God intends a visceral love that "feels with" the other. In short, Jesus' focus on God's compassion suggests a spiritual intimacy with nature. We can only surmise the response of pastoral people to his story about finding a lost sheep and joyfully "lifting it up on his shoulders" (Luke 15:4–6).

In addition to this empathetic appreciation and love of nature, Jesus' proclamation of a new relationship with God implies a rededication to God's creation. Expressions of gratefulness, such as Jesus' prayer for "the bread we need for the day" (Matt 6:11), recall our radical dependence on the earth. His stories of celebrations often involve meals through which relationships are restored. "Congratulations you hungry!" he said, "You will have a feast" (Luke 6:21a). Such celebrations entail consuming the produce of the earth—bread, wine and fatted calves. They require that animals be grazed, seeds planted, and crops harvested.

Finally, in the parable of the sower, Jesus metaphorically connects seed that "fell on the good earth" (Mark 4:3–8) to the arrival of the divine domain. In God's domain "the sun rises on the bad and the good, and rain falls on the just and the unjust" (Matt 5:45b). The ecological vector of this is a vision of God's domain as a realm in the process of becoming. Nature is constantly articulating itself in ways beyond our control. In God's realm, today's situation may not obtain tomorrow. Yesterday's seed has become today's wheat despite the sower's inattention (Mark 4:26–29).

In retrospect, both the stories form the South Pacific and those from the Jesus tradition suggest approaches to ecology that counter if not repudiate Speciesism. Surely Jesus' sensitivity to the birds of the air and the lilies of the field is part of his vision of God's domain, the unity of which includes both empathy for non-human species and a veneration of nature for its own sake. That vision further suggests that the value of the human self is inseparable from its relatedness to the cosmos. Finally, the gospel theme of feasting has ecologically significant implications for our late-modern context. Communion-like celebrations can become occasions of both gratitude and contrition for ecological transgressions. The resulting insights might lead to initiatives aimed at protecting endangered species, promoting clean energy sources, and encouraging environmentally friendly technologies.

But perhaps we should first step back and relearn how to attend to our ecosystem in a compassionate way. Taking a cue from our South Pacific neighbors, we need to discover our own ways to direct warm thoughts toward nature and receive the many kinds of warmth being directed toward us. Perhaps in some mysterious manner we cannot now comprehend, we could begin to recover a capacity to commune with non-human species of plant and animal life. At the very least, myths like the Tale of the *Tavake* and the Dolphin Christ suggest that we need to develop a radically new, holistic consciousness of our natural surroundings. Before we rush headlong into addressing problems we have created, we ought to try reconnecting with the earth itself. Only then will we be able to see ourselves and our Speciesism for what they are.

TALKING POINTS

PACIFIC TALES

- Which one of the four Pacific tales did you find most interesting or significant? Could you relate it to any experiences you've had? Please elaborate.
- Some people feel that Christianity has not been a particularly eco-friendly religion. Do you agree? Why or why not?
- Try to remember a story that you heard from parents, grandparents or someone else when you were a child. Re-tell the story as best you can. What was most important or meaningful about it for you at the time?

- Think about movies or videos you have seen recently. Select one that you feel has a strong moral message. What is this message? Do you agree with it? Why or why not?
- Imagine that you could travel anywhere in the world. Where would you go and what would you do there? How would that experience relate to your everyday life right now?

ISLANDERS, JESUS AND SPECIESISM

- Do you have pets? Do you think they have feelings? Thoughts? Souls? Would you say that you have a relationship with them? Describe that relationship.
- Brainstorm six or seven things you could do to become more aware of your environment on a day-to-day basis. How many of these things could you do with others?
- Do you have a special place or retreat that you go to (whether in your imagination or in everyday experience) for rest, relaxation and re-charging your batteries? If so, picture or illustrate it in a new way. If not, try to envision what such a place might look like and describe or illustrate that. Then share and discuss your concept or illustration with others.
- Do you think Speciesism is a serious problem? If so, how might you go about alleviating it in your immediate community? If not, how would you propose helping to reverse ecologically destructive phenomena like global warming? What can or should churches do about it?
- If you were going to prepare a Sunday school lesson or educational talk on Jesus and ecology, how would you go about it? Think of three open-ended questions you would ask and discuss sayings of Jesus that might be relevant to those questions.

CHAPTER 5

RE-CONNECTING WITH ONE ANOTHER

RACE AND CLASS IN JAMAICA

It was an unexpected culture shock—all the white people looked alike! I had just arrived at Miami International airport after two years of cultural immersion in a village north of Kingston, Jamaica. From 1979 to 1981 my wife and I worked as co-pastors for the Jamaican Disciples of Christ Church.[1] After acclimating ourselves for nearly four months with a Jamaican family in Kingston, we were eventually "stationed" in the small community of Mannings Hill and given oversight of a circuit of four rural parishes.

Although we were really fish out of water and at best inept pastors, the locals tolerated us and even managed to teach us a few things about wealth, poverty, social status, and race relations. To begin with, as the resident "clergy" we were provided with one of the nicer houses in the village. Located on a seven-acre plot, it had four bedrooms, great views of the mountains in the distance, and, unlike most houses in the area, piped water and a flush toilet. We were also virtually the only persons in Mannings Hill with a hot water heater and an automatic washing machine. And most of the time, we were the only ones with a reasonably dependable, private motor vehicle of any appreciable size—that is, one that could carry seven to ten persons at a time. Even though our '66 Rambler was in continual need of repair and subject to inopportune breakdowns, we were able to pay one of the island's most extraordinary mechanics to keep it in running condition.

We were also the only "white" folks in the village. I put quotation marks around the term, "white," because in Jamaica racial categories are not as black and white as Caucasians in the U.S. are accustomed to. There is a complex racial continuum running from, "white and light, to 'olive,' 'light brown,' 'dark brown,' and 'black,'"[2] and one's place on that spectrum is of considerable importance. The lighter one's complexion, the more likely one has a higher social standing—though the correlation is far from precise, since in recent times social standing often has more to do with occupational status.[3]

I don't recall ever seeing a truly "light" skinned Jamaican in Mannings Hill, although some of the guiding lights in the church we pastored were somewhere between "light brown" and "dark brown." The vast majority were "black," including the organist of the Mannings Hill Church, who spoke proudly of his Scottish heritage. In short, it was not uncommon to go for weeks or even months without seeing another person as white as ourselves. I remember one day in particular: I was in Kingston for a routine car tune-up and spotted a white couple walking down the street. It struck me how odd they looked and how unusual it was to see such a sight in a working class neighborhood.

As white "expatriates" from the U.S., then, we were not simply part of a privileged racial caste, but also viewed as members of a privileged social and economic elite. It was assumed by our parishioners that simply because we were from the U.S., we had access to many economic opportunities that were unavailable to most Jamaicans. And in our case this assumption was certainly true, even though we had both grown up in lower middle-class homes, the children of Presbyterian ministers. Strongly encouraged to do well in school, we had entered college at a time when financial aid was plentiful; and had the good fortune to study at Harvard University. To many of our Jamaican neighbors, a few of whom proudly displayed pictures of Queen Elizabeth in their homes, we symbolized American royalty—to be sure, a raw, awkward, unpolished version of the British model, but clearly people of a different world.

And so we were. To further complicate matters, we were among those sixties idealists pejoratively referred to as "hippies." For us this meant—despite the washing machine and the Rambler—that we aspired to a simple lifestyle. In our early correspondence with Jamaican church executives, mistakenly expecting to be based in a remote area, we had floated the idea of using horses for local transportation instead of an automobile. This "horse proposal" was summarily rejected by a hierarchy that was clearly embarrassed that the new Harvard missionaries would even think in such backward, farcical terms. And since Mannings Hill was only twenty miles from the nation's capital, they were of course right. We quickly surmised that our superiors feared any predisposition to culturally inappropriate behavior. For example, I was later reprimanded by a local executive for wearing sandals rather than proper shoes in Kingston. Such attire was unbecoming to a minister of religion in Jamaica, even if off-duty and well beyond his or her church circuit![4]

But while we did live pampered lives in some ways, and occasionally stole off to Kingston on Monday mornings for a poolside breakfast at a hotel, it never occurred to us to purchase a television, lawnmower, or clothes dryer. We insisted on doing our own house-cleaning and yard work even though, as neighbors informed us, the previous pastor hired persons to help out around the house and yard. In fact, we soon learned that this pastor, who moonlighted as a government bureaucrat on week-days, had been a "big man" in the community. In Jamaica, the "big man" was someone you could turn to for favors—a key source for jobs, goods, and cash. Compared to him, we cut a poor figure indeed. How ridiculous I must have looked trying to cut grass the local way, swinging a machete a centimeter above the ground! After the laughter of the neighborhood children subsided, I was grimly aware of adult males watching with criti-cal and even contemptuous gazes. I imagined them thinking that this so-called man of God was too stingy to pay a local to do a job that at least the local could do correctly!

Consequently, it was not long before we became acutely aware of the degree to which many Jamaicans have a multi-faceted "love-hate" attitude toward Americans—especially white ones. On the one hand, we were put on a pedestal as symbols of the good life associated with white skin, wealth, power and freedom. On the other, we represented neo-colonial incarnations of slave masters—hedonistic, hypocritical, untrustworthy and parsimonious folks to tread softly among, to use if possible, and otherwise to avoid. Caught up in this cultural maelstrom, we threw our-selves into our pastoral roles as best we could, trying to establish personal relationships while sensing the awkwardness that often accompanied our efforts to reach out. We were ineffective preachers, but we managed to connect with some of the youth, a few of the visionaries, and an occasional eccentric in the churches we served. But gradually we came to be accepted by a few in the local community as "humble servants," who "spoke up for justice." No doubt the majority considered us hopeless or even disruptive idealists, but for better or worse, we became part of the local scene.

It was this cultural immersion that produced the epiphany in the Miami airport. Having invested myself in the lives, hopes, and dreams of rural Jamaicans, having come to call a few of them friends, I suddenly found myself in a sea of identical white faces! It took a couple days before I could, borrowing a term from hip hop culture, "flip" back into the white world's perceptual modality. And flip I did! The experience drove home to me the degree to which each of us lives in terms of a racial consciousness. We really see only those we identify with; we automatically disconnect from those who do not look like us—or the "us" we think we are. It was, of course, not long before I was my old self, looking through or past or around black and brown folk—unless I stopped myself and intentionally invited the other into my immediate awareness. How sad, how radically inhumane. Speciesism seems bad enough, but to adopt such an astigmatic view of fellow human beings is surely an even greater indecency. Another re-entry shock came from television news coverage: nearly every report of a violent crime featured accusations against blacks! Perhaps it had been that way for years, but since I now saw things with new eyes, it seemed to be weeks before a news story involved a violent white criminal.

Just as race matters, so does economic status. Grocery shopping provided another culture shock, for the economic divide was as great as the racial contrast. Once again, it was not the stores that had changed, but my perceptions. In Mannings Hill, a small shop offered the basics: rice, milk, fruits, bread and the occasional box of cereal. Once back in the U.S., I was overwhelmed at the local Kroger's by an entire aisle stacked with hundreds of boxes of different cereals, brands, types, and sizes. The contrast to rural Jamaica made the superfluity obscene. And though I have now been thoroughly re-acculturated to American consumerism, I still have an occasional twinge of revulsion, a pit-of-the-stomach sensation that we in the U.S. long ago lost our moral integrity in the matter of material consumption. One last cultural shock deserves mention. I was struck by the degree to which the American media avoid discussions of race and class, and all but refuse to mention those words in news stories.[5] The reality of poverty, both at home and abroad, is carefully obscured by the myth that since virtually everyone is middle-class, socio-economic divisions no longer exist.

But perhaps it was seeing great disparities of wealth in Jamaica that heightened my sensibility to economic injustice. In Kingston, luxurious high-rise apartments cast shadows on one-room shacks of tin and cardboard. Thousands of men and boys scavenged the garbage dumps for edible scraps while tourists luxuriated over imported gourmet meals in hotel dining rooms. Even something as innocuous as a late-night visit to a Kentucky Fried Chicken restaurant in a Kingston suburb inevitably involved an encounter of "haves" and "have-nots." For as we bit into our drumsticks, a small crowd of children with large, pleading eyes would press up against the window: "Give us your bones," they would mouth through the glass. And thousands of "rude boys"—angry youth in a nation where unemployment hovered between forty and fifty percent—struggled to survive in street gangs or criminal networks. It was also in Jamaica that I became personally aware of how large corporate enterprises exploit labor.

I had read about ethical quagmires of multinational corporations, especially overseas, but they did not hit home until I met Sister Lewis. Ms. Lewis, a Sunday school teacher at Mannings Hill, was also a skilled seamstress. She specialized in little girl's dresses, fashioning beautiful garments out of long bolts of cloth on a foot-operated machine in her home. She sewed beautiful stitches around the sleeves and edges of the dresses, and embroidered her initials inside the collars. Each dress she made for a large clothing company in Kingston took about five hours to complete, with intermittent breaks for child-care and food preparation. She worked on a contract basis. One day I asked her how much she got for each dress. "One dollar" she said, quickly adding with apparent satisfaction that she had to pay only about twenty cents for the materials.

Shopping in a big department store in Kingston the following month, I saw a dress just like the ones I had seen Sister Lewis sewing. I checked the price tag. It was "ON SALE" for thirty dollars. To compound insult to injury with fraud, someone had almost completely concealed her initials under a "Made in America" label. Why would the company falsify the origin of the garment except to realize the highest possible profit margin? Alas, such marketing practices were successful because many of the shoppers in the store were middle and upper class Jamaicans who, like Sister Lewis herself, embraced the idea that "everything is better in America." "Made in America," implied a garment that was superior to anything that a Jamaican national was likely to produce. In fact, that unfortunate misapprehension was one of the reasons that Sister Lewis could not realistically hope to go into business for herself and be directly and decently rewarded for her labor.

That was over twenty-five years ago, and since then a great deal of consciousness-raising has no doubt enhanced the value of indigenous labor and production among many Jamaicans. But the crass exploitation of textile workers that continues is but one aspect of a larger pattern of the unjust appropriation of the labor and resources in "developing" countries like Jamaica by large, transnational corporations that are often headquartered in the U.S.[6] It has exacerbated the degree to which we in the First World are "disconnected" from those in the Two-Thirds World. We think nothing of buying cheap pants and dresses at stores such as Target, Wal-Mart or Penny's, yet those purchases come at the expense of "what might have been" for people like Sister Lewis and her family of six, who struggled to eke out an existence in a two room shack.

In view of what was even then a growing awareness of racial and class inequities in Jamaica, it is not surprising that Jamaican culture would give rise to collective efforts to transcend those divisions. Perhaps foremost among these is the Rastafari movement. Rastafari has espoused a non-racist, relational self-concept and a non-exploitative life-style which, taken together, challenge the history of racial and economic divisions in Jamaican society. A brief description of these principles and their parallels with the Jesus movement will enable us to examine their relevance for addressing Economism.

RASTAFARIAN CONCEPTS OF
SELF AND LIFESTYLE

Originating in Jamaica in the 1930s, Rastafari has spread to urban centers throughout the world. The term "Rastafari" originally referred to a prince who was crowned Emperor of Ethiopia in 1930 ("*Ras*" was a title of royalty and "*Tafari*" was the family name). Upon coronation, Rastafari assumed the title, "Haile Selassie," which translates as "Might (or Power) of the Trinity."[7] Shortly after we moved to Mannings Hill, I was welcomed to the community by a Rastafarian who lived next door. Glen was friendly and very curious about who I was and why I had come to Jamaica. That evening we discussed a broad range of topics, including the struggle against apartheid in South Africa, political developments in the U.S., the nature of Jesus Christ, and Rastafarian philosophy. Thus began a series of lengthy and stimulating dialogues over the course of the next two years.

Several things impressed me about Rastas from the outset. To be sure, it is difficult to generalize about an entire group, but the vast majority of the Rastas I encountered were unusually altruistic. More times than not when our aging Rambler broke down in the countryside, it was Rastafarians who came to our aid. One time a Rasta improvised a fan belt from the leather belt in his pants, a repair that worked long enough to get the car to our mechanic in Kingston a week later. Another time, when the oil cap disappeared, a Rasta replaced it with a slice of sugar cane that worked remarkably well. Above all, the Rastas I encountered never asked for or accepted payment for such emergency services.

What I found most impressive was not their talent and ingenuity, but their willingness to drop what they were doing and discuss their beliefs and practices. Furthermore, I came to find them remarkably pacific in the face of repeated insults and personal affronts, for indeed many Jamaicans make no secret of their dislike for Rastafarians, and journalists routinely portrayed them as deviants, drug addicts, or even dangerous criminals. On several occasions, I overheard villagers in Mannings Hill calling Glen and his Rasta friends derogatory names. But I never once heard Glen or his friends raise their voices in anger or react harshly to the name callers.

Once, when he had been laid off from his job at a mill, Glen asked local Jamaican Disciples of Christ church members for permission to farm a small portion of unused church lands behind his shack. Although village church leaders approved the request, church executives in Kingston turned it down. I was outraged, but Glen's response was to forgive those he called Babylonians—"for they know not what they do." I began to see that Rastas commonly displayed attitudes at least as "Christian" as did the Christians themselves! Accordingly, I set out to learn more about them, and eventually wrote my doctoral dissertation on the ethics of the movement.[8] Among many fascinating features, two proved particularly interesting: their concepts of interpersonal identity and lifestyle—symbolized respectively by the Rasta terms *I-n-I* and *livity*.[9]

RASTAFARIAN IDENTITY: *I-N-I*

When Rastas wish to indicate the first person singular, rather than saying "I," they use the expression, "*I-n-I*." It connotes the Rasta belief that each one of us is inextricably linked to a whole network of other agents or "I's." Depending on the context, *I-n-I* can also be used as the first person plural, denoting two or more Rastafarians or even the movement as a whole. Perhaps the most important signification of the term is that as *I-n-I*, one's personal ego is inseparably joined to some other "I" in the form of *divine* agency or God (variously characterized as *Jah, Jah-Rastafari, Haile Selassie-I*, Conquering Lion of the Tribe of Judah, or King of Kings).[10] The unity between one's self and divinity is conveyed in Rasta poetry when "Rastafari" is pronounced with a decided emphasis on the final vowel, as in RastafarI. It is also reflected in the Rasta idea that the Roman numeral "I" in the title *Selassie I* does not connote "the first" as much as it evokes the "I" of the *I-n-I* relation.

Moreover, to refer to oneself as *I-n-I* is, as one Rastafarian put it, to refer to one's brothers and sisters as "the same as himself."[11] Thus, when Rastas refer to themselves as *I-n-I*, they are instantaneously connecting themselves to those brothers and sisters who identify with the movement. It is precisely in this sense that the term evokes a radically *social, relational* self-concept. One's individual identity is intertwined with one's group identity. Rastas even speak of a sense of knowing each other intimately—as if from inside the other's consciousness—as "vibrations." Certain ways of looking, speaking, gesturing and moving express vibrations.

Paradoxically, the *I-n-I* who is united to Rastas everywhere is at the same time empowered to be a *sovereign self*. The image of kingship, as expressed in the title of the Rasta poem, "I Man Kingman, Dreadman Rule,"[12] is re-appropriated by Rastas and applied universally to all *I-n-I*, who become "kings" (men) or "queens" (women). In a complete inversion of the colonial dependency syndrome, the obsequious "me" of the Jamaican popular cultural idiom is transformed into a free, self-governing *"I-n-I."* As the "lion" who in the Jamaican context is king of the urban jungle, *I-n-I* rediscovers and reasserts a sense of pride and dignity in his or her blackness.[13] At the same time, the struggle for racial self-esteem is seen, as depicted in one Rasta poetic image, in "black and white."[14]

But the black lion king does not stand alone. *I-n-I* act in solidarity with brothers and sisters who live in abject poverty. In Rasta poetry, *I-n-I* become the immortal *black buds* (black birds) who give themselves unselfishly to the poor, or "human scavengers."[15] As proud, *sacrificial agent*, the *I-n-I* self proclaims a prophetic understanding of history. In the symbol of "Peta wailin in de wilderness," Rastas become black modern-day counterparts to the Biblical prophets, calling for equal rights and justice. In a world circumscribed by violence, *I-n-I* call for peace and counsel restraint.[16]

Finally, *I-n-I*—who are linked to God (*Jah*) and other Rastas, and who exude a proud black consciousness, struggle with the oppressed, prophesy a new day and promote peace—are also *rooted in nature*. This organic connection is evoked in a series of additional new linguistic creations akin to *I-n-I* and known as "I-words." For example, the term, *I-ration* (creation), implicitly links oneself (the "I" of the relational self) to the created world. Similarly, *I-land* (island of Jamaica) suggests a fundamental connection of the self to Jamaica. Rasta lyrics also express this linkage to nature in the symbolism of the drum, sound, fire, wind and earth. In the words of the Rasta poet Farika Birhan, Jamaica is *"I-land* in the sun," *"Earthshaka"* (earth-shaker), and "Babylon *Braka"* (breaker of Babylon). . . . to which all nations must come."[17] Consequently, although repatriation to Africa (the belief that one day Rastas in Jamaica will be enabled to return to Africa and live an idyllic existence) is still important to many Rastafarians, there is an increasing concern for how one can live authentically in the Jamaican context.

RASTAFARIAN LIFESTYLE: LIVITY

I-n-I, as persons who are intrinsically related to transcendent agency, other selves and nature, seek to model *livity*—an integrated, self-reliant lifestyle. For Rastas, *livity* is associated with what Rastas call an *I-tal* (vital) ethos—living in a simple, pure and organic way in harmony with nature. *I-tal* living is exemplified in Rastas' physical appearance, commitment to the "yard" (neighborhood), use of herbs, process of reflection, artistic forms, and modes of production.

Rastas are highly visible because of their distinctive hairstyle. Citing the Biblical injunction, "They shall not make baldness upon their head" (Lev 21:5),[18] Rastas do not cut their hair, but allow it to grow naturally into long matted strands or "locks." Locks are symbolic of the lion's mane, and Rastas view the lion as a consummate African symbol of the freedom, power and sovereignty of *I-n-I*. Locks facilitate the reception of "vibrations" which enhance solidarity amongst Rastas. Moreover, as *dreadlocks* the Rasta hairstyle evokes a conflict-ridden, multifaceted relation between *I-n-I* and the white, Eurocentric elite. The sight of dreadlocks is intended to conjure up sentiments of Black Nationalism, prophetic denunciation and apocalyptic exultation.[19]

To be dread is frequently associated with living in "yards" (enclosed inner-city compounds) or "camps" (semi-urban temporary settlements) that foster grassroots communal relationships with others in the lower economic classes. While Rasta poets sometimes express a nostalgic longing for life in the country, a more frequent theme is nurturing the kind of sociality associated with a rural lifestyle in the urban context. Rastas vehemently resist government efforts to relocate them into high-rise apartment complexes, because such "developments" function to separate them from the neighborhood ethos of the yard. Life in such high-rise projects is viewed as encouraging pretensions of upward mobility and economic superiority—in our terms, pretensions toward Economism—that spark tension and conflict among the poor. The Rastafarian commitment to the yard underscores both *I-n-I's* resolve to dwell with the poor and the contemporary focus on living in urban Jamaica rather than migrating to the African continent.

Rastas are perhaps most identified with smoking marijuana, commonly known as *ganja* in Jamaica. *Ganja*, also called "holy herb," "*kali*" and "sacred weed," is a strain of marijuana (*cannabis sativa*) that has been used among Jamaicans in the countryside for cooking and medicinal purposes for many generations. Citing scriptural sanctions such as Ps 104:14, "He causeth the grass for the cattle, and herb for the service of man," Rastas view marijuana as a means for socio-religious enlightenment or *I-Sight*. Many Rastas use marijuana primarily to facilitate an intellectual process known as "reasoning." Reasonings are ad hoc dialogues on virtually any topic, with the aid of the Bible, newspapers, and other written materials. They may become complex Socratic exercises in which *I-n-I* transcend ordinary, everyday perceptions and arrive at new understandings of reality. The anthropologist Carole Yawney has reconstructed reasonings on the topics of "coming to know Santa Claus" and "the Pope as the head of the mafia."[20] To the extent that reasonings entail critical reflection on Eurocentric ideologies, they challenge the limits of established western beliefs and values.

The prophetic intellectual tenor of Rastafari is reflected in its poetry and song lyrics. Internationally, Rastafari is perhaps best known in connection with reggae music. Originating in Jamaica in the late 1960s, reggae is characterized by deep bass rhythms punctuated with heavy drumbeats. Many of the most prominent reggae artists have been Rastafarians, and many reggae lyrics originally espoused Rastafarian themes, denouncing the hypocrisy of the established order, and heralding the coming of a new society,[21] and developing the poetic vocabulary of *I-words* alluded to above.[22]

As creative autonomous selves, *I-n-I* are engaged in a variety of such self-reliant enterprises as agriculture, fishing, woodworking, knitting, painting, printing, transportation, and the growing and marketing of marijuana.[23] These activities reinforce the essential independence of amorphous small group yards and camps. But such has been the growth and expansion of the movement that some Rastas are now professionals—teachers, university lecturers, and lawyers. Most *I-n-I*, however, eschew life in the fast lane and aspire to the simpler, more self-reliant lifestyle associated with the *I-tal* ethos. Indeed, middleclass lifestyles are viewed as morally dangerous because they can numb one's consciousness of *Babylon*, another key term in Rasta ideology. *Babylon* refers to any affluent society of self-absorbed individuals who worship idols and live decadent lifestyles at the expense of the poor. In Jamaica, *Babylon* is associated with the upper echelons of Jamaican society, especially any institution seen as oppressive, like the police, established churches, or official media. Internationally, the term *Babylon* conjures up images of military complexes, transnational corporations, and religious hierarchies (like that of the Roman Catholic Church) that are perceived to dominate the poor and the marginalized. *Babylon's* agents not only lack self-understanding and *livity*, they are devoid of vision.

On the other hand, the Rasta term *Ithiopia* pertains to a transformative vision of dignity, religious communion, equal rights and justice that lies at the heart of *livity*. As the antithesis of *Babylon*, *Ithiopia* signifies transcending negative self-images, racism, religious hegemony and economic and political domination. Through cooperative work on the land and the sharing of resources, Rastas believe, they have partially achieved and can anticipate a fuller realization of *I-land*. Guided by the *Ithiopia* vision, *I-n-I* cultivate postures of engaged non-acceptance in the midst of *Babylon*. Given their expectation of *Babylon's* eventual demise, *I-n-I* nurture an attentive patience.

The postures of engaged non-acceptance and attentive patience predispose Rastas toward a non-violent "peace and love" ethic. As noted earlier, *I-n-I* are also inclined to assist strangers in need, and are sometimes found mediating disputes between non-Rastas. One startling development in this connection is the Rasta stress on strong father-son bonds: in direct contrast to the matricentric Jamaican family structure,[24] sons often appear alongside their fathers in the workplace.

RASTAS, JESUS AND ECONOMISM

But what, might one ask, is the possible relevance of Rastafari for life in modern America today? It is relevant for at least two reasons. First, it represents a genuine, contemporary cultural alternative for those who are poor, black, and young (in Jamaica the vast majority), and for the lighter-skinned and middle class as well. That is, as a viable cultural phenomenon in the global village, it represents not only a blueprint for a moral life, but one presently modeled by our neighbors in the Caribbean. Second, as a countercultural movement that both critiques and transcends the dominant moral alternatives in Jamaica, Rastafari can provide a living example of how the early Jesus tradition attacked and transformed the dominant moral patterns of its culture. Since there are strong affinities between the Jamaican Rastafarian movement of the late twentieth century and the Palestinian Jesus movement of the first, I shall examine each of these radical social phenomena in turn and then conclude the chapter by showing how both movements provide insights for confronting Economism.

One of the most intriguing things about the Rastafari movement is its persistence into a fourth generation. According to traditional social scientific wisdom, similar cultural and religious movements have either withered away after the founder died or evolved into an established institution. Early researchers of Rastafari therefore predicted that it would either prove to be a passing cultural fad, or develop into a recognizable church or political party.[25] But rather than disappear or become a conventional social institution, Rastafari continues to thrive as a counter-cultural movement. How is that possible?

Since this is hardly the place to offer a detailed answer to that question,[26] suffice it to say that Rastafari has been accepted by a significant part of the Jamaican population.[27] This is due in no small part because it is a home-grown phenomenon that has incorporated yet transcended important features of the two dominant moral traditions in Jamaica since the colonial era: the Anancy Folk and Missionary Christian traditions. Briefly, the Anancy Folk tradition refers to a corpus of indigenous knowledge that emerged in Jamaica during the long history of slavery and has persisted into the current neo-colonial period. To an appreciable degree it has arisen from and finds expression in a cycle of Jamaican folklore that features an artful trickster named Anancy.[28]

Like the machinations of picaresque figures in many folk traditions, Anancy's exploits are replete with concealment and chicanery. He often appears as a spider who is capable of changing into a man. Although he is evasive and cunning, his antics are efficacious strategies for survival. A recurring theme is his ability to cause calamities and then get off unde-tected; even when he murders, rapes, or maims, he inevitably escapes ret-ribution. Even as a tiny spider, Anancy outwits ferocious lions and tigers. He's the outsider, the little guy who outsmarts the well-connected and the powerful. For the great mass of Jamaicans, who both economically and culturally occupy the bottom level of a two-tiered system of haves and have-nots, he is the popular anti-hero.

It is nonetheless clear that Anancy's escapades, especially the more perverse ones, are not intended to represent models for moral behavior. He reflects, in some senses, both the best and worst in human interac-tions, someone to be both emulated and repudiated, both a positive and a negative role model. Take for example his love of leisure and disdain for labor. Due to a legacy of slavery and dehumanizing toil, the Afro-Jamaican self strove to salvage a sense of self-esteem by developing strategies of resistance. Anancy's clever avoidance of work and corresponding pursuit of leisure represents a predictable response to subjugation. Yet while his survival techniques reflect the yearnings of the oppressed, he nevertheless manipulates circumstances and people to his personal benefit. In the story of "*Yunk-Kyum-Pyung*," for instance, Anancy becomes a wicked ruler.

Anancy does not prophesy about the future, and although references to an afterlife occur in the tales, what matters most is dealing with pres-ent events in the light of past experience. But Anancy narratives are not confined to ordinary time and space. It is quite possible to fly to the four corners of the earth while remaining on the island of Jamaica. Africa and the Caribbean are interchangeable, and Anancy interacts not only with animals and humans, but also with spirits and ghosts known as "duppies." Indeed, in this tradition, humans, animals, the souls of the deceased and other spirits co-exist in a fluid continuum of space and time. Like the threads of the spider web he traverses, Anancy is interconnected with all other beings in creation.

Like their fabled trickster, Rastas are rooted in the created world. Living according to the *I-tal* ethos of *livity*, the *I-n-I* self is thoroughly involved in nature. Their dual emphasis on an organic relation to the land and re-creative activity that integrates work and leisure recapitulates the unity of experience in the folk tradition. But by virtue of reasoning with marijuana, each *I-n-I* also stands on her or his own and asserts a degree of intellectual autonomy not usually associated with folk narrative. For example, Rastas question such elements of the folk tradition as duppies and demeaning conceptions of women that conflict with their sense of reality or justice.

But Rastas also reflect Anancy's common touch and value close bonds among people. The social, relational dimension of the *I-n-I* concept has strong affinities with the rich experience of community evoked in Anancy stories. Like Anancy, *I-n-I* speak the idiom of the common folk, interact with them in the marketplace, and live among them in yards and camps. They join in and identify with the pain and privations of the people. And since the folk tradition does not portray Anancy as a savior figure (indeed, he is not above leaving the listener in the lurch), most Rastas do not look to Selassie to set them free. Hence, while Christians approvingly quote the Beatitudes or the parables of Jesus, Rastafarians do not as a rule cite teachings of Selassie. Selassie is not so much an exalted moral exemplar as he is a symbol of ancestral identity, solidarity, and royal power who resisted the Babylonians.

Unlike their mythical alter ego, *I-n-I* espouse a redemptive project that transcends the scope of their roguish folk-hero: they struggle against Babylon. While Anancy is often quick to take advantage of another's weaknesses, *I-n-I* strive to live by an ethic based on peace, love, and a principled avoidance of exploitation—an ethic in which they try to refrain from profiting by stepping on others. And although the folk tradition does not include either an explicit or implicit critique of the established social order, Rastafarian literature is replete with calls for fundamental social change in the interest of justice. *I-n-I* see themselves as prophetic agents, and affirm an unfolding intentionality in history. On the other hand, the folk tradition shows non-human and human agents continually interacting in cyclical, episodic adventures lacking any progressive telos. Rastas may revere the memories of ancestors and the living dead who are so important to the Anancy tradition, but their ultimate concern is of a higher order: it is to confront and survive *Babylon*—which they believe will eventually self-destruct—while beginning even now to realize *Ithiopia* in this world. Thus, while affirming their roots in the past—even back to the dawn of creation—Rastas are oriented toward a prophetic future. In this and other ways, their movement builds on, stretches, and expands the folk tradition in a way that gives it a new moral directionality.

The Rastafari movement has also engaged and, in my view, moved beyond its only real rival for moral ascendancy in Jamaica, the Missionary Christian tradition. For most of its early history, Missionary Christianity in Jamaica was identified with the overseas work of white Protestant European and North American churches. Although the Roman Catholic Church and Anglican Churches had close ties with the colonial elite, Roman Catholics were a decided minority in an essentially Protestant arena. Therefore, Missionary Christianity in Jamaica essentially means the Protestant Missionary tradition.

All the missionaries were enthusiastic evangelizers. While representing a broad spectrum of theological perspectives, they all proclaimed that God was revealed to humanity in the person of Jesus Christ, who offers salvation to all. The Bible was the central and usually the sole testimony to this proclamation. Human beings were sinners—that is, they existed in a state of apartness from God—but were individually accountable to that Supreme Judge.

The missionaries also identified the Good with God. Since God was wholly good and was incarnated in Christ, the latter could "make no compromise with anything that was not good."[29] Indeed, Christ personified the ideal pattern according to which one ought to live. Thus, as his followers' chief moral guide, he was very different from Anancy, who was a morally ambiguous source of both inspiration and amusement. In addition, the Christian notion of the sinful self was significantly different from the view of self in the folk tradition. In the latter, the self was thoroughly interconnected with all other agents in the world, not separate or fundamentally distanced from a monotheistic god who was the locus of ultimate value. Further, Anancy's antics and adventures had neither tragic overtones nor irreversible consequences.

Moreover, the European and American missionaries were strongly influenced by a western conception of gradual linear progress. They seemed preoccupied with problem-solving and project planning. The goal was not just to change individual lives, but to "civilize" a culture. In *Building with Christ in Jamaica*, the metaphor of "building" is used to describe missionary activities,[30] and U.S. Disciples of Christ missionaries were quick to interpret indigenous Jamaican efforts to develop organizational responses to problems as signs of reaching maturity.[31]

Finally, while promoting evangelism, allegiance to Jesus Christ, belief in an individualistic notion of sin, and a predilection for problem-solving, most of the missionaries frowned upon emotional displays of religiosity. Preferring somber and sedate liturgical expressions, they discouraged loud clapping, shouting, jumping or wailing, activities that were characteristic of indigenous religious traditions. It was a losing battle: one missionary remarked in consternation, "The church has been struggling for two hundred years to repress the emotions of Jamaicans!"[32]

Although the ethical worlds of Rastafari and Missionary Christianity differ in many points, three deserve specific mention. First, the Rasta self does not exist in a state of sin or apartness from God, because the "I" of the *I-n-I* relational self is integrally linked to God (*Jah*). Thus problems of human conduct result from inadequacies in consciousness, not from an ontological dichotomy between creature and creator.[33] Also, given the multi-vocal and essentially open-ended character of reasoning with marijuana, both the content and form of *I-n-I's* faith claims are subject to change in accordance with individual revelatory insights. In Rastafari, then, it is simply not possible to expect adherence to established formulations of belief.

Second, although Rastafarians and Christians share a concern for redeeming the world, Rastas actively involve themselves in the everyday struggle of the poor for survival in that world. While the Christian missionaries often sanctioned the prevailing economic and political status quo, *I-n-I* denounce it as a representation of *Babylon*. *I-n-I's* concern with the issue of multinational corporate exploitation indicates the extent to which Rastafarians have moved beyond the reformist social agenda of the missionaries. Where today's successors of the early missionaries at best promote a "liberal" social gospel, Rastas affirm a "liberation" ethic, and view conflict as a creative resource, not as an aberration to be eschewed. Where the mainline missionaries stressed a gradual, linear progressivism—a methodical building up of the kingdom of God in the world— Rastas call for a more dramatic end to *Babylon* and the ushering in of a radically new era with untold possibilities for human ennoblement.

Third, while Rastas and the more progressive of the Christian missionaries would agree on the importance of reason in faith and life, *I-n-I* claim that by reasoning with marijuana they transcend ordinary conceptions of rationality. Reasoning with the aid of the holy weed, they believe, affords deeper insight (the "*I-sight*" mentioned earlier) into the nature of reality than is attainable by ordinary reflection, Scripture reading, or prayer.

With all this in mind one begins to see that the contemporary Rastafarian movement has a number of parallels with the Jesus movement adumbrated by the Jesus Seminar. Rastas bear witness to the emergence of a powerful personal and social identity that enables *I-n-I* to struggle against both the materialism and narcissism inherent in the American dream, and the limited horizons of the folk tradition. Just as Jesus preached against many of the social and economic conventions of his age, Rastafari represents forms of sociality that challenge what passes for the good life in *Babylon* today. And, although there are important differences between the ethical worlds of Rastafari and the Jesus movement, an appreciation of the former can help us to develop a fresh appreciation for the latter. Indeed, the more one listens to Rasta poets and singers and becomes acquainted with the core symbols and practices of the movement, the better one can imagine how the Jesus movement became a dynamic, prophetic countercultural force nearly two thousand years ago.

Indeed, one of the most striking things about the leader of that movement is that he seldom talks about himself or his mission, but proclaims the divine domain.[34] Whereas the New Testament writers preach Jesus,

Jesus himself preaches the Kingdom (or "Kin-dom") of God.[35] And just as the Rasta concepts of *I-n-I* and *livity* represent alternative ways of being conscious of self and lifestyle, many of Jesus' sayings appear to have a similar function: they proclaim counterintuitive wisdom and subvert or invert conventional moral understandings.[36] "Whoever tries to hang on to life will forfeit it, but whoever forfeits life will preserve it" (Luke 17:33).[37] Social status will be reversed in the Kingdom: "The last will be first and the first last" (Matt 20:16). Much as Rastas spurn the powers and principalities of *Babylon* for the vision of *Ithiopia*, Jesus frames our existential predicament as one of a choice between opposite loci of value. "No one can be a slave to two masters. No doubt that slave will either hate one and love the other, or be devoted to one and disdain the other" (Matt 6:24). Contrary to the world's expectations for wealth and happiness, "You can't be enslaved to both God and a bank account" (Matt 6:24).

Jesus' counterintuitive values are nowhere more evident than in his references to economic life. At virtually every turn, Jesus challenges the conventional assumption of economic success as a primary value: "How difficult it is for those who have money to enter God's domain . . . . It is easier for a camel to squeeze through a needle's eye than for a wealthy person to get into God's domain" (Matt 19:23, 25). His parables castigate the human preoccupations with financial security: "There was a rich person who had a great deal of money. He said, 'I shall invest my money so that I may sow, reap, plant and fill my storehouses with produce, that I may lack nothing.' These were the things he was thinking in his heart, but that very night he died" (Thom 63:1–3). It is now time to relate some of these teachings to what is perhaps the most ominous moral threat of our age—the religion of Economism.

One of the pitfalls of worshipping the economy as our ultimate concern is that economic success requires establishing a "permanent" residence. If you doubt this, just try obtaining credit—or even a job—without a relatively permanent address. Furthermore, owning a home is not only the primary source of equity for many people, but is widely regarded as an essential element of the American dream. But from the day we close on our home, we become enslaved to a mortgage that obliges us to pay for our home several times over in interest. In effect, we ransom a sizeable portion of the next twenty-five or thirty years of our working lives to the mortgage holder.

Then, from the moment we move into "our" homes, we worry about a decline in real estate values. This anxiety can drive a wedge between us and neighbors whose financial resources, cultural non-conformities, or personal idiosyncrasies may negatively affect real estate values in the neighborhood. Hence, even against our better instincts we might shun present or potential neighbors who are not like us.

In the face of such fears, Jesus recommends that we "Be passersby" (Thom 42).[38] His most committed followers are urged to adopt a nomadic mode of life: "And Jesus said, 'Foxes have dens, and birds of the sky have nests, but this mother's child has nowhere to rest his head'" (Luke 9:58). We are to lead a "liminal"[39] existence, disengaged from personal attachments, social status, or institutional approbation (Matt 12:48–50; Luke 14:26). As liminal selves, we live in transition between the lives we led before "going along the road" with Jesus and the yet to be realized outcome of the journey. Our challenge is to do better than the wealthy would-be follower who went away dejected (Mark 10:17–23).

Rastas pose a difficult problem for Jamaica's census takers, because they are frequently on the go between camps and yards, spending a few weeks with one circle of brothers or sisters and then relocating for a while with another small group. And even those *I-n-I* based in urban areas retain a strong urge to work the land and grow their own food in the countryside. They cluster together in semi-rural areas for occasional festivals or "grounations." Because of their "dread appearance" (the wearing of dreadlocks), simple dress, and marijuana smoking, Rastas are often unwelcome in the homes and communities where they grew up. And as members of a religious group that exists in tension with both indigenous folk movements and the Christian Churches, they occupy an ambiguous spiritual limbo. In this sense, their social alienation resembles that of the early Christians, whose faith set them apart from the popular Roman and Greek religions as well as the major Jewish sects of the time.

For such passersby, Rasta or early Christian, the larger society's definition of good moral character is at best problematical. The value of home ownership we noted earlier is an important element of the religion of Economism because it represents a bourgeois sensibility—a sense of being a good middle-class citizen. This self-perception requires building a reputation as someone who embodies the default or received moral code, but entails the associated danger of becoming self-righteous. And that fault Jesus ranks second only to greed in the catalogue of moral transgressions. In the parable of the Pharisee and the toll collector (Luke 18:9–14), Jesus absolves the latter, who confesses his fault and pleads for mercy, but condemns the former as a pious fraud: the toll collector went home "acquitted" and the Pharisee did not.[40] Both stood under judgment, but the Pharisee's blindness to his own impiety made him arrogant. Jesus' dramatic insistence on the need for humility stands as a corrective to our middle-class penchant for taking pride in such petty virtues as keeping up a nice lawn, providing the kids with a costly private education, or dutifully attending church on a regular basis.

Seen from the perspective of a liminal worldview, the Pharisee errs in equating his moral worth with an established moral character that has been built up over time. But the liminal self is in transition from the past and is in some sense "not yet." This is not to argue that achieving a good moral character is unimportant, but rather that it is a "project-in-process." In the parable, the Pharisee's prayer is rejected not because of sinful deeds, but because he thinks his well-established moral character ("I fast twice a week, I give tithes of everything that I acquire") somehow renders him morally superior to "that toll collector over there."

Another vital point appears in Jesus' statement that "What goes into you can't defile you; what comes out of you can" (Mark 7:15–16). This did much more than challenge contemporary purity regulations; it undermined common assumptions about what constitutes good behavior and stressed the importance of proactive moral responses. We cannot rewrite the past, but for liminal selves who are projects-in-process, what has already happened is never the last word. It doesn't continue to defile us—not only because our moral characters are already compromised, but also because character is always a work in progress. Therefore, the true measure of our moral life is what comes out of us—how we respond to our received moral traditions.

Just as that ecstatic prophet known as John the Baptist—who allegedly sported "a mantle of camel hair"[41] and lived on locusts and raw honey—challenged his first-century hearers, he stands as an affront to clean-cut, affluent Americans, those whom John Kenneth Galbraith labeled "the contented majority." Similarly, the Jesus who reportedly allowed his disciples to eat without washing their hands (Mark 7:1–5), gather grain on the Sabbath (Mark 2:23), and heal on the Sabbath (Mark 3:1–5), subverts more than an ethic based on purity codes: he raises vital questions about the ethical standing of the social and religious rituals of conventional, middle-class life.

But this doesn't sound like the Jesus we have grown up with. Where is this "Jesus-Seminar Jesus" coming from? Why does he seem to have such a radical, iconoclastic edge? Part of the answer lies in his early associations with the aforementioned wandering preacher, John the baptizer. In Mark's account, we first encounter Jesus when he is being baptized by John; and since John is mentioned in all four of the canonical gospels, we can assume that his relationship with Jesus was important for the early Christian movement's understanding of who Jesus was and what he was about. In Mark's account, Jesus' ministry begins only after John has been arrested—in what may be a prefiguring of Jesus' fate.

In any event, just as John the baptizer is not interested in hearing about blue blood or ethnic purity ("Don't even start saying to yourselves, 'We have Abraham for our father" [Luke 3:8]), Jesus seems not overly attached to his own family. As Jesus the "passerby" instructs his followers, "If any of you comes to me and does not hate your own father and mother and wife and children and brothers and sisters—yes, even your own life—you're no disciple of mine" (Luke 14:26). And Jesus the prophet gets no respect "on his home turf and among his relatives and at home" (Mark 6:4).

Apparently Jesus also noted John's condemnations of financial improprieties like price gouging ("Charge nothing above the official rates" [Luke 3:13]) and extortion ("No more shakedowns! No more frame-ups either!" [Luke 3:14]). Like the autonomous *I-n-I*, John has not bribed officials, and therefore is not beholden to political figures; indeed, he takes it upon himself to criticize King Herod's marriage to Herodias. Of course, the cost of a discipleship that confronts Economism is high: lacking political connections, both John and Jesus are vulnerable to arrest, imprisonment, and execution.

One of the core problems with the religion of Economism is that it aspires to a non-ultimate locus of value. In H. R. Niebuhr's terms, it is the stuff of a henotheistic faith, where one has trust in and loyalty to one god among many others.[42] Rastas, on the other hand, are headed toward an open-ended *telos*, an *Ithiopia* of radical equality, equity, non-racism, love, peace and justice—none of which money can buy and none of which is fully attainable in the present world. Jesus also proclaims an ideal that is mysterious and only indirectly described.[43] Like the elephant in the Buddhist story mentioned in Chapter Two, God's imperial rule is "spread out upon the earth, and people don't see it" (Thom 113:4); indeed, it is "right there in your presence" (Luke 17:20–21).

Positively, it is like a hidden treasure that one "sells every last possession" to obtain (Matt 13:44),[44] or a priceless pearl, to buy, for which a merchant sells "everything he has" (Matt 13:45/Thom 76:1–2). It is as powerful as the "leaven that a woman took and concealed in fifty pounds of flour until it was all leavened" (Matt 13:33/Luke 13:20–21).[45] The divine domain is characterized by growth, expansion, and buoyancy. There is a subtle, but significant "creation of space." In the parable of the empty jar, the kingdom can be envisioned as the empty space that results from the spilling of the meal (Thom 97:1–4). Also, like the tiny mustard seed slowly taking root in the soil and the leaven concealed in the flour, the spilling of the mill goes unnoticed. Thus, God's imperial rule is a "behind-the-scenes" creating of space which makes room for something to happen.[46] Human efforts may be involved—for in the parable of the growing seed Jesus refers to a "harvest time" when the "farmer sends for the sickle" (Mark 4:26–29)—but ultimately the divine domain reflects the way God graciously works through nature. Unlike the god of Economism, the God of Jesus transcends a closed universe of supply and demand. This God cannot be measured, bought or sold.

Indeed, Jesus bears witness to a God who "causes the sun to rise on both the bad and the good, and sends rain on both the just and the unjust" (Matt 5:45)—not a deity who employs some rational, social, or economic calculus in his distribution of blessings. Another problem with the religion of Economism is that people inevitably have to compete with one another for jobs. Today's students are encouraged to learn how to "market themselves" to prospective employers. They are coached on how to outshine other applicants for the same position. Sooner or later they become caught up in interminable games of one-upmanship. But contrary to the presuppositions of Economism, God shows no favoritism for middle-class, law abiding, church-going, responsible citizens. In fact, Jesus repeatedly proclaimed a God who is "generous to the ungrateful and wicked" (Luke 6:35).

The generous character of the divine domain is revealed in the Prodigal Son parable (Luke 15:11–32), in which the Father celebrates the return of his errant son, and in the parable of "the laborers in the vineyard" (Matt 20:1–15), where the proprietor pays each worker the same amount even though some have worked longer hours than others. The tension in both parables is rooted in perfectly reasonable concerns about the fairness of the protagonists' actions. While the older son in the prodigal parable may have just cause to complain that his father has taken him for granted, he is so fixated on his own jealous feelings that he cannot rejoice at his brother's restoration to life. Because he is not living as a passerby, and because he insists on comparing himself to his brother, he cannot appreciate his father's gracious forgiveness.

Indeed, one wonders whether our habituation to Economism has obscured the very concept of "grace." From the viewpoint of Economism, the vineyard owner in the parable seems manifestly unjust. Neither big business nor big labor would deem it fair to pay those who worked a full day the same as those who worked only an hour. But Jesus employed an entirely different frame of reference; he saw his fellow humans as nomadic selves living a liminal existence. We must, he said, abandon our "punch the clock" mentality (even if we have to punch it for a living) and be thankful for the bread we receive, and welcoming to latecomers. Responding to God's graciousness, the liminal self does not feel superior to others,[47] for it does not dwell on comparisons—which, after all, are always relative to our own individual, and often quite limited and biased, standpoints.

Further, while the key actors in the religion of Economism are producers and consumers, Jesus associated God's imperial rule with children, outcasts, and the poor. He says that God's domain is peopled with children (Mark 10:14) and that we have to be able to accept God's domain "the way a child would" (Mark 10:15). The child's vulnerability and ready acceptance represent correctives to the calculating and defensive postures associated with Economism's religious zeal for getting ahead. God's domain is also connected with attacks on demons: "But if by God's finger I drive out demons, then for you God's imperial rule has arrived" (Luke 11:20). In his world demons were blamed for a wide range of physical and mental afflictions; in ours, the word commonly connotes such self-delusions as greed, envy, and jealously—impulses that hamper our ability to abide by the very moral conventions we espouse.

But above all others, Jesus insists, the poor are inheritors of the kingdom: "Congratulations, you poor! God's domain belongs to you" (Luke 6:20). His message for the rich is not so good: "I swear to you, it is very difficult for the rich to enter Heaven's domain . . . it's easier for a camel to squeeze through a needle's eye than for a wealthy person to get into God's domain" (Matt 19:23–24).[48] The rich who think that because of their investments they "lack nothing" are in for a rude awakening (Thom 63:1–4). Jesus' glowing assurances to the poor and dire prognosis for the rich subvert Economism's stories of success and well-being.

In conclusion, it is clear that the message of the divine domain offers to itinerant disciples on the fringes of worldly structures of wealth and power both a countervailing praxis and a beacon of hope. If we take Jesus' moral injunctions seriously, we must repudiate haughty self-aggrandizement, especially ostentatious displays of dress, titles, and social status (Luke 20:45–46; Matt 11:7–8). The flashy lifestyle of the upwardly mobile will be out of place. We won't be siding up to "those who wear fancy clothes," because they are found "in regal quarters" (Matt 11:7–8). While we may not yet be willing to abandon home ownership and circulate freely as passersby, we can at least become less anxious about material values. In fact, in a provocative and outlandish way, Jesus goes so far as to counsel against all such concerns (Luke 12:22–28), and promises fulfillment to those who but ask, seek and knock (Matt 7:7–8). While no doubt an extreme exaggeration, this promise points to an ennobling dimension of faithful living that discredits Economism's willful pursuit of individual success.

The central thrust of the moral teaching of Rastafari and Jesus is simply that a global neighborhood requires a neighborhood ethos. This will entail developing new networks of "allies" comprising persons of different races and social classes. Recognizing that race and class are social constructs, allies will work together to re-construct relationships along cross-cultural or even "intercultural" lines,[49] and thus create communities free of arbitrary divisions. But given the very real legacies of racism and classism as "systems of advantage"[50] in U.S. society, little progress will occur until these systems are named and addressed. The Rastafarian critique of *Babylon* and Jesus' implicit critique of the kingdoms of this world both suggest the need for a full-fledged, critical examination of the American Empire as a system of oppression based on race, class, and gender. Of course this will not be easy and it will invite hostile as well as benign responses. But just as Rastafarians appeal to the relational self-concept of *I-n-I*, allies will need to affirm the essential humanity that reconnects them with significant others. Like Jesus' invocation of God's power to cast out demons, or a sovereign Rasta's celebration of the power associated with the lion's mane, allies will need to employ their solidarity as human beings to overcome their sense of marginality.

Together, we can nurture a prophetic sensibility that is open to creative acts of solidarity with movements of the poor. This may entail migrating back into urban communities, working overseas, or encountering the poor in our daily activities. We can also contribute to social change by supporting such efforts as the Fair Trade Movement, the Anti-Sweatshop Campaign, and other initiatives for corporate social responsibility. Wholehearted participation of this sort may even spark new linguistic or narrative traditions (such as the emergence of the *I-word* vocabulary in Rastafari, or the parabolic sayings of Jesus) that produce useful shifts in conventional concepts and interpretive frameworks. Such acts of solidarity with the marginalized may also give rise to more self-reliant forms of behaviors: riding buses, bicycling to work, or car pooling; exchanging knowledge about financial planning, health care, or parenting; refurbishing parks, sidewalks, and street corners; or participating in civic celebrations, neighborhood recreation, and collective work projects.

In these and many other ways we can and must reconnect with one another by creating community with those who are marginalized in the global neighborhood. The first step is to resist the temptation to compare ourselves to others; the next is to rein in our desires for upward mobility. We will then need to challenge one another to move beyond conventional beliefs and values to repudiate colonial mission legacies, to embrace more inclusive moral visions. This will require flexibility of mind and steadfastness of purpose. We will have to discard treasured creeds, formulaic behavior patterns, and counterproductive ritual expressions. We might take a cue from Rastafarians, who manifest a characteristic calm and detached patience by reasoning together, with or without herbal assistance, in the midst of the Babylonian rat race.

TALKING POINTS

RACE AND CLASS IN JAMAICA

- Without looking at the following questions, complete the sentence below:
'I am _____.
How did you respond to this exercise? Did you make any mention of race, class or gender? Why or why not? Discuss your answers with a small group. In retrospect, what role does each of these categories play in your own self-understanding?

- As a child, when did you first become aware of being "white," or if you are not white, what was the first time that you remember being aware that you were dealing with a white person as such? Describe that experience. Was it painful? Pleasurable? Growing up, how did you "learn" to be the race you are today?

- Do you think there is such a thing as "white privilege"? If so, talk about three examples in your experience. If not, how do you explain the fact that so few non-whites head fortune five hundred companies? Coach NFL teams? Are among the top fifty golfers on the PGA tour?

- Select two articles from a daily newspaper of your choice, one about an international event and one about a local event. How is the issue of social class dealt with in each article? Is it mentioned directly? If not, what is implied about the class status of the persons mentioned in the article? What voices do you hear being represented in the article? How does the treatment of class differ in the two articles, if it does?

RASTA CONCEPTS OF IDENTITY AND LIFESTYLE

- List the five persons who you feel closest to right now. How often do you see or speak with these persons? What do you talk about? Do you share basic values? If so, what are three of the most important ones?

- Think about your spiritual life. Does it make sense to you personally to speak about a "relationship with God" or a "connection with a higher power" or an "openness to a vital force"? If so, try to describe what that relationship or connection is like. When do you have it most? How does it make you feel? What do you do to enhance it? And if not, is there anything in your experience that transcends strictly human encounters, or are you a thoroughgoing secular humanist? If so, what gives meaning and/or purpose to your life?

- Draw a large circle, divide it into seven wedges, and label each as one day of the week. Now, fill in your primary activities during an average week. After you've finished, reflect on the lifestyle represented. How many activities involve work, leisure, sleep, play, day-dreaming, thinking/pondering, eating? How many cost money—and how much do

you spend on each? Which would you like to give up? What's missing
that should be there? How many of these things do you do alone? How
many with other people?

- In certain ways, Rastafarians as a whole are quite self-reliant, especially
  those who grow their own food. Do you think self-reliance is possible
  in modern America? Why or why not? What are some things you could
  do to become less dependent on other energy sources, such as automo-
  tive fuel or electricity.
- What is the "*Babylon*" in your experience? What do you consider to be
  the embodiment of evil, inhumanity, or selfish disregard of others? Talk
  about how this might be constructively dealt with.

RASTAS, JESUS AND ECONOMISM

- How do you relate to your neighbors? Do you know them by name,
  occupation, hometown, shared political, social, or cultural interests?
  In what ways are your neighbors different from you . . . ethnically and
  racially? Are all of you in the same socio-economic strata? Do you tend
  to vote the same way? If you could encourage new neighbors to move
  in, what characteristics would you be looking for?
- How do you think the historical Jesus survived during the time of his
  ministry? How did he find enough to eat? Deal with medical emergen-
  cies? Keep in touch with people in other places? Could you imagine
  yourself living today as Jesus did? Why or why not? What people today
  most exhibit the itinerant life of Jesus?
- Can you see Economism as a religious force—that is, as representing
  some people's ultimate concern? How do its temptations impact your
  life? How would you relate it to current events? The fighting in Iraq?
  The Middle East? The threat of future hurricanes and heat waves?
- Make two lists of material objects that you either currently possess or
  would like to possess: (1) the ten things I have that I couldn't live without and (2) the ten things I would really like to have but do not presently possess. Then compare your lists with those of others. Remembering
  that these lists represent your opinions about "needs" versus "wants,"
  ask yourself how many of the things on both lists everyone in the world
  should or could have. What amendments might you want to think
  about as a result of this exercise?

CHAPTER 6

RE-CONNECTING WITH
THE ENEMY

MUGGINGS, POWERLESSNESS AND GRATITUDE

Right after the events of 9-11, it was uncanny how seldom we heard anyone say, "Love your enemy"! The nation's focus was on striking back, getting even, and launching an offensive "war" against the new number-one enemy, "the terrorists." In the 2004 elections George Bush and the Republicans remained in power by employing the rallying cry, "Fight them over there, or we'll have to fight them over here!" Labeling the new military initiative a "war" rather than a multi-lateral international police action, the Bush-Cheney Administration sought unequivocal backing for increased military funding, blanket approval for secret courts, protocols for torturing "enemy combatants," and a broad national mandate for "homeland" security.

Ordinary citizens of nations at war, however, commonly indicate no personal hatred for the people of the "enemy" nation. In the Second World War, for example, it was not the German people who were our enemies, but rather the Nazi regime that had usurped control.[1] Foot soldiers are but pawns in a struggle between military-industrial elites whose political apologists generate various "explanations" (weapons of mass destruction, rogue regimes in need of reform, or liberating the oppressed) to ease any moral qualms of the respective populations. Sometimes official pronouncements prove invalid and the public cries out for an end to the killing, but in the initial stages of most wars, the "hawks" have little difficulty in stirring up war fever.

The current U.S. administration has from the start insisted that the present conflict is a "different kind" of war, for it is directed not against the people of other nations, but "rogue regimes" and collections of "bad guys" who are so bent on our destruction that any settlement of issues by rapprochement or negotiation is impossible. Further, since this is a different kind of war, *it has to be fought differently.* The Administration has suspended a number of long-standing conventions regarding intelligence collection, sharing information with the press, treatment of prisoners, protection of human rights, and interrogation procedures. But in a war on terrorist networks rather than nation states, how are we to conceptualize the enemy? Are these networks or their individual members to be considered evil? And shall we suspend our normal inability to see the ordinary citizens living in enemy-controlled territory as our antagonists? What about those who aren't shooting at our troops or planting roadside bombs, but who may occasionally harbor or support those engaged in terrorist activities? Do they now become "enemies?"

In this new, ill-defined "war on terror," things have gotten very personal. Individuals however tenuously identified with certain organizations have now become enemy combatants. If any such individual threatens us, then we can respond as if attacked by a nation state and strike back in self-defense against the perceived enemy as well as any allies, family members, neighbors, or other victims of "collateral damage." But why is a nation's impulse to retaliate in kind so strong? Since as individuals we instinctively respond to an attack by striking back, and since the war on terror entails responding to attacks by persons rather than nations, it might prove useful to reflect on personal experiences of being attacked.

Over the course of my life, I've been mugged twice. The first time was in Washington D.C. Two men approached me and one struck me square across the face with brass knuckles (I still have a slightly crooked nose as a reminder). His accomplice had a knife and threatened to slit my throat if I yelled. I didn't yell. The other attack occurred on a remote beach in the U.S. Virgin Islands, this time at gunpoint. I had fallen asleep on the beach and suddenly awoke to a rustling in the bushes behind me and a scene out of an old western movie. Two men with their lower faces covered by red bandanas and pistols in hand were running toward me. They thrust me face down into the sand and told me to keep my eyes shut and not to turn around. As they grabbed my radio and started to run off, I froze, waiting for a bullet to smash into my skull, but no shot was fired. Probably a radio was not worth the risk a homicide investigation might generate. Though these experiences happened long ago, the memories are quite vivid; violence is like that.

Both events, of course, produced immediate and powerful feelings of having been violated—not only physically, but also emotionally, psychologically, and even spiritually. In the initial seconds after the D.C.

mugging, I recall pushing myself up out of a pool of blood, my head spinning, and lights popping on in a house across the street. A woman's head appeared at a window and she asked whether I needed help. "Yes," I said. "Well, come over here," she replied, "and I'll call the police." When I got to her door, she invited me inside and gave me a damp cloth to wipe my face and stop the bleeding. A neighbor rushed over, shouting, "It's not because you're white, it's not because you're white!" I nodded. She went on, "I've been robbed twice in the last month. Nobody's safe here!" Then I looked up. It was a two-story house. At the top of the stairs, six or seven children had assembled, and the smallest ones were actually shaking. It must have been quite a sight—a white man in the living room of a black household in the middle of the night. And it occurred to me that these kids had seen violence before, maybe lots of violence. The older ones just stared, wide-eyed. They weren't shaking.

Then the white police officer arrived. "What were you doing?" he asked. "Walking to the bus stop after the game," I said. The old Washington Senators ball park was four blocks away. He was skeptical. Minutes later we were speeding away in his car. After a torrent of racist expletives and reprimands for being so stupid to be on foot in this "hell hole," he told me that four people had already been murdered that night. Throats were slit. This area of D.C. had the highest homicide rate in the whole country. I was lucky to be alive.

As I replayed the evening in my mind that week, I felt disoriented and perplexed. I remembered that just after being struck in the face, I had momentarily met the eyes of the mugger with the knife raised in his hand. I can still see those eyes—angry, fearful, and distant. Snatching my wallet out of my pants, I pleaded with him, "Just take the money!" There was a split second of hesitation, and then, shoving me down into the pavement, he said, "Okay, just shut up about it!" There was something in the tone of his voice when he said the word "okay" that made me wonder. Maybe for an instant he viewed me as a creature like himself. Maybe in that flash of recognition, that split second of decision when he had complete power over life and death, something human clicked. In any event, hard as it may be to understand, I began to feel grateful that he had spared my life. And while I hoped that he would be stopped from hurting anyone else, I didn't hate him or want to hurt him.

On the other hand, there was the police officer. He had come to my aid, yes, but he was so filled with racist venom and hatred for everyone in this neighborhood, not just the muggers. He was like a soldier in a war who had demonized the enemy. "They" weren't human. It was "us" against "them." It was kill, or be killed. But I hadn't been killed. And a sister in the neighborhood had invited me into her home, helped nurse my wound, and called for help. The moral calculus was far from simple. Could it be that the knife-wielding mugger still possessed an ounce of humanity? Maybe, years ago, like the older youth I had seen staring at me from the staircase, he too had stopped shaking. Caught up in a climate of daily violence, perhaps he had been forced to numb himself in order to survive. As he grew into a young adult, who had been his role models? Were some of the children I had seen in the house headed toward a similar life of crime? And could it be that beneath all the policeman's bravado and racist stereotypes lived a loving human being who was drowning in a sea of violence? Could counseling and exposure to less violent surroundings restore a deeper sense of humanity? And would alternative strategies—in addition to dealing after the fact with individual crimes—help address the culture of violence in our nation's capital? All of a sudden, I had more questions than I could answer.

Five years later, in the immediate aftermath of the Virgin Islands incident, I remember having an overwhelming feeling of powerlessness. It was not simply that those robbers had invaded my space and stolen my radio, or even that they had scared me out of my wits, but that they had done so with such impunity! I reported the crime to local authorities, but they were quite pessimistic about apprehending the offenders. "Happens all the time," they said. "There's hundreds of these boys. You need to be more careful."

This time my reaction was not a feeling of gratitude that my life had been spared, but one of humiliation and vulnerability. For the first time in my life I thought about buying a hand gun. I wanted power—a weapon with which to defend myself the next time someone threatened me with physical violence. I finally decided not to go there, because I came to understand that violence is rooted in the dialectic of powerlessness and power. And, in some inexplicable way, refraining from violence, at least in my cases, entailed the brokenness of grace. The real problem was not inner city black males, white racist police officers or Virgin Islands bandits; it was the specter of powerlessness and a life devoid of dignity and grace. These nascent insights were later to be confirmed and deepened when I worked in one of the most violent arenas of the post-World War II era, urban South Africa.

CONFLICT AND VIOLENCE
IN SOUTH AFRICA

From 1994 to 1997 I taught ethics at the University of Durban-Westville (UDW), an historic black university located in one of South Africa's largest metropolitan areas. Situated in a hilly suburb east of downtown Durban, the campus was sandwiched in between two black townships.

Since early 1994, when the African National Congress movement led by Nelson Mandela won control of the government in the nation's first real democratic election, there had been a campaign to transform South Africa's entire educational system. Once again I was representing main-line American churches,[2] this time with a twofold assignment: (1) to provide an overseas mission link between the Disciples and U.C.C. churches in North America and higher education in Africa, and (2) to play a constructive role in the larger transformation process in higher education in South Africa. Life on the University campus mirrored the conflicts in the country at large, and during my tenure in South Africa I experienced those conflicts at home as well as on campus. Following a brief exposition of these conflicts and their underlying causes, I will discuss ethical themes that emerge when South African students talk about conflict, show their relation to the Jesus tradition, and examine the problem of Militarism in the light of these themes.

BREAK-INS, CAR-JACKING & ARMED GUARDS

Soon after arriving in South Africa, I spoke with my colleagues about renting a house. My wife and I were surprised that their first and paramount concern was security. While we were interested in something roomy, airy, relatively secluded, and close to the University, our new colleagues worried about whether there were high fences, secure bars on windows (and the fewer windows the better!), electronic surveillance systems, and nearby police presence. Indeed the obsession with security seemed universal, but especially among "whites" (Afrikaners and British) and "Indians" (those who identified culturally with India).

We finally settled on a three-bedroom house in a neighborhood that had recently become "colored"—a term denoting persons or groups of mixed racial identity. It was near the top of a hill in a beautiful, tree-lined section, not far from the University, and tucked down below street level. Because it was situated across the street from a wooded area, it felt relatively remote despite its semi-urban surroundings. To us, it seemed to offer maximum privacy along with an aesthetically pleasing setting. But our university colleagues saw it as an invitation to burglary or worse. They especially didn't like the way the house was only partially visible from the street, and described the burglar bars as "flimsy" and hardly worth the metal. They shook their heads, intimating that even with an alarm system (which they assumed we would have installed) we were sitting ducks. We thought they were paranoid.

We couldn't have been more wrong! The first break-in occurred during our first trip out of town. Prying off a few bars afforded easy entrance through one of the bedroom windows: gone were a television, stereo

set, radio, small kitchen appliances, luggage, clothes, most of the food
in the fridge, jewelry, and miscellaneous personal items. The house was
pretty well ransacked. I suddenly had the sinking feeling that it had been
a mistake to come to South Africa in the first place. It was not like the
abstract powerlessness I felt after the Virgin Islands mugging; now I was
deeply frightened by a specter of violence that threatened to overwhelm
me. In this setting buying a weapon seemed not only useless, but coun-
ter-productive. We learned that many of these burglaries were done by
gangs of youth who were themselves armed. What would one gun be
against a marauding group of bandits? Besides, robbers were especially
intent on stealing weapons: wouldn't a gun on the premises invite future
robberies? Our anxiety level was further increased when South African
acquaintances assured us that had we been in the house, we might well
have been killed.

As a result we instituted our own little "homeland security" system.
Thicker burglar bars were bolted into cement casings around the windows
and a motion-detection system was installed to survey most of the inside
of the house. A UDW theology professor actually suggested that we install
a live electric wire on top of the existing wall, but we blanched at the
possibility of electrocuting a six year-old who was trying to steal a loaf of
bread. The principal effect of what we did was that it at least gave us the
illusion that we had some control over our lives. It was an expensive illusion, however, and we realized that most South Africans could not afford
even this amount of security—to say nothing of theft insurance on all the
rented electrical appliances.

Then, two months later, while dining in a nearby restaurant, our car
vanished. The police who filled out the missing vehicle form told us that
it was the third car-jacking in that area in the past hour. The thieves'
usual practice was to cruise streets near restaurants or shopping centers,
and when several customers in the same area had parked their cars and
gone about their business, the thieves would radio a truck waiting in the
vicinity and simply haul off the vehicles. It didn't matter that our steering
wheel was secured by a bar lock; five or six men would simply lift the car
onto the truck. No window smashing, lock-bar sawing or hot-wiring were
needed. When we asked about when we might expect to get our car back,
the officer smiled and said that it would probably be for sale in another
country within twenty-four hours!

During the next two years we had two more full-fledged break-ins, and
at least three attempts to get into the garage—an adjoining but separate
structure. Both break-ins occurred in broad daylight, and both times the
alarm systems were blaring when we reached the house. Police told us that
the thieves used special saws to cut through the thick burglar bars. A few

days after the third break-in, I decided to hide in the house after my wife and daughters had gone for the day. Hearing someone trying to force a door open, I cautiously approached and opened it just in time to see two boys of no more than nine or ten, scurrying away into the bush across the street. Maybe all these break-ins had been the work of children being trained by adults in the criminal arts.

A month later, after the garage door had been pried open, setting off an alarm, I ran outside in time to see an older youth, maybe sixteen or so, racing down the street. Following this episode, a senior colleague had some strong advice. He insisted that I hire two armed guards to keep the house under constant guard, assuring me that local guards were accustomed to twelve hour shifts, worked for very small wages, and would be a sufficient deterrent for most petty thieves. On closer questioning, he admitted that they were sometimes bribed to look the other way, but the promise of bonuses combined with frequent replacement of guards would probably prevent being robbed by them or their accomplices.

In retrospect, the craziness of this whole approach to dealing with robbery and violence hits home only when one is removed from the situation. For the longer we lived in South Africa, the more accustomed we became to the presence of armed guards. Several supermarkets had gun towers in their parking lots where lone riflemen reminded me of lookouts at American prisons. The disturbing thing was that after a while I began to feel safer knowing that they were up there and that virtually every gated community had a guard house in front.

But could the guards be trusted? The lesson to be learned was that locks, bars, alarms, and armed guards could never put an end to robbery and violence. If the thieves were desperate enough, they would find a way to thwart your security system. And if you walled yourself off in a gated community, you not only lived in fear every time you went out into the real world, but increasingly distanced yourself from the real world that you could not do without. That is to say, when one considered the ensemble of "hired help"—the cleaning staffs, gardeners, child care workers, hairdressers, masseuses, private tutors and the omni-present guards—no one could actually wall themselves off from the real world after all.

ASSAULTS, HOSTAGE-TAKING AND THE COMBAT FORCE

While I was confronting burglaries at home, life at my workplace was also fraught with violence and conflict.[3] Like many educational institutions in South Africa, UDW was a child of apartheid, a social policy that established separate worlds based on racial and ethnic differences. Instituted by whites, who represented less than ten percent of the nation's population, apartheid institutionalized segregation in housing, education, jobs and politics. In the process, whites consolidated their control of the economy, all of the engines of government and all of the gateways to higher education.

UDW was established in 1961 as the "University College for Indians," and registration was initially restricted to Indians. Over succeeding years, students and staff began to chip away at the apartheid bureaucracy. In 1974, a whites-only governing Council was replaced by a mixed race body, and in 1977 some non-Indian students were admitted to the University. During the 1980s, many apartheid advocates were replaced with younger anti-apartheid faculty, a staff association was formed, and black[4] student enrollment began to grow. By 1996, more blacks were registered at the University than Indians.

Buoyed by the vision of a "New" South Africa,[5] student expectations were running high, even though the legacy of apartheid was alive and well on university campuses. In most South African tertiary institutions, the majority of professors were still white. At UDW, where Indians controlled the bureaucracy, tensions ran high between Indians, whites and black Africans, and conflicts among different ethnic groups further complicated the situation. During my brief tenure at UDW, students continued to struggle against the apartheid legacy in numerous "mass actions" including class boycotts, physical assaults, and the trashing of campuses. In 1995, some faculty and staff received death threats, homes were burglarized, students barricaded roads leading into campus with burning tires, classes were cancelled and the rector's office was ravaged.

In 1996, these conflicts escalated. Staff went on strike, the acting rector and two vice-principals were reportedly taken hostage, and classes were cancelled for days at a time. Then, in May, a coalition of students and staff who referred to themselves as the "Transformation Alliance," initiated a campus-wide boycott of classes. In an attempt to take over the University, they blocked the rector from entering his office, and he in response latter requested that the Council close the University indefinitely. When a private security firm, Combat Force, was hired to seal off the main campus with a ring of razor wire, a few students pelted their heavily armed security guards with stones and erected burning barricades. The guards retaliated with teargas and rubber bullets, injuring several students and staff. Calm was eventually restored when Combat Force was replaced by a police contingent. An *ad hoc* meeting of stakeholders reached a compromise that allowed the campus to reopen two weeks later, and a judicial Commission of Inquiry was appointed by the government to investigate the crisis. As the academic year limped to a conclusion, sporadic violent protests and work stoppages continued, and the Commission was unsuccessful in obtaining workable concessions from either staff or students.

This brief snap-shot of turmoil at UDW poses fundamental questions. What were the underlying reasons for the conflict? Why was disorder so widespread and flagrant? How had things become so chaotic? And remember that this turmoil was unfolding against the background of the almost miraculous election of Nelson Mandela, and the emergence of a new democratic, multi-racial government. With the end of one of the most powerful totalitarian regimes in history came the hope that peoples of different races and cultures could live in peace; that democratic institutions could enfranchise the heretofore excluded majority; and that wealth and power could be more equitably distributed. In the most general sense, the gaps between such hopes and the actual conditions on campus represented the flash points of conflict. By examining each of these "gaps" in turn with respect to the values of South African students and moral insights derived from the Jesus tradition, we can gain fresh insights for reconnecting with the enemy in the context of America's present impasse.

RACIAL, ECONOMIC AND POLITICAL ROOTS OF CONFLICT

While the local media provided daily coverage of campus turmoil, they offered little in-depth analysis of the underlying causes of disturbances. The violence was routinely blamed on a handful of student dissidents, agitators in staff unions, or sinister off-campus political operatives. Aside from the occasional quote from a student leader, students were rarely if ever heard from, and almost no scholarly research on their value orientations was done. Yet it was the students, the so-called "lost generation"[6] of black South African youth, who were pushing the hardest for transformation. While at UDW, I interviewed a number of them about the sources of their discontents.[7] They spoke about many interrelated factors, but three over-riding concerns were racism, economic inequality, and political marginalization.

Students decried what they described as racial stereotyping, racial exclusiveness, and a mentality of superiority among those who viewed themselves as elite racial and ethnic groups. Blacks cited numerous cases in which Indians and whites were given preferential treatment. Indians complained that since the 1994 elections they had become "the new blacks." Black students referred to high levels of ethnic conflict, especially between Zulus—the majority black group at UDW—and other African ethnic groups, particularly Sothos and Xhosas. African students of all ethnic groups reported ongoing violence stemming from television viewing in residence halls. In one case, Zulus assaulted Sothos for switching from a Zulu language program to one in Sotho. And in addition to racial and ethnic incidents, black students often found the university an alien world, for despite the black majority, an Indian legacy still permeated the campus. As one black student put it, "When I'm at UDW, I think I'm in India."

Racism usually had economic overtones. For instance, the avoidance of student residence halls by Indians led some black respondents to express the view that "maybe non-blacks don't want to mix" or "are afraid of intimidation," but an even stronger sentiment was that "Indians don't want to live here." They were people who had "so many cars" and "nice clothes." As one respondent said, "It is simply about economic power."

On the whole, black students were continually preoccupied with basic economic issues: money for fees and transport, money to buy food, money to send home to feed children, money to repay loans. Many found themselves in a "debt trap," devoting inordinate amounts of energy simply to paying the interest on loans. And most spoke of countless street corners back home where young men were "sitting around with nothing to do." They might feel that they had at least some chance for a useful and rewarding career, but their responses evinced a deep sense of uncertainty about employment opportunities when they graduated . . . *if* they graduated.

Following the turmoil of '95 & '96, the University set up various workshops and "transformation forums" on campus, but students often lacked representation on panels or in discussion groups, and when they were invited to participate, the agenda seldom addressed their questions or issues. Even when they could help shape an agenda, they said, the needs and concerns they expressed were not taken seriously. The apartheid legacy was such that academics, administrative functionaries, and Council trustees could not imagine that they had anything to learn from those at the bottom of the pecking order.

While the majority of black students may have aligned themselves with the government's ruling political party, the African National Congress (ANC), they still felt marginalized when it came to internal campus politics. For example, during the upheaval described earlier, the need to appoint a new head of the university led to a bitter dispute. Strong student support arose for Professor Itumeleng Mosala, a former president of the Azanian People's Organization (AZAPO). A theologian and chief director of higher education in the government, he was the only indigenous South African finalist for the position. But since many South Africans associated AZAPO with radical political agendas, the University Council decided not to appoint him. And although many students, blacks and Indians alike, were aligned with the African National Congress (ANC), Mosala's student supporters suspected that ANC party leaders had pressured Council members. As one supporter put it, the 1996 boycott of classes, "was all about Mosala!"[8] In any event, when news of the Council's decision became known, students were particularly disheartened. Not only had they no voice in this decision, but it served to reinforce a general sense that in matters concerning academic appointments their viewpoints were never taken seriously.

THE NEW SOUTH AFRICA,
JESUS AND MILITARISM

In response to these experiences of racism, economic inequity, and political marginalization—and emboldened by visions of a New South Africa—university students generated a number of positive, constructive ethical ideas.[9] Although there is not space here to develop them in detail, it will be helpful to articulate three overarching themes: relationality, empowerment, and alterity.[10]

Relationality symbolizes the profound spirit of communal cohesion and solidarity in traditional African social experience. It is expressed by the Xhosa phrase *ukunxulumana* (side-by-sidedness), which evokes the sense in which persons fundamentally exist as social beings who stand beside one another. It is most directly and dramatically experienced in compelling face-to-face friendships with other persons. It pertains to a complex web of social reality, including the extended family and the wider community. Even in the modern context of the New South Africa, it evokes a sense of dwelling in a holistic cosmos of divinities, spirits, ancestors, animals, objects, and contexts that shape and define who one is and what one does. Relationality links the self to the farthest temporal and spatial horizons of human experience.

Empowerment refers to the sense in which this universe of relationality is infused with vital force or power. The African theologian, Gabriel Setiloane, refers to this power as *seriti*. *Seriti* is "like an aura around the human person, an invisible shadow or cloud or mist . . . . while physically its seat is understood to be inside the human body, in the blood, its source is beyond and outside the human physical body."[11] Such power is an all-pervasive, energizing and motivating dynamism that is generative of relationality. The self is "vital force in participation; and participation is made possible by *seriti*."[12] Thus, the moral life in all of its relationality is understood in terms of the struggle to increase the power of vital force in the cosmos.[13] With reference to interviews with African students, it is manifest in autonomous selves who voice complaints and exercise political power. It is the impetus behind "Africanization,"[14] fueling a desire for capacity building on a number of levels. For instance, students sought to develop marketable job skills, enhance political skills for participation in the emerging democracy, and also develop research skills for lifelong learning. Ironically, interviews disclosed that students felt most individually empowered through the creative displays of song, dance, and drama employed in mass actions—the same ones that administrators and academicians abhorred.

Alterity refers to the discovery of personal meaning in terms of others. This sense of being "other-oriented" is succinctly captured by the Zulu expression *umuntu ngumuntu*, which roughly translates "A person is a person through (or by virtue of) other persons."[15] The concept of alterity connotes a sense of responsibility for others that presupposes a deep capacity for empathy. The most pervasive complaint of students at UDW was that those in authority didn't care about their plight. The principle of alterity thus tacitly invoked involves prioritizing the needs of one's neighbor and, if necessary, self-sacrifice on his or her behalf.

Such an other-oriented sensibility invites all people into a matrix of relationality and therefore entails respect for persons of other races and ethnic groups, as well as the practice of non-violence. In a focus group, several Zulu women spoke of situations in which Indians had discriminated against them, but then went on to describe instances in which Zulus had also "intimidated" and "boxed" (physically struck) Indians. And while they narrated these altercations with a jovial, even gleeful spirit, the women acknowledged the ultimate futility of this way of acting. After the laughter died down, they admitted that "The fighting is not good," "We have to get beyond stereotypes," and "We need to know each other."

Taken together, these three themes—relationality, empowerment and alterity—represent a South African ethic of transformation. The side-by-sidedness of relationality, when yoked with the empathy of alterity, implies a re-envisioning of society along the lines of the close personal relationships associated with life in a family. Of course, this new grouping does not involve a biological or homogeneous nuclear family, but rather a heterogeneous, inter-racial, inter-ethnic social entity. In such a "rainbow family," the focus is on face-to-face communication about vital matters of everyday life, and the acknowledgement of diverse personal histories, languages, cultural celebrations, and religious worldviews. Such an ethos leads to an interest in journeying into the other's neighborhoods, vicinities and countries of origin.

So pervasive is the legacy of apartheid that empowerment requires studying the history of resistance. First, today's black South African youth seek to appropriate the struggle against colonialism that is implicit in the poetry, song, story, and dance of African peoples. Second, empowerment necessitates a re-construction of reality. One of the poignant but also matter-of-fact results of the Truth and Reconciliation Commission's initiative—a town by town pilgrimage into stories of persecution, confession of wrong doing and forgiveness—has been simply the acknowledgment of the oppression of the apartheid era. Narratives of beatings, torture, and murder serve to fill in and preserve the public record of what actually took place. Third, empowerment is linked to public demonstrations against social injustices—protests that disrupt the normal course of events in order to shift attention to alternative visions. Fourth, and perhaps most significant, empowerment entails social reversals that produce a redistribution of the power that is consolidated in a few hands.

Finally, in the "new" South Africa, alterity implies a closing of the gaps in the "worlds apart" mentality of apartheid. It mandates a "crossing over" of racial, ethnic, economic, and class barriers. When yoked with empowerment, alterity implies giving "voice" to the "unheard voices" by encouraging the oral testimonies of Truth and Reconciliation hearings; and by the writing, publishing, and performing of music and literature created by township youth. It requires creating "moratoriums for moral reflection," including workshops, retreats and forums where policy documents are re-assessed and new initiatives are born.

And a thoroughgoing alterity, at least in the South African context, entails a fresh appreciation of the significance of religious experience in the public domain. To champion a reductionistic, social-scientific, secular worldview is to ignore the constructive moral potential latent in African spirituality, the African Initiated Church's movement, and interfaith dialogue. The Truth and Reconciliation meetings have produced poignant scenes in which victims of torture, rape, and the murder of loved ones were moved to forgive the offender after hearing him or her confess and repent. Difficult as it may be to believe, this has happened time and again as the stories of oppression have been told and offenders have come forward.

Such examples of reconciliation naturally bring to mind the Jesus of the gospels. Indeed, the African principles of relationality, empowerment and alterity have close affinities with Jesus' teachings about family, non-violent resistance to oppression, and lifting up the marginalized. As we examine some of these passages, we begin to discern the depth and complexity of Jesus' point of view regarding those whom we usually regard as "enemies." Therefore, let us briefly consider a few relevant texts.

The historical Jesus would make our contemporary champions of family values blush when he challenges a follower to hate "father and mother and wife and children and brothers and sisters, and even his own life" (Luke 14:26). Not only does the family headed by Mary and Joseph play no explicit role in his teachings, but his relationship to his parents and siblings appears to have been tenuous at best. And although he had women followers, Jesus apparently remained unmarried until his death—at an age when Jewish men were expected to have a wife and children.

In fact, Jesus proclaims as his "family" a group of followers who have joined him in a social and religious movement. Many find Mark disturbingly blunt: upon learning that his mother, brothers and sisters were looking for him, Jesus responded, "My mother and brothers—whoever are they?" (Matt 12:48). Then he looked at those seated around him in a circle and said, "Here are my mother and my brothers. Whoever does God's will, that's my brother and sister and mother." (Matt 12:49–50). Thus Jesus both expands and in effect undermines conventional understandings of kinship codes by invoking a more expansive vision of family.[16] His movement does not represent a rejection of the close and intimate relationships associated with kinship, but rather enlarges the sphere of such associations.[17]

Moreover, Jesus' involvement in his own movement, and perhaps his growing reputation as both miracle worker and itinerant prophet, made his family and neighbors suspicious of him. Mark tells us he drew such a crowd in Nazareth that his family "came to get him" because, ". . . they thought he was out of his mind" (Mark 3:21). The writer of the gospel of John reports that, "Many folks were saying, 'He's out of his mind and crazy. Why pay attention to him?'" (John 11:4). When Jesus preaches in the local synagogue, the hometown folks are skeptical: "Where's he getting all this?" "Who gave him the right to perform such miracles? This is the carpenter, isn't it? Isn't he Mary's son? And who are his brothers, if not James and Judas and Simon? And who are his sisters, if not our neighbors? And they were resentful of him" (Matt 13:54–56). And Jesus replied, "No prophet goes without respect, except on his home turf and among his relatives at home!" (Matt 13:57).

In short, to challenge kinship codes and to expand traditional conceptions of family is to invite scorn and derision—to risk being labeled mad. Yet regardless of being spurned by those he grew up among, Jesus continued to preach and model a radical idea of family as a form of relationality among those who seek the kingdom of God. It is interesting to note that Jesus becomes "the enemy" in his hometown in the very process of expanding the concept of family in the wider world. In becoming part of Jesus' family, we too may come to be seen as the enemy by family and friends.

And to be sure, Jesus was the leader of a resistance movement. He juxtaposed the kingdom of God with the empire of Caesar, and his announcement of the kingdom of God had unmistakably political connotations. Since the Greek term *basileia* (dominion or royal power) would clearly have suggested the Roman Empire,[18] to speak of *basileia tou theou* (the kingdom of God) is to pit "the sovereignty of God against the power of whatever political empire was then in place."[19] In fact, as Funk argues, Jesus' aphorisms frequently contrast visions of an earthly, Davidic kingdom and God's realm. Asked when the long-awaited kingdom would come, Thomas' Jesus says that God's realm will not match expectations for a Davidic restoration; rather it "is spread out upon the earth, and people don't see it" (Thom 113:4). Or, as Luke records Jesus' answer to a similar question, "You won't be able to observe the coming of God's imperial rule . . . [o]n the contrary, it is right there in your presence" (Luke 17:20–21).

Nonetheless, it is important not to depoliticize Jesus. In the ancient world, religion and politics were not viewed as separated from one another,[20] at least not to the extent that they are so understood by many of us today in the U.S. As Horsley points out, the Jesus who is seen by some contemporary scholars to defer to the authority of the Roman Empire has been reduced to a merely religious figure.[21] Those who seek to spiritualize Jesus tend to interpret the oft-quoted passage, "Give Caesar the things that are Caesar's, and give God the things that are God's" (Matt 22:21), as if Jesus were referring to two realms of obligation that were entirely separate from one another. But in ancient Palestine, the state (that required taxes) and sanctioned religions (that required faithful allegiance) were fundamentally interrelated.

In view of the anti-imperial thrust of Jesus' social identification and teaching, then, the passage might well be interpreted as a scornful rejection of Caesar's reign. Such a reading imagines a Jesus who asks for a coin with Caesar's face on it—he does not himself produce such a coin. And when the coin bearing Caesar's image and the caption "son of God" is provided, Jesus dismissively says, "Yes, give that to Caesar." The subtext is clear: if you traffic in his currency and submit to his authority, then, by all means give him his tribute. But if you are one of Jesus' followers, give your allegiance to God. Since God is sovereign over all of creation, including all of the land and the fruits of the land, then to give God "the things that are God's" is to support with one's tithes and allegiance whatever promotes God's reign on earth. Needless to say, the Roman Empire that oppressed and persecuted Jews in a number of ways would not have been on that list. In any event, as Horsley adroitly observes, ". . . if Jesus' questioners and listeners all assumed . . . a separation of Caesar and God into utterly separate spheres, then how could the question have possibly been part of a strategy to entrap Jesus?"[22]

Like many South African freedom fighters during the apartheid era, Jesus was executed by the state; unfortunately, many suppose he was killed at the behest of "religious" authorities. Perhaps taking their cue from Luke's gospel, many scholars and clergy gloss over the fact that Jesus was the victim of a Roman political execution, crucifixion being a standard Roman way to intimidate those who contemplated rebelling against the state. Furthermore, the careless habit of lumping together the many and diverse Jewish factions of Judea and Galilee under the simplistic rubric of "Jews" ignores their wide differences in social location and historical experience, and especially the "extreme gulf that existed between rulers and ruled in the ancient world."[23]

Indeed, Jesus' mission arises in an era marked by periodic eruptions of popular unrest and outright revolts by both Galileans and Judeans against the Roman imperial order. It also takes place in the historical context of the previous five centuries of foreign rule at the hands of the Assyrian, Babylonian, Persian, and Hellenistic empires. As Horsley notes, under the successors of Alexander, the Greeks imposed their political ideas and practices on Judean aristocracies, who adopted the Greek language and patterned their societies after the Greek *polis* (city-state).[24] The priestly aristocracy in Judea even conspired with the Seleucid emperor in Syria to change the Temple-state in Jerusalem into a Greek style city-state. All of this happened even before the Roman Empire expanded its control into the Middle East and, finally, into the remote territory of Palestine. To make a long story short, Empires ruled with iron fists, oppressive taxes, imprisonment, torturing dissidents, executing rebels, and demanding total allegiance to the emperor.[25]

Against this background, Jesus' teachings point toward a divine domain that stands in judgment of the Roman Empire's rulers and indigenous accomplices, and that reflects a widespread hope for the renewal of God's ancient covenant with Israel. As Horsley sees it, Jesus condemns rulers for oppressing the people in Palestine, and teaches that Roman rule was being brought to an end through performances of exorcisms that evoked liberation.[26] Focusing his ministry on village communities, Horsley says, "Jesus proclaimed an alternative social order of cooperation and social justice free of oppression."[27]

Perhaps most significant of all is Jesus' proclamation that God's realm is home to the indigent and the downtrodden, not the wealthy and powerful. "Congratulations you poor! God's domain belongs to you" (Luke 6:20). "It's easier for a camel to squeeze through a needle's eye, than for a wealthy person to get into God's domain" (Matt 19:24). "How difficult it is for those who have money to enter God's domain" (Mark 10:23). "You can't be enslaved to both God and a bank account" (Matt 6:24).[28] "Jesus said to them, 'I swear to you, the toll collectors and prostitutes will get into God's domain, but you will not" (Matt 21:31b). Nowhere does Jesus say, "Congratulations you rich! God's domain belongs to you!" In the context of the Jesus movement, empowerment is the shining hope of the poor, the sinner, and the hated toll collector.[29] One implication is that in order to be empowered for life in God's realm, we too will need to be "alert for" (and even "aligned with") the power that comes from being despised—and therefore the more difficult to avail ourselves of the more affluent we become. In the divine domain, the poor, the physically challenged, the outcast, and the prodigal son are all empowered with new hope because conventional understandings are turned upside down. In the parable of the dinner party (Luke 14:16–23), it is "the poor, and crippled, the blind, and the lame" who are invited to the feast.[30]

In such a realm, Roman values of honor and pride (we Americans might invoke "success" and "saving face") are seen to be dishonorable and shameful. In Jesus' movement, achievement is not getting ahead of the competition, moral "one-upmanship," or exacting a pound of flesh for transgressions. Rather, the goal of life is what we see pictured in the parable of the Prodigal Son (Luke 15:11–32): redemption from shame and failure into wholeness. Indeed, Jesus calls us to shift our attention from comparing ourselves through microscopic economic lenses of our own devising to appreciating mysterious grace (as in the parable of the vineyard laborers, Matt 20:1–15). Furthermore, he frequently exhibits a non-judgmental compassion for those who violate conventional mores (as in the story of the adulterous woman, John 7:53–8:11).

Finally, like the black African youth who is empowered to protest against vestiges of apartheid, Jesus models a courageous opposition to economic and political injustices. And by permitting his disciples to eat with unwashed hands and gather food on the Sabbath, he repudiated the oppressive dimensions of purity codes that were ostensibly religious, but represented the political and economic power of the Temple authorities. In any event, Jesus' most dramatic demonstration against imperial rule is his turning of the tables upside down in the famous "temple incident."[31]

After disrupting the operations of the money changers and the pigeon merchants (whose functions were essential to Temple operations), Jesus is reported to have issued a sharp challenge to the priestly regime: "Don't the Scriptures say, 'My house is to be regarded as a house of prayer for all peoples'?—But you have turned it into 'a hideout for crooks'!" (Mark 11:17). More than simply call attention to religious profiteering, Jesus actually interfered with the Temple's dubious business practices during the most profitable time of the year. One wonders whether he could have mounted this protest by himself: must not the temple incident have been a carefully planned operation carried out by a dedicated group of dissidents under his direction? Since the Jerusalem high priests worked in close collaboration with their Roman imperial sponsors, it would not be far-fetched to interpret this protest demonstration as an act of political rebellion. Further, if indeed he recited sayings of Isaiah and Jeremiah (Mark 11:17) that harkened back to earlier struggles against oppressors, Jesus would have been reviving the ancient theme of resistance to all imperial rule.

Surely enough has been said to make the case that where the empire is concerned, Jesus takes sides. Even if it is argued that God is impartial about political agendas, Jesus does not appear to be neutral about the

oppression of his people.[32] There are enemies and they can be identified, especially Roman imperial rule. Jesus opposes various forms and
expressions of it, and he ultimately pays with his life for such opposition.
However skeptical one may be of the notion of life after death, the continuing witness to Jesus' teachings—perhaps especially his resistance to
imperial rule—by the first century movement that told the story of his
resistance, represents a kind of resurrection.

And much as South African students found a new dimension of
freedom in concern for "others," the Jesus movement bears witness to
an empowerment linked to self-giving love (*agape*) that extends even to
antagonists—something one might term a "love-the-enemy" ethic. Even
as he leads resistance to oppressors, Jesus says, "You are to be as liberal
in your love as your heavenly Father is" (Matt 5:8). "If you love those who
love you, why should you be commended for that? Even the toll collectors do as much, don't they?" (Matt 5:46). Rather, he says, "Love your
enemies . . . pray for those who abuse you . . . love your enemies, and do
good, and lend, expecting nothing in return" (Luke 6:27–28, 35).

As practical advice, such sayings seem ridiculous. Our economy would
collapse if everyone lent on request and expected nothing in return. And
who can possibly be expected to repay injury with benevolence? Several
of Jesus' teachings highlight the degree to which his followers must have
struggled to live out this love-the-enemy ethic. "When anyone conscripts
you for one mile of service, go along a second mile" (Matt 5:41).[33] By law, a
Roman soldier could require a Jew to carry his supplies for one mile—but
no further.[34] In this context, Jesus' injunction might well embody a sly
strategy to surprise and perplex a soldier while at the same time intimating the oppressive nature of the conscription. Surely it was not intended
as a universal ethical maxim.

Similarly, he is quoted as saying, "I tell you, don't react violently against
the one who is evil; when someone slaps you on the right cheek, turn the
other as well" (Luke 6:29a).[35] This could have referred to altercations with
neighbors, but a more likely setting is a Galilean peasant being smacked
across the face by a wealthy creditor or a Roman soldier. The piece of
advice that follows is likewise gnomic: "If someone is determined to sue
you for your coat, give that person the shirt off your back to go with it"
(Luke 6:29b).[36] Poor peasants in debt to moneylenders or Roman tax
collectors would understand this teaching as a way of mocking the cruel
demands laid upon them by those who were directly or indirectly agents
of the empire.

In sum, understood in the context of a people at the mercy of Rome's
explicit program of confiscation, these seemingly impractical sayings of
Jesus begin to sound quite down-to-earth. And though far from universal

ethical norms, they can still represent powerful resources for subverting an oppressive imperialism. Indeed, they may even imply a strategic norm for dealing with enemies. The version of the Golden Rule attributed to Jesus says simply, "Treat people the way you want them to treat you" (Luke 6:31). Our western penchant for individualism relates this to everyday encounters with other persons, but as Funk points out, "on the lips of Jesus in Galilee in the first century, the focus may well have been on the oppressors of the group"—most likely "the Romans and the upper classes among the Galileans."[37]

Fast forward to today. What would happen if the U.S. government and its military apparatus treated members of the al-Qaeda movement or Hezbollah the way it would want them to treat members of the U.S. government? It certainly wouldn't imprison them unlawfully, torture them, or indiscriminately attack their communities or their relatives. Rather it would try to initiate dialogues with them, afford fair trials to suspected wrongdoers, and refrain from bombing civilian targets. And yet the Bush-Cheney Administration adamantly refuses to talk with representatives of al-Qaeda or Hezbollah, rejects the protocols of the World Court, and either launches or supports aerial strikes on villages where al-Qaeda or Hezbollah operatives may have surrounded themselves with non-combatant civilians.

But Administration supporters would no doubt argue that, of course, we do not treat those deemed "terrorists" as we ourselves would like to be treated. They are, after all, pathologically fanatical killers. And if that were all, we might at least be persuaded to have pity for them. But according to the defenders of the American Empire, these so-called "terrorists" are representatives of an evil that threatens the civilized world; and by so labeling them we can justify doing unto them precisely what we do not want them doing unto us. Jesus' commentary on such proposals is instructive. In the parable of the Samaritan (Luke 10:30–35), he presents the paradigmatic expression of his "love-of-enemy" ethic by making "the enemy" a moral exemplar.[38] The foe becomes friend.

The story tells of a Jew who has been beaten and robbed and left for dead by the roadside. A Temple priest, one of the rich and powerful, hurries by without lifting a finger to help. Similarly a Levite, a servant of the temple cult, ignores the victim and hastens on his way. Perhaps their chief concern is maintaining purity; perhaps they fear an ambush; perhaps they simply refuse to become involved. Then, Jesus tells his listeners, a Samaritan happens by—one of those people all good Jews had for centuries despised. And to the listeners' considerable shock and discomfiture, the Samaritan not only nurses the man's wounds and carries him to an inn, but he "goes the extra mile" by paying for his care.

While this parable can be read from a number of vantage points,[39] viewed in its narrative context, it is a response to an inquiry about the identity of our "neighbors." Immediately after saying that we are to love our neighbors as ourselves, Jesus introduces an enemy alien as a better neighbor than the priest and the Levite. By presenting the Samaritan as an ethical model, Jesus invites his listeners to disregard ethnic and tribal divisions. This new view of an old "enemy" also suggests that prominent and even devout "neighbors" can sometimes be greater enemies than the agents of whatever imperial power holds sway. Elsewhere, Jesus says, "Look, I'm sending you out like sheep to a pack of wolves. Therefore you must be as sly as a snake and as simple as a dove" (Matt 10:16). That is, you must be aware of what is really happening, and still manifest a self-less love toward the snakes next door.

At the center of such love is the need for forgiveness. If we hope to find mercy for our misdeeds, we ought to show the same kindness to those who commit wrongs against us. Jesus says simply, "Forgive and you'll be forgiven" (Luke 6:37c). But if we don't forgive others, there will be hell to pay. In the parable of the unforgiving slave (Matt 18:23–34), an extraordinarily forgiving master cancels a debt equivalent to ten million dollars. The wildly exaggerated figure indicates that this is not intended as a simple matter of fact tale. And, by introducing such a ridiculous figure, the story teller not only underscores the seriousness of the debt, but also satirizes the master. Only a very inept master could be in a situation where a slave accumulated a ten million dollar debt under his watch, and such a master is so absurdly wealthy that the listener wonders if he could be anything but corrupt himself!

In any event, when the slave couldn't pay it back, he pleaded for mercy, and out of sheer compassion the master cancelled his debt. But immediately the slave brutally demands repayment of a hundred dollars owed him by a fellow slave. When the later pleads for mercy, the first slave has him thrown into jail. Morally outraged, other slaves tell the master what has happened. He too is outraged: "I canceled your entire debt because you begged me. Wasn't it only fair for you to treat your fellow slave with the same consideration as I treated you?" (Matt 18: 32–33).

Fast forward again to life today. One of the hallmarks of a moral perspective is the capacity to put oneself in another person's shoes, or the ability to see ourselves as others see us. When as children we did something wrong to another child, our parents would prick our conscience with the challenge, "How would you feel if John or Mary did that to you?" But can we not do this as a nation? What happens when we imaginatively put ourselves in the shoes of people of other countries and take a good look at our national behavior from overseas? The short answer is that we begin to see ourselves as "foreigners" see us. And when foreigners look at us, what they see is a paradox.

On the one hand, they see a land of wealth and unparalleled economic opportunity, political freedom, and the good life. As a Jamaican youth once put it to me, "In America, you have the three V's: Visa, Volvo and Video." Such things—a line of credit, an automobile, and the latest electronic technology—are unknown to most of the world's peoples. Wherever I have traveled in the "developing world," people are clamoring to emigrate to America. I don't know how many times I've heard people say, "Everything is better in America." "Can you sponsor me for an immigration permit?" "Can you send money for airfare to America?" We are the envy of the world.

On the other hand, when they look at America, they also see a big arrogant bully, a colossal military power. In the idiom of Rastafarians, we're a Babylonian Vampire, sucking the blood of the innocent. For an increasing number of youths abroad, especially Muslim youth, we are the Satan of the global neighborhood—dangerous, capricious, unscrupulous, and mean-spirited. Foreigners see a profligate nation who pollutes the global neighborhood yet refuses to take responsibility, a warmonger who has been in more wars and killed more people in the past century, than the combined nations in Bush's "axis of evil." Time and again incredulous people have asked me, "How can you Americans preach democracy and freedom when you continue to provide military support to the world's worst tyrants? "How can you call for nuclear disarmament and yet continue to build up the largest military arsenal in the world?"

In addition to adopting the South African principle of alterity and thus trying to see ourselves as others see us, we need to become less self-absorbed and more concerned with the desperate needs of others. From the moral point of view a global neighbor can do no less. The crucial issue is neither "How secure am I?", "Where will my oil come from in 2025?", nor "Can I maintain my parents' standard of living?" These are legitimate and important concerns, but whether we like it or not, they must *and will* be answered in the context of a more basic question: "What is happening with my neighbors?" And to answer that question we need to know something about them. What makes them tick? What issues are they struggling with? I remember an international conference held in Jamaica between North American mission executives and Caribbean church leaders. After much discussion, the North Americans asked in all sincerity, "Tell us, what can we do for you?" The unanimous response of the Caribbean leaders was, "Get to know us. Get to know who we are and what we have to offer to you. Don't look at us as a charity case, potential immigration problem, or threat to your way of life. Talk to us."

Right after 9-11 a number of my students at TCU asked in exasperation, "What was the point of the attacks? What were the terrorists trying to do?" One of my students was a former U.S. Marine pilot. In an introductory religion class, he explained that the U.S. was disliked by many people in the world. This came as a shock to several students in the room. Then a Muslim student in the class explained that senseless acts of terrorism are not sanctioned by classic Islamic social teaching and go against the whole thrust of the moral teaching in the *Qur'an*. I found it ironic that week, listening to countless news broadcasts, that not a single interview addressed the issue of why the terrorists had hijacked the planes. We didn't have much of a clue and still don't, because we haven't asked the people who could give us the answers. We seem to care little for what their motives were, what led them to sacrifice their lives, or how they view the past and the future.

While the 9-11 attacks were not, according to Islamic teaching, legitimate acts of jihad, they did represent the desperate acts of a militant faction at the edges of a complex Islamic socio-religious movement that has been in conflict with the western world at least since the Crusades of 1096–1212. They arose in the context of the killing of 17,500 civilians during Israel's 1982 invasion of Lebanon. They followed upon years of bombardments and state-sponsored executions of Palestinians—actions which, like the 2006 air raids on Lebanon, have been in large part financed by the U.S. They represent a perverted, tragic act of violence, but one that is rooted in years of crushed hopes and violent struggle for the basic justice of the Palestinian peoples.

If we can see the awful devastation of the Trade Towers as in some way remotely connected with a people's struggle for justice, however deplorable the means, it changes our view of those responsible. Yes, as terrorists they should be brought to justice, but justice cannot be an imitation of their terrorism. Killing and maiming innocent Afghans and Iraqis is not the answer, for that renders us as morally bankrupt as the perpetrators of 9-11.

Addressing people who considered themselves paragons of virtue and piety, Jesus once remarked, "You see the sliver in your friend's eye, but don't see the timber in your own eye. When you take the timber out of your own eye, then you will see well enough to remove the sliver from your friend's eye" (Thom 26:1–2). Similarly, our moral outrage against the 9-11 terrorists, against any acts of terror, should not blind us to our own complicity. We cannot eliminate violence or terrorism overseas until we recognize and deal with its domestic roots. This means acknowledging and carefully examining the racial, economic, and political injustices that contribute to such conflicts. It means confronting our colonial legacy.

Just as South Africa's Truth and Reconciliation Commission has sought to name and exorcize the demons of the apartheid era, we in the U.S. need to come to terms with the genocide of Native Americans and Mexicans, slavery and lynchings, the imprisonment of Japanese Americans during WWII, and continued racist and classist practices—all of which remain largely buried in the national psyche. We need to counteract the willful and ongoing distortion of reality by jingoist neo-conservatives who seek to control the nation's news media. We must become aggressive activists in promoting affirmative action and eliminating poverty.

To love the enemy is to experience a change of heart—to move beyond anger, fear, hurt and suspicion. It is to embrace the enemy as part of a new "rainbow family" in which there is face-to-face communication that acknowledges different histories, languages and personal narratives. But it also demands sacrifice and struggle. Taking a cue from Jesus, as we seek to model a deep, intercultural, interfaith relationality, we will become vulnerable to being labeled as the enemy by the Empire's defenders. For if you are not with Caesar, you are against him. Following Jesus' anti-imperialistic message, we will need to remove our support from the Empire. For some this will entail tax resistance, conscientious objection, or non-participation in ceremonies that glorify national authority and power.

Furthermore, to be a disciple of Jesus is to move among and alongside "the least of these" in the global neighborhood—discovering the strange and mysterious power of the poor, the physically challenged, and the ideological outcast. We may even be called to take stands with such victims of imperialistic incursions as Palestinian freedom fighters, Iraqi rebels, or innocent bystanders. If this be treason, then following Jesus is potentially treasonous. Such discipleship may incur serious penalties, for we live in as powerful and cruel an empire as Jesus found in Rome. It is of course not at all clear what form such acts of solidarity will take today. But all who are serious about moral behavior must be ready to act when a "temple incident" presents itself. As the repercussions could be quick and severe, we may risk life and limb in upsetting business as usual, but we will be bearing witness to a gracious and hope-filled divine domain.

To love the enemy is the ultimate act of gracious living. To reconnect with the enemy is to become an angel of grace—that is, to experience a profound vulnerability while resisting the temptation to respond defensively. It is to transcend self-preoccupation by looking deeply into one another and trusting what cannot be seen or is as yet unknown. It demands a readiness to forgive, just as we ourselves have been often forgiven, for just as violence stems from oppression, so grace bespeaks liberation. Grace is the calm still center in the midst of violence. It is what enables us to empathize with the pain, ignorance, and need of the outcast in our midst. To live gracefully is to be "at home," to be in a "safe place" where even bombs and torture cannot threaten.

But on a more immediate and practical level, what can we do about the U.S. investment in the so-called "war on terror"? Clearly, it is time for a radical new direction in U.S. foreign policy. We are nearing another presidential election. Perhaps a first step is to elect representatives and a President who realize that a self-destructive American Empire is *not* in our best interest simply because it does not contribute to peace and security in the global village. It is time to identify, promote and support leaders who are not only serious about learning from others in the global village, but who are first and foremost willing to address the demons within themselves and their neighbors before lashing out in fear and ignorance toward so-called demonic elements in faraway places.

In the final analysis, only when we begin to recognize and expel our own demons do we come to recognize that they are not so different from those we imagine in foreign "enemies." When we seek forgiveness for our own transgressions from brothers and sisters at the edges of the global village, it becomes surprisingly easy to forgive those "foreigners" as well. And then we are no longer so vulnerable, so powerless—for we have begun to experience grace.

TALKING POINTS

MUGGINGS, GRATITUDE AND POWERLESSNESS

- What is your personal experience of violence? Talk about a specific incident in your life or in the life of someone you know in terms of What? When? Where? and Who? Describe your feelings after the fact.
- Imagine that you are writing a letter to a stranger named "Mary" about grace. What experiences, symbols or metaphors would you draw on? Now write the letter and read it aloud with friends.
- Brainstorm on the word "enemy." When you reflect on it, what persons, images, groups or patterns of thought and actions come to mind? Make a collage of this brainstorm, using colors, pictures or phrases from magazines and newspapers. Compare and contrast your collage with those of others.

CONFLICT AND VIOLENCE IN SOUTH AFRICA

- Recall your days as a student in primary or secondary school. What were the school's rules or policies about violence? Make a short list of "No-No's." How many of these rules are related to property? To persons? What were the punishments? Did the punishments fit the crimes? How or how not?

- Conduct an informal survey of violence on television. Working in a team, pick three popular television shows. Make a commitment that each of you will watch all three shows during the week, with pen and paper in hand. Note every instance of violence you see on each program, whether verbal, physical, or other (e.g., a silent stare of hate). Share your surveys with each other. What do they suggest about the range and scope of violence in the media?

- What are some of the root causes of violence in the world today? How does religion play a part as a catalyst for violence? How could religion be a source for non-violent healing?

THE NEW SOUTH AFRICA, JESUS AND MILITARISM

- Of all the persons you know, who stands out as a quintessentially 'moral' person? Jot down three moral traits, attributes, or qualities that this person embodies. Now relate these three moral features to the African ethical themes of relationality, empowerment and alterity. What differences or similarities do you find?

- Imagine that you are part of a production team that is creating a one-act play that is a contemporary re-enactment of the temple incident described in Mark 11:15–17. Your job is to create a drama in which Jesus or a Jesus stand-in appears in your community today and does something comparable to the temple incident in Jerusalem. How do you script this Jesus figure? Where and how does he carry out his protest? If possible, enlist youth to help produce and then perform the play. Discuss the moral implications of your play.

- Do you think the U.S. today is an empire? Why or why not? In either case, given the tension in Jesus' sayings between the divine domain and Caesar's imperial rule, can the church—or even groups of humanists who take Jesus' sayings seriously—accept American militarism? If an American President really tried to be a contemporary disciple of Jesus, what would his or her foreign policy look like? How would such a Commander in Chief approach the crises in the Middle East? In Iraq? Share your ideas with others.

CHAPTER 7

CONCLUDING REMARKS

IMPLICATIONS FOR SOCIAL ETHICS

For those readers interested in social ethics, it will be important to relate what has been said about an ethic of re-connection to the four dominant strands of ethics outlined in Chapter Three. For those who care little about such theoretical points, I offer in the following section of this chapter a few practical implications of this ethic for confronting the unholy trinity of Speciesism, Economism and Militarism. Admittedly, as a treatise on social ethics, this book has been a rather limited, exploratory exercise. I have only begun to develop themes of an alternative, subversive ethic for life in the late-modern, global village, and have but suggested what is possible if we begin to view the moral teachings of the historical Jesus in the light of radical social movements and the narratives of indigenous peoples in other lands.

Nevertheless, I view this exercise as a point of departure for more elaborate reflections on how the moral perspectives of marginalized persons in the U.S.—especially African Americans, Hispanics, Native Americans, Asian Americans, the poor, homosexuals, the physically and mentally challenged, and non-citizens—provide constructive resources for social ethics in the North American context. But as in the case of the historical Jesus, to appreciate the prophet from afar is often easier than to acknowledge the wisdom of one's neighbor. My hope is that by attending to the moral perspectives of cutting edge "foreigners," that we will be better positioned to "hear" and even embrace the moral insights of cutting edge "locals." With several such insights now in mind, let me recapitulate and deepen the earlier critique of the prevailing, dominant streams of ethics in North America today by commenting briefly on each.

COMMUNALISTS

Our ethic of re-connection stretches the more or less culture-specific boundaries of the communalist. By emphasizing that the community *is* the global village, it challenges both the retreatist and the parochial tendencies of the communalist; for even as it nudges moral agents closer together in the global neighborhood, it does so in ways that undermine the insularity of the nuclear family. South African relationality, the vibrations shared between and among *I-n-I*, and Jesus' remarks about repudiating parents and siblings—all these call into question the primacy of hearth and home, kith and kin, clan and tribe, and stress the wider nexus of our social relationships.

Second, our ethic mandates solidarity with the "least of these" in the global village community. *I-n-I* champion the cause of the disinherited, South African freedom fighters call for economic justice, and Jesus unequivocally congratulates the poor. Even Pacific myths bear witness to the saving power and strength of the underling who normally sits at the margins and from whom nothing extraordinary is expected, and in the Legend of Tagimoucia the commoner marries the heroine who in turn risks much to marry him. While communalists *may* express a concern for such solidarity, the socially situated character of their existence in a relatively homogeneous community militates against a full-fledged, thoroughgoing solidarity with those beyond the community's contours, let alone the marginalized.

Third, our ethic of re-connection calls into question the ideologically specific character of the communalist's worldview. In the global village, one encounters numerous rationalities as well as religious perspectives, and the fact that some of these may be more or less incommensurable with one another should not be taken as an intractable problem for ethics. On the contrary, encounters between fundamentally different rationalities should be seized as creative opportunities to develop new perspectives. And like the counter-intuitive wisdom of Rastafari and the Jesus movement, such perspectives will be expressed more in terms of open-ended symbols and enigmatic parabolic sayings than they will rely on propositional or creedal formulations of doctrine. In a global arena of interacting perspectives, many traditional theological and philosophical problems that depended on iron-clad doctrinal claims will no longer arise. The so-called, "scandal of particularity," for example, simply evaporates.

NEOCONS

The love-of-enemy aspect of a re-connection ethic erodes the fear that drives the neocon's mission to strengthen and "defend" the empire. First, it implies that the neocon's mission cannot be simply imposed on others, but rather must be viewed in relation to the many missions of our global neighbors. Nor can it presume to nullify the missions of other nation states. For example, a military invasion to effect "regime change" would be anathema to such an ethic. Aggressive regimes like the current U.S. administration would have no sanction to oppress or dominate others in the global neighborhood. Rather, an ethic of re-connection would lead to the creation of a greatly strengthened international policing force that could impose all sorts of economic and political sanctions and exert considerable moral pressure on offending groups or nations. In such a world, moral persuasion might well achieve results that we can hardly imagine in our current geo-political order.

Second, viewed from the perspective of an ethic of re-connection, the neocon's vision of the American Empire appears as a late-modern version of Jesus' *mammon*, *I-n-I's Babylon*, or the apartheid ("worlds apart") mentality that confronted the South African freedom fighter. It is a dangerous vision because it is exclusive, celebrates a groundless exceptionalism, and is ultimately genocidal. At bottom it represents a henotheistic faith that accepts the state as its primary deity. In fact, *everything*—including civil and moral law, human rights, conceptions of justice, religious freedom, and even the economic well-being of the contented majority—is at risk to be sacrificed on the altar of national security. In order to preserve and enhance the luxurious lifestyles of the global village's ruling elites, neocons will increasingly have to rely on force to put down the rebellions of millions of their neighbors. So-called "limited" nuclear strikes are not out of the question. But an ethic of re-connection—one that begins by labeling the empire for what it is—radically interrupts, undermines and finally begins to subvert the capacity of neocons to impose their imperialistic vision on the planet.

Third, a re-connection ethic implies a readiness to be *con-verted* by the moral examples of those we tend to demonize. If the Samaritan, or "foreigner," is by definition "evil," or part of an axis of evil, then we cannot imagine how our salvation is bound up with, let alone dependent upon, that alien agent. This paradox may be one of the most difficult implications of our ethic to grasp. I'm reminded of an encounter in the summer of 2003 with rural artisans in India who were displaying and selling large, hand-painted scrolls depicting various ancient and modern stories. Traditionally, these scrolls functioned in part as "texts" of mythic lore as well as news briefs of the events of the day. They would be unfurled in village after village and the stories would be sung in the indigenous dialect. In this way, even illiterate villagers in remote regions of the continent had access to current events.

One of the scrolls told the story of 9-11 as seen through the local art-
ist's eyes. In this version, Osama Bin Laden is shown calmly fleeing C.I.A.
jet planes in the Afghanistan mountains. At the bottom of the scroll, he is
pictured with a halo illuminating his face, safe from the bombs exploding
outside. An ethic of re-connection demands that we at least think about
such "texts" and allow them to initiate fresh reflection on our own rendi-
tions of the meaning of 9-11 and its aftermath. For example, to a world
that has seen American raids on Afghanistan and Iraq result in tens of
thousands of deaths and the disruption of hundreds of thousands of lives,
might Hezbollah play the good Samaritan?

LIBERALS

A re-connection ethic in the global village strikes at the heart of the liberal humanist's treasured individualism, vaunted rationalism and empty
relativism. While liberals speak out for and occasionally speak to the marginalized "other," they rarely stand in the trenches with the "have-nots."
But good neighbors in the global village have to leave their comfortable
cocoons and give up their preoccupation with individual autonomy to join
with and share in the exhaustion of the oppressed.

Second, our ethics represents a correction to the liberal's notion of linear progress. Indeed, from the vantage point of an ethic of re-connection,
Babylon continues to smother *Ithiopia*, apartheid still casts a shadow over
the sputtering "New" South Africa, and *mammon* always stands ready
to seduce seekers after the divine domain. The liberal's easy optimism
must give way to the cautious hope of those who recognize that conflict
is a creative modality of change, and that a long struggle is the necessary
preamble to reconciliation.

Third, our ethic entails an embrace of *religious* enthusiasm that the
liberal eschews and for the most part fears. To re-connect with our neighbors in the global village is to move beyond the parameters of enlightenment rationalism and to encounter levels and depths of spirituality that
are virtually unknown to the liberal elite. As we see in the narratives of
Pacific Islanders, it is to re-connect with other species and the earth itself.
As with the South African notion of relationality, it is to recognize that
our very selves are intertwined with ancestral spirits who are still present
here and now. As with the Rastafarian self-concept of *I-n-I*, it is to view
ourselves as intrinsically linked to transcendent power. And as with Jesus,
it is to recognize that the divine domain is an unseen presence among
us. In a time when resurgent fundamentalism threatens to overwhelm
the liberal's ideals of social order and religious polity, an ethic of re-connection impels us to reach out to and engage the soul of the other who
confounds and angers us. Perhaps the Rasta's *livity* and the radical charity

of Jesus' teachings represent potential forms of *praxis* that could lead to rapprochement with fundamentalists of all varieties. The liberal humanist may yet have something to learn from the fervid traditionalist.

POSTMODERNISTS

Finally, to use hurricane Katrina as an analogy, an ethic of re-connection sweeps through and upends the baby boomer postmodernists' unquestioning embrace of technological innovations, privatistic pursuit of self-realization, and tendency to compartmentalize social issues. The Rastas' *I-tal* ethos, the parabolic simplicity of Jesus' metaphors, and natural symbols of Pacific narrative all point to a "species life" quality of living that is independent of today's technological consumerism. America's postmodernist rejection of master narratives coincides with the creation of a moral vacuum in which the status quo forces of production are given a free reign, ethically speaking. Thus, the cries of those in movements at the margins—from those advocating more monies for AIDS research, to those concerned about hydrocarbon emissions—are generally not given any more moral credence than those seeking to use precious financial resources for cosmetic surgery or luxury automobiles. An enlightened ethic of re-connection refrains from imposing any new master narrative and mandates that we *listen to* and actively *engage with* those prophetic voices on the margins who have morally compelling messages to share with us.

Second, the postmodernist's "feel-good," "me-first" focus on individual well-being is fundamentally challenged by a re-connection ethic that calls us out of our comfort zones and social clubs into real world give-and-take relations with those in actual distress. In short, an ethic of re-connection would suggest a different ending to the story of the life-saving station in Chapter Two. It would entail, at the very least, a serious encounter with the persons of color—the "immigrants"—who were shipwrecked off the coast. Perhaps a new life-saving station would be built, but this would only be the first in a series of new paradigm shifts. For the immigrants would in all probability bring new ideas, dreams and visions to those at the life-saving station. They might begin to ask why there were so many ship wrecks in the first place. They might institute measures to prevent future tragedies. They might demand legislation that would enable ships to enter safer harbors to the north or south. They might provide training assistance to develop a new "sea corps" of volunteers who would return to the lands of their origins to teach future immigrants new, safer navigation methods. In short, the whole function and nature of the life-saving station itself could radically change! But such change would require moving beyond the known, the familiar, and the comfortable.

Third, in a global village postmodernists who cling virtuously to single issues are fundamentally estranged from the *potpourri* of diverse issues that form an interconnected whole. With an ethic of re-connection we will, as Parker Palmer pleads, "think the world together"—but must do so both in concert and in conflict with those of different nationalities, races, ethnic groups, social classes, and worldviews. Rejecting the postmodernist's belief that nothing ultimately coheres, we will listen carefully to those from the margins who have found some provisional "space to stand on" or existentially useful "survivalist meaning system"—some "criteria for judging *Babylon*." We will pay special attention to how such neighbors make sense of the whole, and with newly-found charity make courageous moral judgments. Without such an ethic of re-connection, the postmodernist is, ethically speaking, stranded in a nihilistic atomism from which there is no escape.

In sum, an ethic of re-connection, derived from the vantage point of agents who are genuinely "other" in the global village serves to dissipate the insularity of the communalist, repudiate the arrogant exclusivism of the neocon, counter the romantic optimism of the liberal, and subvert the narcissistic, consumerist myopia of the postmodernist. It bears witness to a new way of treating one another. It stresses reaching out and getting to know our global neighbor, letting down our guard, letting go of fear, and seeking ways to cooperate on the dividing issues of our time. It will require solidarity with kindred spirits in the creation of new values, novel spiritual experiences, and deeper understandings. It points toward a re-imagining of the world as an interconnected whole, the good as something we can't buy, and the self as intrinsically made up of a multiplicity of others.

IMPLICATIONS FOR THE MORAL
CRISES OF OUR TIME

Americans have a penchant for the practical. We tend to ask, especially about philosophical or religious books, "So what?" "What difference does it make?;" or, in the words of the hilarious 1970s television commercial, "Where's the Beef?" Let me, then, bring into sharp relief three substantive insights which have emerged from our quest for moral wisdom from Jesus and other foreigners.

First, *we do not need the bulk of our military apparatus*. Mammoth cuts in U.S. military appropriations are absolutely critical to the peace and security of the global village. The money would be better spent on the establishment of international policing institutions and peace-keeping forces; new reconciliation and restorative justice initiatives; and educational and research ventures that help prepare U.S. citizens to speak other languages and better understand the cultures of other peoples. My hunch is that if we truly seek to launch an "anti-terror" program, something like the above will be much more effective than the present course of ad hoc, unilateral military actions that simply serve to stir up hatred against the U.S. We can begin this process by supporting initiatives such as control of the small arms trade and nuclear disarmament.

Second, *we do not need to support the luxurious lifestyles of the wealthiest of United States citizens.* Sharp reductions in "corporate welfare" coupled with more progressive tax policies would help bring about a more equitable distribution of wealth. For example, we could re-examine the big tax breaks and infrastructure dollars that are made available to corporate giants such as Wal-Mart. And we could work to restore 1960s personal income tax brackets, in which the wealthiest of Americans paid a fairer share of taxes.

Third, *we should stop embracing every new technological development irrespective of its contribution to the quality of our lives.* On a personal level, this could mean leaving the I-pod at home, turning off the cell phone, folding up the laptop, and opening car windows. We all need to slow down, walk to more places, and reduce our consumption of fossil fuels. Most of us would also benefit from less multi-tasking and could easily dispose of half of the things we own. I submit that by doing so, we will actually be happier and enhance the quality of our lives.

The great irony is that, viewed from the perspective of indigenous oral wisdom, the Jesus movement or contemporary cutting edge movements, none of these three ideas are particularly radical at all! In fact, Jesus and Rastas would no doubt look askance at *any* military appropriation, the *very concept* of a middle-class lifestyle, and our near *religious devotion* to technological gadgetry. What I am proposing, rather, is a more middle-of-the-road, modest formula for U.S. citizens who wish to contribute toward moral well-being in the global village. That these three ideas will strike most readers as hopelessly idealistic indicates how *unrealistic* we Americans have become in the twenty-first century.

For by any measure of commonsense, we cannot sustain our military-industrial colossus without both destroying our country's economy and inviting more and more military reprisals from abroad. Nor can we continue to indulge our virtually unlimited appetite for goods and services while our balance of payments worsens, the national debt escalates and the U.S. dollar is taken hostage by foreign creditors. Finally, and most significantly, we cannot realistically anticipate that our descendants seven generations hence will inhabit a sustainable planet if the polar ice shelf is melting away, global warming is spiraling out of control and billions of inhabitants are struggling to survive.

Clearly, these are huge issues to tackle, and they beg another practical question: "Where do we begin?" We need to start from where we are, with our own conscious awareness of ourselves, the local institutions that matter to us, and the familiar societies in our regional communities. Let me suggest three exercises.

(1) The critical self-examination implicit in Jesus' teaching about the log in one's own eye and the Rasta denunciation of luxurious lifestyles suggest the need for a heightened awareness of how social location affects ethical reasoning. In particular, we need to become more conscious of how race and class shape our own perceptions of poverty, suffering, and freedom—and what is possible and desirable regarding our own lives. For instance, we need to take a hard look at how rampant consumption contributes to economic injustice and ultimately to military oppression.

(2) I-n-I's protest against Babylon, South African youths' critique of a "worlds-apart-mentality" and Jesus' rebuff of elitist pretension all imply that we need to question the underlying values and socially privileged character of our churches and schools. True prophets will center religious education on the denunciation of oppressive structures, mentalities, and lifestyles. Only after a thoroughgoing de-construction of ecclesiastical and educational bureaucracies will we produce more socially responsible institutions.[1] Perhaps we should take our cue from the Rastas' leisurely, informal reasoning in small groups, or from Pacific Islander banter around the *kava* bowl. We need to create "liminal" spaces in our church and academic calendars—moratoriums when business as usual is replaced by reflection and reassessment.[2] However eccentric it may seem, one wonders whether the judicious use of such substances as marijuana and *kava* might sometimes prove of value in building mutual trust. Rastas are probably right in seeking a higher consciousness in order to see priorities and values more clearly. At the very least, striving for something akin to *I-Sight* will lead us to challenge everyday consciousness as the paramount reality.

Be that as it may, even a cursory exposure to alternative groups such as Rastafari and the Jesus movement should nudge us toward engaging in face-to-face encounters with the poor everywhere. From a Rastafarian perspective, it would be important to gain firsthand knowledge of the underground marketing economies of the "have-nots" who operate outside the world of banks, debit cards and checkbooks. If we take the Rasta indictment of Babylon seriously, we will need to avoid a too facile equation of "the ethical" with "the professional," and re-evaluate the essence of the good life and right social relationships.

(3) The Rastafarian emphasis on transcendent agency in *I-n-I*, young South Africans' stress on the spiritual dimension of relationality, the Pacific

Islander use of transformational symbols, and the Jesus movement's focus on the divine domain—each of these implies that ethical discourse needs to take religion seriously. While the modern West is essentially secular, being part of the global village means dealing with a broad spectrum of religious behavior. We must therefore avoid imposing on other religions reductionist interpretations that both denigrate the reality and power of religious consciousness and ignore its unifying potential. Since 9-11 we have witnessed primarily the divisive role of religion, but it is also a powerful force for bringing people together. For example, religion can give rise to interfaith dialogues and generate vital discussions about our common humanity. Indeed, in the parable of the Samaritan, Jesus challenges us both to respond to and to exhibit a radical form of altruism. And the stunning paradox of his dictum, "The last shall be first and the first last" calls on us to do the unexpected in the post 9-11 era—even to the point of loving our enemies.

By way of conclusion, let me attempt to summarize the ethical demands we face by highlighting the implications of the Jesus movement for our self-understanding, our common destiny, and the demands of discipleship in everyday life.

WHO WE ARE

As passersby sympathetic to the spirit of Jesus' movement, we are "relationship-seeking beings." Like *I-n-I*, we are interdependent with all other beings in the global village. We therefore reject the ideologies of unrestrained individualism and Speciesism. We Americans must view our heritage of core traditions with wary and discerning eyes; we must be "sly as snakes and as simple as doves" (Matt 10:16/Thom 39:3), guided as much by future expectations as by past experience. Our ethics will therefore be pulled in the direction of the divine domain that both is and is yet to be. At the very least, that means resisting strict identification with current corporate or political institutions. While we can appreciate love of country and the tug of hearth and home, we must be alert to how either patriotism or family loyalty may become a roadblock to moral integrity.

WHERE WE ARE HEADED

Speciesism, Economism and Militarism are dead-end paths in the global village. As passersby who identify with alternative social movements, we seek a modality of living that is both more mysterious and less comfortable than that produced by traditional morality. Although we have trouble picturing this divine domain, it exists all around us as an aliveness and uplifting movement that is bringing about extraordinary happenings. It is an aura of grace poured out over good and bad alike that dissipates grudges, envy, and jealousy. It is a spiritual realm in which childlike acceptance and vulnerability rule the day, pernicious delusions are swept away, and the poor become proprietors.

RULES OF THE ROAD

As passersby in social solidarity with the dispossessed, we expect reversals and stand ready to abandon outmoded understandings, institutions, and relationships. As members of a rag-tag movement, we will join hands with unlikely and unkempt fellow travelers in order to move forward as communities. We will be less naive about our inevitable entanglement in corrupt practices and institutions than those under the spell of Economism. We will adopt a more nuanced response to violence than those enamored with Militarism. While those blinded by Speciesism continue to assault the eco-system, our commitment must be to sustain the earth, to initiate small-scale agricultural ventures, and to develop low-cost cottage industries. Whatever the means, we will simplify our lifestyles and minimize consumption. Then, buoyed by the optimism of the poor and the outsider, we will discover new ways of responding to poverty, fear, and ecological distress in the post 9-11 world.

And though passersby, we will be followers of the Prince of Peace. This means somehow re-connecting with our enemies, and the first step is to get to know them. Such a "knowing"—perhaps an adaptation of Rastafarian "I-Sight"—will no doubt entail what Thomas Kuhn termed a "paradigm shift."[3] In traditional religious language, we will need to undergo a "con-version" of perspective. I believe that the impetus for the shift must and will come from interacting with marginalized persons both within and beyond U.S. borders. Just as the Jesus movement reached out and embraced one and all—the poor, the sinner, the Samaritan, and even the Roman centurion—so it is our calling to make common cause with diverse persons, whether they be our neighbor or our enemy.

Such a movement, reflecting the increasingly pluralistic society of both the United States and the global village, will prepare the experiential ground for a radical new understanding of ethics. And because the moral teachings of the historical Jesus represented a subversive and anti-imperial wisdom for his time and place, they may yet serve as a point of departure for launching the paradigm shift we so desperately need if we are to re-connect with the earth, with one another, and with the enemy.

NOTES

PREFACE

1. The speech, "An Enlightened Faith for an Enlightened Age," was delivered on March 3, 2004, as the Keynote Address of the spring meeting of the Westar Institute held in New York, N.Y.

2. The First Axial Age is the period roughly between 800–200 BCE. Armstrong has utilized the concept in her cross-cultural, comparative work in religious studies. See her classic work, *History of God*, and her recent study of the Axial Age, *The Great Transformation*.

3. The Greek phrase "*basileia theou*" has traditionally been translated into English as "kingdom of God" (see Cobb, "Commonwealth and Empire," 142). Although earlier in his career Funk translated the term "reign of God," in recent years he shifted to the less hierarchical "divine domain."

4. The Second Axial Age extends roughly from the dawn of the modern scientific revolutions that followed the late medieval period up to the present day and into the future.

5. See Palmer, *Courage to Teach*, 35f.

6. The roots of our alienation run deep and have been exacerbated by the U.S. response to 9-11, which I shall discuss shortly. In our daily lives, it has come down to extolling what the British sociologist Bauman describes as "the life-mode of a shopping-mall stroller as the paragon of happy humanity and the good life" (*Life in Fragments*, 283).

7. In this book, unless otherwise indicated, I will use the expression "American" to refer to citizens of the United States, with a particular eye to those in the contiguous forty-eight states, while mindful that the term "The Americas" includes all the many peoples and cultural traditions of South, Central and North America, including those areas of the Pacific—especially Hawaii—that have strong political links to the U.S.

8. *Webster's New World College Dictionary*, 4th ed., s.v. "speciesism."

9. Cobb describes this term in *Earthist Challenge to Economism*. For an understanding of religion as an ultimate concern, see Tillich, *Shaking of the Foundations*, 57. For a characterization of religion as a "means toward ultimate transformation," see Streng, Lloyd, and Allen, *Ways of Being Religious*, 9–12.

10. *Webster's New World College Dictionary*, 4th ed., s.v. "militarism."

11. Whether or not one is enamored with Al Gore, the motion picture he narrates, *An Inconvenient Truth*, vividly illustrates how we U.S. citizens bear an inordinate responsibility for global warming.

12. Galbraith, *Culture of Contentment*, 10.

13. The song "A Little Help from My Friends" appeared on the Beatles' album, *Sargent Pepper's Lonely Heart Club Band.*

14. In appropriating the term "McDonaldization," I draw on Ritzer's account of the concept in *McDonaldization of Society.*

15. Obviously, no one can approach biblical or other texts with an entirely neutral or "objective" frame of reference. We all read biblical texts through our own lenses and the scholars of the Jesus Seminar were not exceptions to this rule. They tended to look for a rather iconoclastic, non-apocalyptic, wandering sage as they worked their way back through different layers of Jesus material dating to the second and first centuries of the Common Era. So it is not surprising that they tended to find such a Jesus! But by taking distinct and rather unambiguous stands on which of the sayings of Jesus are most authentic, they bequeathed to ethics a list of morally loaded sayings that is both manageable (they are relatively few in number) and provocative (they tend to have a countercultural edge).

16. These three focal points—self, other and good action—are basic elements of ethics. See Gustafson's discussion of parallel base points in *Christ and the Moral Life*, 1–2. By focusing on the nature of such fundamental points, this book represents an investigatory exercise in foundational ethical analysis.

CHAPTER ONE

1. Rushworth Kidder, President of the Institute for Global Ethics, cautioned against a response of revenge, lockdown, and isolationism in a letter to friends of the Institute in September 2001. See the Institute's website, www.globalethics.org.

2. The actual withdrawal was in June 2002. See Swomley, "Nuclear Arms," 25.

3. *Kansas City Star*, March 9, 2003.

4. Yarri has documented numerous instances of encroachments on civil liberties in "Suspension of Rights."

5. In the first year after 9-11, between 1,500 to 2,000 individuals were detained in the U.S., but the identity of most of them was kept secret. See Cole, "Let's Right Terrorism," 37–38.

6. "America as Sparta," *Boston Globe Online*, March 12, 2002.

7. A "pre-emptive" strike is one in which a state attacks an enemy which is perceived to be an imminent threat. The Bush Administration, especially in the early build-up to the Iraq War in the fall of 2002, frequently argued that Iraq represented such a threat because of its supposed arsenal of "weapons of mass destruction" and its apparent capability to utilize such weapons. In the eyes of a number of critics, however, the eventual U.S. assault on Iraq was a "preventive war" rather than a pre-emptive strike because there was not reliable evidence that such weapons of mass destruction existed, or existed in sufficient numbers, or that there was a capability for utilization of such weapons. The distinction is a crucial one because, while there is a long-standing moral tradition of just war theory that is at least not necessarily incompatible with a pre-emptive strike approach to conflict, it would be a stretch to use just war theory to justify a preventive war. I am indebted to a TCU colleague, David Grant, for first informing me about this distinction.

8. See Maura Reynolds, "Pre-emptive Force Part of U.S. Security Policy," *Fort Worth Star-Telegram*, December 11, 2002.

9. In a videotape broadcast, Osama Bin Laden took responsibility for organizing the 9-11 attacks. See Douglas Jehl and David Johnston, "Bin Laden Says He Ordered 9-11 Strikes," *Fort Worth Star-Telegram*, October 30, 2004. However, questions are now being raised about the scope of responsibility for the attacks. See for example, Griffin, *Christian Faith and the Truth Behind 9/11*. For an account of U.S. complicity in ushering the Bin Laden family out of harm's way immediately after 9-11, see Unger, *House of Bush, House of Saud.*

10. See the detailed account of this and other post 9-11 military initiatives, especially regarding U.S. efforts to militarize outer space, in Johnson, *Sorrows of Empire*, 79f.

11. Eight weeks prior to the U.S. invasion of Iraq, Hans Blix took great pains to challenge "several of the Bush administration's assertions about Iraqi cheating and the notion that time is running out for disarming Iraq through peaceful means." See Judith Miller and Julia Preston, "Chief Inspector Rebuts Assertions Made By U.S.," *Fort Worth Star-Telegram*, January 31, 2003.

12. See Karl Rove's comments in Jay Root, "Bush Assured of War Stance, Strategist Says," *Fort Worth Star-Telegram*, March 21, 2003. For an excellent account of the Bush-Cheney administration's shifting public relations campaign regarding Iraq see Everest, *Oil, Power and Empire: Iraq and the U.S. Global Agenda*.

13. The supposed link to al Qaeda later came under intense scrutiny and has largely been discredited as bogus. See Douglas Jehl, "Pentagon Reportedly Skewed C.I.A.'s View of Qaeda Tie," *New York Times*, October 22, 2004. For a recent, insider political analysis concerning the on-going war in Iraq, see Miller, *Blood Money: Wasted Billions, Lost Lives and Corporate Greed in Iraq*. For a more conservative perspective see Diamond, *Squandered Victory: The American Occupation and the Bungled Effort to Bring Democracy to Iraq*. For a readable, less technical, but highly informed political analysis, see Packer, *The Assassin's Gate: America in Iraq*.

14. In the latter stages of the 2004 Presidential campaign, George W. Bush began to speak in terms of "the transformational power of liberty" and of a mission to free the world of tyranny. See David E. Sanger, "In Bush's Vision, a Mission To Spread Power to Liberty," *New York Times*, October 21, 2004. With respect to the actual motives which may have been involved in the decision to go to war, see Manochehr Dorraj, "Behind the Question of War," *Fort Worth Star-Telegram*, February 2, 2003. See also, Woodward, *The State of Denial*.

15. According to a study by a research team at the Bloomberg School of Public Health at John Hopkins University, "an estimated 100,000 civilians have died in Iraq as a direct or indirect consequence of the March 2003 United States-led invasion." Elisabeth Rosenthal, "Casualties: Study Puts Iraqi Deaths of Civilians at 100,000", *New York Times*, October 29, 2004. That figure represented only the first eighteen months of the war. For more recent estimates, see the website: www.iraqbodycount.net.

16. By the summer of 2004, the number of American troops in Iraq was averaging about 138,000. "Deployment: 6,500 Soldiers Ordered to Extend Stay in Iraq," *Fort Worth Star-Telegram*, October 30, 2004. Those troop levels increased during the "surge" of 2007 and stood at roughly 160,000 at the time of this writing. For recent incisive scholarship on the war, see Peter Galbraith, *The End of Iraq* and Ricks, *Fiasco: The American Military Adventure in Iraq*.

17. Senior American officials acknowledged that the insurgency "has significantly more fighters and far greater financial resources than had been estimated. . . . When foreign fighters and the network of a Jordanian militant, Abu Musab al-Zarqawi, are counted with home-grown insurgents, the hardcore resistance numbers between 8,000 and 12,000 people, a tally that swells to more than 20,000 when active sympathizers or covert accomplices are included. . . ." See Eric Schmitt and Thom Shanker, "Estimates by U.S. See More Rebels with More Funds," *New York Times*, October 22, 2004.

18. Since the 2004 presidential elections, several books have appeared that provide both specific and wide-ranging analyses of the war on terror. See especially, Wright, *The Looming Power: Al-qaeda and the Road to 9-11*; and Coll, *Ghost Wars: The Secret History of the CIA, Afghanistan and Bin Laden*. For an insider account from an intelligence agent who had to remain anonymous at the time, see Anonymous, *Imperial Hubris: Why the West is Losing the War on Terror*.

19. I draw this insight form Revering, "'God Bless America': Patriotism and Political Theology." For a recent study that examines the relation of acts of violence—most spectacu-

larly the attack of 9-11—to religious processes, see Rennie and Tite, eds., *Religion, Terror and Violence.*

20. I first became aware of the ubiquitous character of the prioritization of the term, "comfort," during an annual field trip experience to a tourist resort in the Fiji islands. In 1990, along with faculty and students of the Pacific Theological College, I visited an area of Fiji that supplied domestic labor and grounds keepers for one of Fiji's luxury hotels. In a meeting with mid-level Fijian managers of the hotel we were informed that most of the hotel's customers were "comfortable." It struck me that this was an interesting choice of words. In this context, where the average tourist was anywhere from 500 to 1,000 times as wealthy as the typical housekeeper who catered to their needs, it was odd to hear "comfortable" instead of "affluent" or "rich."

21. Despite a considerable sympathetic outpouring from many Europeans—especially the British, for the plight of those harmed by the 9-11 attacks, public opinion polls throughout Europe also registered concern about many aspects of the U.S. response to those attacks. Majorities of the populations in France, Germany and Russia registered strong resistance to the U.S. war on Iraq in public opinion surveys. See Fawn Vrazo, "Nations Offer Condemnation, Support for War," *Fort Worth Star-Telegram*, March 21, 2003.

22. See the excellent brief historical sketch of the centuries-old conflict between Islam and western civilization in Lewis, "Revolt of Islam," 50–63. Confronting the discontinuities of history would also entail re-visiting the Vietnam War. In this connection, see the superb collection of essays, Gardner and Young, eds., *Iraq and the Lessons of Vietnam: Or How Not to Learn from the Past.*

23. In this connection, Defense Secretary Rumsfeld's attempts to marginalize the heretofore primary actors in European affairs (especially France and Germany) as constitutive of an "old Europe" which was now giving way to a "new Europe" (containing some Eastern European allies), alienated leaders throughout Europe.

24. For a perspective on the bubble that U.S. policy makers reside within, see Chandrasekaran, *Imperial Life in the Emerald City: Inside Iraq's Green Zone.* There is also a strong but generally unacknowledged positivist bias reflected in the way discussions about political affairs are framed in the media. That is, there is an assumption that such affairs concern sets of facts or viewpoints that can be reported in ways which are more or less value neutral and therefore do not concern morality as such. See Isikoff and Corn, *Hubris: The Inside Story of a Spin, a Scandal and the Selling of the Iraq War.* See also my critique of this bias in another context in Johnson-Hill, "Unheard Voices," 1–20.

25. This anxiety is especially prevalent among women. A recent study found that ninety percent of the 1,925 women surveyed "said they felt financially insecure, even women who identify themselves with strong characters" and make "over $100,000" annual salaries. See Kara McGuire, "Survey: Women Feel Financial Uncertainty," *Fort Worth Star-Telegram*, August 23, 2006.

26. Edmund L. Andrews, "Economy Improves, but Not Optimism," *New York Times*, October 26, 2004.

27. Barbara De Lollis and Sue Kirchhoff, "U.S. Airways: Workers Should Not Count on Pension," *USA Today*, October 8, 2004.

28. See Maria M. Perotin, "A Bigger Slice of the Pie: Workers Can Expect the Cost of their Health Care Coverage to Climb Again Next Year," *Fort Worth Star-Telegram*, October 24, 2004.

29. Robert Pear, "Social Security Payment Will Increase, as Will Medicare Bite," *New York Times*, October 20, 2004. Rising health care costs disproportionately affect the elderly. See Draut and McGhee, "Retiring in the Red."

30. It should be noted that most of the economic currents now visible in North America are also impacting the global South as well. For a perspective on the global economy from the standpoint of a prophetic understanding of Christian faith, see Gillett, *The New*

Globalization. For an account of a specific national economy, see Manley, *Jamaica: Struggle in the Periphery*.

31. Draut and Silva, "Borrowing to Make Ends Meet," 19. The figures cited are 2001 dollars.

32. See Brubaker, *Globalization at What Price?*, 7. Brubaker draws this statistic from the 1998 United Nations Development Report.

33. Brubaker, *Globalization at What Price?*, 7.

34. Brubaker, *Globalization at What Price?*, 7

35. See the Pulitzer Prize winning account of Shipler, *Working Poor*.

36. For information about the causes and contours of economic inequality, see the collection of essays in Ackerman, Goodwin, Dougherty and Gallagher, eds., *The Political Economy of Inequality*.

37. See especially, chapter five, "Unshared Goods: Hunger and the Global Economy," in Childs, *Greed: Economics and Ethics in Conflict*, 63–76. For a recent account of how liberal capitalism is incompatible with the traditions of Christian faith, see Long and Fox, *Calculated Futures: Theology, Ethics and Economics*.

38. See Sider's trenchant analysis of global inequities in *Rich Christians*, esp. chaps. one and two.

39. Several alternative proposals have appeared in the past four years. See Barone, *Radical Political Economy*; Nelson, *Economics for Humans*; and Barrera, *God and the Evil of Scarcity*. In a more technical, theoretical work, *Business and Economic Ethics*, Arthur Rich systematically develops an ethics of economic systems from a Christian theological perspective that charts a middle way between the "savage deregulations" of market driven economies and "regulated" Marxist economies.

40. In *Economic Compulsion and Christian Ethics*, Barrera argues that people are unwittingly coerced in exchange economies, such that they do not behave as free rational agents.

41. The following section represents an expansion and development of part of my article, "Was Jesus Green?" 3–8. Although not everyone will agree with his politics, Al Gore's *An Inconvenient Truth* is an undeniably persuasive, statistically rigorous, account of climate change and global warming. For detailed statistics see the web sites—http://www.climate-crisis.net/ and http://www.climatecrisis.net/thescience/. Also, for National Geographic facts on global warming see http://news.nationalgeographic.com/news/2004/12/1206_041206_global_warming.html.

42. Rasmussen, *Earth Community*, xii.

43. Dougherty, "Genes, Ethics and Religion."

44. In *When the Rivers Run Dry: Water—The Defining Crisis of the Twenty-first Century*, Pearce argues that a worldwide water shortage is the most fearful looming environmental crisis. See also, Brown, Kane and Roodman, *Vital Signs*, 15–21.

45. Rasmussen, *Earth Community*, 4. The Worldwatch Institute web site has a plethora of statistics on threats to the environment. See http://www.worldwatch.org/node/3982.

46. See the recent, cross-cultural report of the Intergovernmental Panel on Climate Change by clicking on http://www.usgcrp.gov/usgcrp/links/ipcc.htm and http://ipcc-wgl.ucar.edu/wgl/wgl-figures.html. The scientific data on the dramatic nature of climate change is now overwhelming and beyond dispute, in spite of political commentary to the contrary.

47. Dye, *Understanding Public Policy*, 170.

48. The social ethicist Gibson Winter describes this metaphor as the "mechanistic" paradigm of the techno-society in *Liberating Creation*. However, there are also good examples of efforts to chart a new course which reconciles environmentalist concerns with new technologies. See esp. Hawken, Lovins and Lovins, *Natural Capitalism: Creating the Next Industrial Revolution*.

49. Although the nature and extent of global warming is still debated by some commentators, a recent comprehensive four-year study of warming in the Artic conducted by nearly 300 scientists shows that heat-trapping gases are contributing to profound environmental

changes. See Andrew C. Revkin, "Arctic Study Brings Warning," *Fort Worth Star-Telegram*, October 30, 2004.

50. In *Energy at the Crossroads: Global Perspectives and Uncertainties*, Vaclav Smil argues not only that our dependence on fossil fuels must be reduced because it damages the biosphere, but also because it presents an increasing security problem as the world relies on more expensive supplies and Middle Eastern crude oil. Smil's book outlines "energy linkages" —the effect energy issues have on the economy, on quality of life, on the environment, and in wartime.

51. In *The Omnivore's Dilemma: A Natural History of Four Meals*, Michael Pollan examines what he calls "our national eating disorder," by tracing four meals—beginning with a McDonald's lunch—back to their species origins. Although Pollan does not develop the implications of his research for social policy, the reader will probably never look at a Chicken McNugget the same way again. See also McDonough and Braungart, *Cradle to Cradle: Rethinking the Way We Make Things* for a new design paradigm that offers practical steps on how to innovate within today's economic environment.

52. On the international scene, major constructive approaches to ecological stewardship are gaining traction under the umbrella of the term "sustainability." In *The Sustainability Revolution*, Andres Edwards describes a growing worldwide coalition of various sectors of society around common themes such as the need for economic restructuring that respects principles of nature, the restoration of life forms and intergenerational perspectives on solutions.

53. Goudzwaard, Vander Vennen and Van Heemst provide a parallel account of the crises that we face in *Hope in Troubled Times: A New Vision for Confronting Global Crises*, but offer resolutions that arise from and are strongly influenced by First World social locations. At a more philosophical level, thinking beyond "business as usual" requires thinking beyond the modernist paradigm. See Winter, *Liberating Creation*, esp. the last chapter.

CHAPTER TWO

1. I am indebted to my PhD mentor, the late Howard Harrod, for this understanding of the nature of ethics.

2. This way of characterizing ethics draws on the initial chapter of Gustafson's *Christ and the Moral Life*.

3. An excellent translation of the complete Nichomachean Ethics can be found in McKeon, ed., *Introduction to Aristotle*, 308–543.

4. H. R. Niebuhr describes the multifaceted nature of the self in his classic work, *Responsible Self.*

5. See the description of how one way of doing ethics—the "hermeneutical-dialogical comparison" approach—implicitly stresses a concern for the other, in Twiss and Grelle, eds., *Explorations in Global Ethics*, 17.

6. See Roof's discussion of "late modernity" as an alternative to "post-modernity" in *Spiritual Marketplace*, 325, note 11.

7. Clinebell, *Basic Types of Pastoral Care*, 138.

8. The story is found in Pali Buddhist literature. It also appears in Jacob, *Second Handful of Popular Maxims*, iv-v, 63; and in other publications. I am indebted to Andrew Fort for linking me to list serve correspondence with Amod Lele concerning the origins of this story. Amod Lele attributes her information to Katherine Ulrich.

9. Fisher, *Living Religions*, 134.

10. Here I am not adopting a "realist" position about "the elephant" under discussion. Rather, I am claiming that we do have "conventions" that some people take to have moral force, and which therefore have practical validity. To the degree that I am concerned to ground ethics in experiences of life itself, I share Don Cupitt's focus on "life" (see Cupitt, *Life, Life*).

11. See Holloway, *Godless Morality*, 156.

12. McQuilkin would represent this school of thought. See his *Introduction to Biblical Ethics*.

13. My re-telling paraphrases Clinebell's version (see *Basic Types*, 13–14).

14. In outlining these strands of moral tradition, I draw heavily on the somewhat dated but still relevant typology articulated by Betsworth in *Social Ethics*.

15. Berger and Luckmann, "Secularization and Pluralism," 73.

16. Weber, *Protestant Ethic*, 182. Even worse, Weber asserts, these specialists imagine that they have "attained a level of civilization never before achieved" (182).

17. Our contemporary existence in a late-modern world with what are generally termed as postmodern technologies should be distinguished from the term "postmodernism," which is associated with various interpretations of our postmodern predicament (see Wolfe and Gudorf, eds., *Ethics and World Religions*, 19).

18. See Holland and Henriot, *Social Analysis*.

19. Barnet and Muller, *Global Reach*.

20. For an incisive narrative of how this domination has evolved, see Johnson, *Sorrows of Empire*.

21. Hobsbawm, *Age of Extremes*, 9.

22. Wittgenstein, *Philosophical Investigations*.

23. With the turn away from a representational (or designative) theory of language—in which scientific language is conceptualized as picturing nature—truth appears relative or context-dependent.

24. Locke, *Science as Writing*.

25. MacIntyre, *Whose Justice?*

26. See Roof, *Spiritual Marketplace* and Leaves, *God Problem*.

27. Margolis, *Fabric of Self*.

28. Margolis, *Fabric of Self*, 8.

29. Margolis, *Fabric of Self*, 9.

30. Margolis, *Fabric of Self*, 11.

31. Margolis, *Fabric of Self*, 11. Margolis goes on to develop three combined forms of self-image—the reciprocator, the called self and the civic self. But the three alluded to in the text above are the primary constructions.

32. Such a three-fold imaging of self, and the image of the exchanger self in particular, represent a serious problem for more modernist approaches to ethics which presuppose a unified, centered self that is really capable of entering into and keeping long-term commitments. For an excellent and incisive account of sexual ethics from a modernist perspective, see Farley, *Just Love*. However, given her sensitivity to contemporary experience as a source of ethics, she presses toward a late-modern perspective, especially when she argues that there are circumstances in which some permanent commitments may cease to bind: "Sometimes the obligation must be released, and the commitment can be justifiably changed." (305). I submit that in today's late-modern period, that such a shift from traditional Roman Catholic moral teaching is much more comprehensible if understood in the context of decisions that are taken as a result of the dynamic interaction of different images of self.

33. See *Responsible Self* for an example of H. R. Niebuhr's relational approach.

34. See Kammer's excellent treatment of these issues in *Ethics and Liberation*, 30–32, 82–89, 118–121.

35. Gill outlines three of these alternatives (liberalism, communalism and postmodernism) in *Christian Ethics*, and I draw heavily on his analysis in this section. However, his account of three options is only one way of describing our contemporary moral landscape in the West and is not meant to be exhaustive. For instance, I also include what has become a fourth mainstream alternative, "neoconservatism." This ethical option has surfaced especially in the last quarter of the twentieth century and has been particularly associated with what Daniel Shor has described as the "cartel" that shapes decisions in George W. Bush's administration.

For a different account of the ethical alternatives, see the survey in Crook, *Introduction to Christian Ethics*. Crook also alludes to African American and Feminist approaches, but these more radical perspectives do not feature prominently in his own ethics.

36. This burgeoning literature is already overwhelming in its range and variety. For representative overviews and accounts of these perspectives, see Parsons, *Feminism and Christian Ethics*; Welch, *Feminist Ethic*; Cannon, *Black Womanist Ethics*; Riggs, *Awake, Arise and Act*; Sanders, *Empowerment Ethics*; McAuliffe, *Fundamental Ethics*; Ellison, *Erotic Justice*; Mohr, *Gay Ideas*; Dussel, *Ethics and Community*; Bonino, *Toward a Christian Political Ethics*; De La Torre, *Doing Christian Ethics from the Margins*; García, *Dignidad: Ethics Through Hispanic Eyes*; Paris, *Spirituality of the African Peoples*; Trimiew, *Voices of the Silenced*; Lee, *Marginality: The Key to Multicultural Theology*; Tinker, *Spirit and Resistance*, and Weaver, ed., *Defending Mother Earth*.

37. Rawls, *Theory of Justice*.

38. For a "postliberal" vantage point, see Liechty, *Theology in Postliberal Perspective*.

39. See Gilman, *Fidelity of Heart*.

40. See Marx, *Towards a Phenomenological Ethics*.

41. See Schutz and Luckmann, *Structures of the Lifeworld*, 2 vols.

42. "Cultural narratives" are the stories a culture tells about itself. In the following section, I draw heavily but not exclusively on Betsworth's typology of narrative moral traditions in his *Social Ethics*.

CHAPTER THREE

1. In this chapter, I will focus on the *dominant traditions* in American history. Thus, the title of the chapter could just as well have been, "Our (White, Anglo, Affluent, Straight and Mostly Male) Moral Heritage." This section represents an appropriation, reworking and expansion of central parts of my paper, Hill, "The Boy Scout and the Mafia Boss."

2. See H. R. Niebuhr, *Kingdom of God*.

3. Consider the model behavior of Abram in yielding the choice of territory to Lot in Gen 13:1–18. According to Brueggemann, such kinship *shalom* evokes "a dream of God that resists all our tendencies to division, hostility, fear, drivenness and misery" (*Living Toward a Vision*, 16).

4. See Deut 9:15 and Numbers 25.

5. See the story of Abigail's peaceful intervention in I Sam 25:1–39. Janzen refers to this as a "wisdom model story," one of five major types of ethical model stories in the Hebrew Bible. See his *Old Testament Ethics*. The Pilgrims tended to eschew the royal model stories in part because they were in rebellion against European monarchies.

6. See the role of Elijah in I Kings 21.

7. Luke 1:52–53.

8. MacIntyre, *After Virtue*.

9. Smedes, *Mere Morality*.

10. Hauerwas, *Community of Character*; and, Hauerwas and Willimon, *Resident Aliens*.

11. Winthrop, "A Model of Christian Charity," 83.

12. Betsworth, *Social Ethics*, 26, 49–50.

13. Betsworth, *Social Ethics*, 35f.

14. Galbraith makes this point forcefully in *Culture of Contentment*, 2f.

15. See Riggs, *Awake, Arise & Act*.

16. Betsworth, *Social Ethics*, 36.

17. Rather than viewing the "mission of America" story as the communal dimension of the American Enlightenment (as Betsworth does), I consider it as more of a direct outgrowth of both the Biblical model of the elect who are given (and seize) the Promised Land and of the nationalistic fervor of the colonists in revolt against the British.

18. Betsworth, *Social Ethics*, 17, 109. This narrative emerges in relation to deism and the revolutionary politics of the French Enlightenment. The more pragmatic themes of the Scottish Enlightenment in America's own enlightenment story of progress do not take center stage until after the revolutionary period (see Betsworth, *Social Ethics*, 53).

19. Betsworth, *Social Ethics*, 110.

20. Betsworth, *Social Ethics*, 111.

21. Hudson, *Religion in America*, 60–194.

22. Tuverson, *Redeemer Nation*, 157.

23. Betsworth, *Social Ethics*, 124–25.

24. Strauss, *Natural Right and History* and Strauss, *Rebirth of Classical Political Rationalism*.

25. Bloom, *Closing of the American Mind*.

26. Kristol, *Reflections of a Neoconservative*.

27. See Baum, ed., *Neo-Conservatism*.

28. Barnett focuses on "connectivity" and calls for a shift of our strategic interests away from a "Leviathan" approach to winning the peace (concentration on winning traditional wars against sovereign states with overwhelming military hardware) to a "Systems Administration" model (dispatching thousands of trained peacekeepers to win post-war conflicts). Thus he expands the neocon agenda in new directions. But these strategic "transformations" are all in the service of preserving America's long-term military superiority and spreading democracy to the world (*Pentagon's New Map*).

29. In addition to Hispanic sources listed in chap. 2, n. 36, see Boff, *Cry of the Earth*. See also, Dalton, *Moral Vision of César Chávez*.

30. See Betsworth, *Social Ethics*, 53–80. The following account summarizes Betsworth's key points regarding the gospel of success in America.

31. See Mead, *Nation with the Soul of a Church*.

32. Galbraith, *Culture of Contentment*, 80.

33. See McGuffey, *McGuffey's Fifth Eclectic Reader*, 231.

34. Carnegie, "Wealth," 653–664.

35. See Walzer, *Spheres of Justice*.

36. See Lind, *Up from Conservatism*.

37. Kant, *Critique of Pure Reason*.

38. Pollit, *Reasonable Creatures*, 31–41.

39. Rand's philosophy of ethical egoism is outlined in *For the New Intellectual* and *Virtue of Selfishness*. Although Rand is identified as a conservative in contemporary political paradigms, understood from the perspective of the modernist paradigm associated with the Enlightenment, she is a classic liberal.

40. Kurtz, *In Defense of Secular Humanism*.

41. See Rorty's critique of liberals in *Achieving Our Country*, 38.

42. This refers to a majority of those who actually go to the polls in democratic countries—even though they frequently constitute a minority of a nation's population as a whole. See *Culture of Contentment*, 10.

43. These value orientations have affinities with the non-traditional ways of being religious described in Streng, Lloyd and Allen, *Ways of Being Religious*. I have combined Streng's seventh and eighth modes of religiosity in my "techno-consumerist" moral orientation. I also draw heavily on Betsworth's account of the story of well-being in *Social Ethics*, 81–106. Individuals frequently combine two or more of these ways of seeking well-being, but generally accent one in particular.

44. Lasch describes the heavy demands modern Americans place on personal relationships in *Culture of Narcissism*.

45. Betsworth cites O'Neill and O'Neill, *Open Marriage* as an example of this moral orientation.

46. Derrida, *Margins of Philosophy* and *Ecriture et la Différence.*

47. For an account of both trajectories, see Griffin, ed., *Founders of Constructive Postmodern Philosophy.*

48. Habermas, *Theory and Practice.*

49. Tracy, *Blessed Rage for Order* and *Analogical Imagination.*

50. Foucault, *Archaeology of Knowledge.*

51. Taylor, *Erring: A Postmodern A/Theology.*

52. Gutierrez, *Power of the Poor*, 57–58.

53. Thorstein Veblen had a habit of pointing out the tribal nature of the rich and the power-ful—and in such a way that he was repeatedly fired by the academic institutions in which he taught. See Galbraith, *Culture of Contentment*, 81, footnote 2.

54. See a succinct description of this moral grounding in Gallagher's commentary on the case study, "A Conflict of Interest," in Wolfe and Gudorf, eds., *Ethics and World Religions*, 246–252.

55. Dale Stover, "Postcolonial Sun Dancing," 819.

56. Given the enlightenment liberal's penchant for universality, it is interesting to note that even a modernist like the German philosopher Georg Hegel could be drawn to the study of the non-western philosophies of India, albeit in defense of his own master narrative.

57. While certain processes of "globalization" (such as transnational investment and mili-tary alignments) often function to divide nations and peoples from one another, I am arguing for an alternative approach to human interaction in the global village, one that builds on constructive encounters to create greater awareness of what is happening in different com-munities due to global news outlets, people to people exchanges between organizations, the growth of global institutions of civil society, and increased sharing of knowledge and culture through the arts and mass entertainment media. I am indebted to David Pfrimmer for the preceding list of constructive encounters.

58. The following account draws heavily on a three-page section of my longer article, Hill, "Teaching for Transformation," 223–225.

59. Professor Wilfred is Head of the Department of Christian Studies, School of Philosophy and Religious Thought, at Madras University. He is the author of *On the Banks of the Ganges.*

60. H. R. Niebuhr, "War as the Judgment of God," 953–55.

61. Gutierrez, *Power of the Poor*, 57–58.

62. See references to parallel life-altering experiences in Hoehn, *Up from Apathy*, 35–40.

63. *Webster's International Dictionary*, 2nd ed., s.v. "movement."

64. *Random House Dictionary*, 2nd ed., s.v. "social movements."

65. Mathies, "Sati, Understanding and Condemnation."

66. Hicks, *Religion in the Workplace*, 2.

67. Meeks stresses the importance of seeing the surviving documents of Christianity's beginnings as addressed not to individuals, but to communities, and as being primarily con-cerned with "the way converts to the movement ought to behave" (see *Origins of Christian Morality*, 5).

68. Armstrong, "Suggestions for a Second Axial Age."

69. See the excellent study by Prothero, *American Jesus.*

70. Meeks, *Origins of Christian Morality*, 1.

71. Murray Jardine has argued that persons who dwell in literary cultures (virtually all of us Americans!) have particular difficulties linking the objects evoked by literary constructions to particular contexts of concrete practices or narrative traditions (see "Sight, Sound and Epistemology," 1–22).

72. Interview with author, Suva, Fiji, January 15, 1990.

73. Although we Americans tend to be rampant individualists, it is important to remember that there are western scholars who have stressed a relational sense of self. For example, the Asian American feminist theologian Rita Nakashima Brock says that in our heart of

hearts we are "relationship-seeking beings" (*Journeys by Heart*, 4). The theologian H. R. Niebuhr described a complex social self in *Responsible Self*. And in his early work, Karl Marx described human beings as "vital expressions" of social life who have a "species-consciousness" characterized by "free, conscious activity" in which we organize our relationships as social forces (*Economic and Philosophical Manuscripts*, 350).

CHAPTER FOUR

1. I was a Lecturer in Church and Society and later Chair of the Department of Theology and Ethics at the Pacific Theological College (PTC) from 1989–93 & 1998–99, respectively. PTC is the primary ecumenical, degree-granting, protestant seminary in the South Pacific region.

2. In this regard, I am indebted to students who generously shared their work in courses I taught at PTC in phenomenology of religion (1990–92) and contextual theology and ethics (1998).

3. The recent interest in narrative ethics, facilitated by the writings of Martha Nussbaum, is a testimony to the power of the story for ethical reflection. Rather than reasoning deductively from general principles, Nussbaum views the particular and the individual, especially as disclosed in narratives, as the starting place for ethical discernment. See *Fragility of Goodness*. See applications of Nussbaum's approach to Biblical ethics in Barton, *Ethics and the Old Testament* and Janzen, *Old Testament Ethics*. Betsworth applies a narrative ethics approach to interpreting broad traditions in American life in *Social Ethics* (see Chapter Three above). Of course, stories figured prominently in Jesus' moral teachings as well.

4. The Indo-Fijian scholar, Subramani, presents a trenchant critique of the "negative influence" of European fiction about Pacific Islanders in *South Pacific Literature*, 75–94. Social scientists' critiques of Margaret Mead's classic study, *Growing up in Samoa*, demonstrate that anthropologists were also susceptible to romantic stereotypes.

5. Jardine has argued that unlike persons living in oral cultures, those who dwell in literary cultures tend to take objects in three-dimensional visual space as the model of what is really real and tend to regard other kinds of experience as derivative or unreal. Consequently, Jardine argues, some of the moral disorientation and fragmentation we experience in modern life is related to difficulties in linking these objects to particular contexts of concrete practices or narrative traditions (See "Sight, Sound and Epistemology"). Jardine draws on Bernstein, *Beyond Objectivism and Relativism*.

6. A great deal of cross-cultural interaction among South Pacific Islanders occurred even prior to the advent of western colonization. Some historians have argued that ocean voyages in large, double outrigger canoes by Islanders equaled or surpassed the distances covered by voyages in the Atlantic by European sailors during the late Middle Ages. See Campbell, *History of the Pacific Islands*, 11, 13–14.

7. For an abbreviated account of this commonly accepted version, see Amadio, *Pacifica*, 56–57. For an alternative version, see Reed and Hames, *Myths and Legends of Fiji*.

8. In Fijian, "*Adi*" is a term of honor accorded to high-ranking women in a hierarchical social system.

9. *Kava* is a non-alcoholic drink made from steeping the pulped fresh root of a local plant (also called *kava*), or its powdered or dried equivalent, in water. In Fijian, *kava* is also called *yagona*. The term, "*yagona*," refers both to the drink and to the green plant, *Piper methysticum*. Kava is consumed in a leisurely fashion, often outdoors, by small groups of participants seated in a circle around a large bowl called a *tanoa*, in which the *kava* is mixed and from which it is served. Sometimes the *tanoa* is referred to as a *kava* bowl. The tanoa is made of wood, and often ornately carved, for kava drinking is a major pastime in Fiji. On special occasions it entails a great deal of protocol and ceremony, but in everyday practice, it is a relatively informal social activity. For an insider's perspective on and description of *yagona* drinking, see Ravuvu, *Fijian Ethos*, 25–26.

10. As a mark of respect for ancient customs, villagers would touch the *kava* bowl as they walked by it.

11. It was customary for chiefs to marry their young daughters to powerful older men.

12. *Masi* is a beautiful article of clothing made by pounding out the bark of a tree, and is traditionally worn on ceremonial occasions.

13. The following analysis represents an appropriation of material previously published in my article, "Doing Ethics in the Pacific Islands."

14. This is significant because eye contact is a rich and complex form of social interaction in the islands. A slightly raised eyebrow can communicate a world of sentiment, allegiance, disdain or solidarity, depending on the agents and the context. We can only conjecture what transpired between mother and daughter in this emotionally laden, non-verbal exchange, but the mother could be signaling her daughter either to follow her own instincts or to resign herself to her father's expectations. More likely, perhaps, the mother is conveying a complex set of feelings involving grief, regret, remorse, hope and rebellion.

15. *Vakaturaga* refers to actions and personal characteristics that are associated with a person of high status, and evokes respect, deference, compliance, humility, loyalty and honesty, among other virtues. For a detailed discussion, see Ravuvu, *Fijian Ethos*, 18–19.

16. Depending on the antiquity of the myth, it could be argued that this moral tension already existed prior to western impact, or at least prior to missionary Christian influences. In their "Introduction," Linnekin and Poyer stress the tenacity of indigenous notions of identity and morality even in the face of major political and economic changes.

17. A representative example of such analyses is Kirch, *Evolution of Polynesian Chiefdoms* and Bellwood, *Polynesians.*

18. A "liminal" space is one that an agent occupies when in *transition* from one stage or place to another. In the narrative under discussion it connotes a context in which one is momentarily situated betwixt and between, enmeshed in a set of troubling circumstances and their as yet uncertain outcome. Such spaces can serve as "thresholds" for the moral imagination, because they represent momentary anti-structural locations in which one is temporarily distanced from the structures and strictures of ordinary, everyday experience.

19. For a detailed description of *vanua*, see Ravuvu, *Fijian Ethos*, 14–15.

20. Tua's account is very similar to the version provided by Amadio, *Pacifica*, 60–61. Quotations from the myth that are cited in the text are taken from Amadio's version. I will provide an abbreviated version in the following subsection.

21. See Beaglehole, *Social Change*, for a classic ethnographic study of social change processes in the Cook Islands.

22. Although we are not given specifics about the dance in the myth, Cook Islanders reported to the author that the moonlight dance is probably a reference to an erotic dance, known in the local idiom as *Urupiana*. The early missionaries especially despised Urupiana, which was often a prelude to lovemaking.

23. See Beaglehole, *Social Change*, 172–174.

24. See Beaglehole, *Social Change*, 177.

25. While I did find dissenting opinions on this point, most men from Polynesia said that it was not a good idea to go fishing during the time of a full moon. Speculation ranged from the idea that the additional light on the surface of the water frightened the fish away to a belief that fishing at this time was taboo, because one should be honoring the gods rather than attending to one's own needs.

26. See Beaglehole, *Social Change*, 179.

27. Linnekin and Poyer emphasize that these and similar elements are much more formative for Pacific Islander identity than such factors as descent, innate characteristics, or unchanging social and cultural boundaries (see "Introduction," 1–16).

28. Technically, a *kakai* (story of tales) should be distinguished from two other types of oral narrative in Tokelau: *tala anamua* (stories of the past) and *gafa* (genealogical tales). While

the latter are regarded as true by Tokelauan storytellers in the sense of relating to actual events in time and space, *kakai* are believed to be "neither true nor false." See Huntsman, "Ten Tokelau Tales," viii-xvi.

29. A transcript of an original tape-recording of the tale in Tokelauan (as well as an English translation) appears in Huntsman, "Tokelau Tales," 54–63. Huntsman, who recorded at least two other versions of the tale from two Tokelauans in Atafu in 1976, developed the English text of the tale in a rigorous fashion. After she recorded it on tape, a fluent Tokelauan speaker transcribed it into Tokelauan. Later, Huntsman and a least one Tokelauan native speaker then translated the Tokelauan transcription into English.

30. Nukunonu is the largest of the three Tokelau atolls, and the one in which the art of telling entertaining stories (*kakai*) is best preserved. See Huntsman's account of why Nukunonu, as opposed to Atafu and Fakaofo—the other two Tokelau Islands—became the main reservoir of traditional knowledge ("Tokelau Tales," x-xvii).

31. Huntsman, "Tokelau Tales," xviii.

32. In the following account, I provide an abbreviated version of Huntsman's transcript ("Tokelau Tales," 55–63), and all quotations in the synopsis are from that transcript. In order to provide a "word-for-word" flavor of the narrative, I begin the synopsis by directly quoting from the English translation of the transcript.

33. Huntsman does note, however, that this account of Hina's sympathy ("*fakamita*") for birds is "deleted from (or not added to) other versions" of the story. See "Tokelau Tales," 111, note 2.

34. The Tokelauan expression "*fakamita*" translates literally as "(to have) kind thoughts." Huntsman says that *fakamita* ". . . is an example of a very precise Tokelau verb. It means doing something on behalf of another through sympathy for them. The example given me was of someone who intuits that another is hungry or thirsty and takes it upon himself to seek what the other desires (but does not say he wants) on his behalf." Huntsman, "Tokelau Tales," 111, note 2.

35. In this connection, it is interesting to note recent scientific findings suggesting that the bird's cerebrum is like that of a mammal. An international consortium of 29 scientists has reached consensus that bird's brains direct complex behavior, like tool use or vocalization. See Sandra Blakeslee, "Mind of their Own: Birds Gain Respect," *New York Times*, February 1, 2005.

36. "Plaiting" refers to braiding, as in the Tokelauan expression, *Fili te ika* (literally, "wrap the fish"), where *fili* refers to plaiting the coconut leaf around the fish. *Tokelau Dictionary*, s.v. "plait." Plaiting or braiding—weaving together different fibers or hairs—was traditionally an important skill in Tokelau.

37. "*Puka*" is a general Tokelauan name for two types of trees in the *puka* family. See *Tokelau Dictionary*, s.v. "*puka*."

38. Huntsman notes that Hina's craving for fish suggests that she is pregnant because "pregnant women in Tokelau characteristically crave fish" ("Tokelau Tales," 112, note 8).

39. Huntsman provides a transcription of this tale, "The Tale of the Fahua [Tridachna Clam]," in "Tokelau Tales," 45–53.

40. See the "Tale of Nonu," "Tale of Malaulekona," "Tale of Lu and Lekava," and "Tale of Loiloihavaiki," in "Tokelau Tales," 3–43.

41. Huntsman and Hooper, *Tokelau: A Historical Ethnography*, 42.

42. Huntsman and Hooper, *Tokelau: A Historical Ethnography*, 40. Given their mutual concern for understanding institutions and social organizations, Huntsman and Hooper tend to accent the intricacy of *human* relationships that is evoked by the saying.

43. This is not to ignore a Tokelauan *concern for hierarchy* (as entailed in the structure of the fish meeting itself). In fact, rank order is a fact of experience, and it is because of this order that the *Gagale* is perceived as "marginal" in the first place.

44. This account of the story is drawn from Johnson-Hill and Johnson-Hill, "Dolphin Christ," 14–15.

45. Modern western conceptions of what constitutes the realm of the "miraculous" limit our capacity to appreciate the lived experiences of those who do not share our notions of rationality. My argument in this chapter assumes that if we are to truly enter the world of Pacific Islanders, we need to adopt what the phenomenologist Alfred Schutz once described as an attitude of *epoché*—to suspend or bracket our normal expectations of what is possible. In other words, we need to guard against the premature imposition of a particular western consciousness upon those living in non-western contexts.

46. For a fascinating account of the worldviews of our distant ancestors, see Frankfort, Frankfort, Wilson and Jacobsen, *Before Philosophy*.

47. In *Economic and Philosophical Manuscripts*, Marx described the realization of our "species-being" as the actual spontaneous, free and creative expression of our "intellec-tuality." See Marx, *Economic and Philosophical Manuscripts*, 328–330. Although Marx was concerned to recover a holistic understanding of our human potential as rational and creative forms of "species-life," his abstraction of the human species from the natural world predisposed him toward Speciesism.

48. See Primavesi's careful articulation of this argument in *Making God Laugh*.

49. I am indebted to my colleague, Andrew Fort, Professor of Religion at TCU, for the expression, "mental migration."

50. Palmer, *Courage to Teach*, 31–32.

51. In addition to the canonical gospels, at least thirty other accounts circulated in the first two centuries. See Spencer, *What Did Jesus Do?* The Jesus Seminar's primary sources were the synoptic gospels (Mark, Matthew & Luke), which provide accounts of Jesus' adult ministry and contain sayings and descriptions of typical actions, and the Gospel of Thomas. Unlike the synoptic gospels, Thomas consists solely of sayings of Jesus, and offers no reports of his actions. See Meyer, *Gospel of Thomas*.

52. In this regard, I will draw heavily on Borg's description of the inner workings of the Seminar in *Meeting Jesus Again*. However, it should be noted that Borg's formulation of the distinction between these layers represents an early version of that distinction, and tends to suggest a somewhat "realist" view of what he terms "the post-Easter Jesus." In *Christianity Without God*, Lloyd Geering distinguishes between "the Jesus of history and the Christ of faith" (91–92). See also Richard Holloway's assertion in *How to Read the Bible (13)* that, "In other words, though Jesus did not claim to be divine, his followers made the claim on his behalf, after years of meditation on his continuing impact on their lives."

53. See Borg, *Meeting Jesus Again*, 15–17. For Borg's more extensive discussion of the "pre-Easter Jesus" see esp. chap. 2, "What Manner of Man?," 20–45.

54. The fruits of their labors have been published as Funk, Hoover and The Jesus Seminar, *Five Gospels*; and Funk and The Jesus Seminar, *Acts of Jesus*.

55. Two of the more vociferous critics have been Johnson, *Real Jesus* and Wilkins and Moreland, eds., *Jesus under Fire*. Miller provides a defense of the Seminar in *Jesus Seminar*.

56. These red passages, along with those designated pink ("Jesus probably said something like this"), were combined into a brief volume, Funk and The Jesus Seminar, *Gospel of Jesus*. Funk later selected the most salient of these verses to serve as a basis for his portrait of the Galilean sage, *A Credible Jesus*.

57. Thomas Jefferson compiled what he considered to be the non-doctrinal, morally coher-ent, teachings of Jesus in a book entitled, *Life and Morals of Jesus*. In 1835, Strauss wrote *The Life of Jesus Critically Examined*, which represented an attempt to recover the historical Jesus by de-mythologizing the gospel texts. See the summary of developments in the past century in Funk et al., *Five Gospels*, 2–5.

58. For a more detailed description of these ideas, using Chinese religions as a lens, see my article, Hill, "Was Jesus Green?"

59. All scripture quotations are taken from Funk, Hoover and The Jesus Seminar, *Five Gospels*.

60. Borg, *Meeting Jesus Again*, 47.

CHAPTER FIVE

1. We worked as Overseas Staff of the Christian Church (Disciples of Christ) in the U.S. and Canada.

2. See the illuminating discussion of various attempts to classify racial distinctions in Kuper, *Changing Jamaica*, 65. See esp. chap. 10, "Race and Class," 62–69.

3. See Kuper, *Changing Jamaica*, 60.

4. In this sense, nineteenth century American missionaries had certainly succeeded in inculcating western dress standards in Jamaica. Church members often complained about scantily clad tourists who practically "go naked" on the island's beaches. This way of thinking in the church was often linked to a colonial mind-set. Worship services were burdened with archaic liturgical forms. Heavy suits were still standard church wear even in tropical heat.

5. See my discussion of this issue in terms of the coverage of the 1980 Jamaican elections by the multinational news magazines, *Time* and *Newsweek*, in Johnson-Hill, "Unheard Voices," 1–20.

6. For a dated but useful introduction to the exploitative practices of transnational corporations, see Barnet and Muller, *Global Reach*, as well as the later work by Barnet and Cavanagh, *Global Dreams*. One of the best recent studies of these practices is Peters, *In Search of the Good Life*.

7. For the origins of Rastafari, see Johnson-Hill, *I-Sight*, 3–40.

8. Johnson-Hill, "Elements of an Afro-Caribbean Social Ethic."

9. The following description of *I-n-I* draws heavily from Johnson-Hill, *I-Sight*.

10. "Jah-Rastafari" has a dual reference. "Jah" denotes Yahweh, the God of the ancient Israelites; and "Rastafari" denotes Prince Tafari, the prince who was later crowned emperor of Ethiopia.

11. Cashmore, *Rastaman*, 316–317.

12. Faristzaddi, ed., *Itations of Jamaica*, n.p.

13. As I argue in Johnson-Hill, *I-Sight*, it is often necessary to understand Rasta words (as expressed in poetry and song lyrics), in a multifaceted symbolic way. Frequently, they express meanings that confound our understanding if we insist on a one-dimensional or literal interpretation of meaning. In my approach to symbology, I strive to interpret poetic expressions by contextualizing them in terms of carefully constructed concepts of both everyday and religious experiences in Jamaican culture.

14. Smith, *It A Come*, 1–16.

15. Wong [Onuora], "Retrospect," in *Echo*, II, 1–8.

16. Onuora, "Reflection in Red," in Burnett, ed., *Penguin Book of Caribbean Verse*, 84–85.

17. Faristzaddi, ed., *Itations of Jamaica*, n.p.

18. Since Rastas generally cite the King James Version of the Bible, I will use that translation when referring to Rastafarian quotations of biblical scriptures.

19. Nettleford, "Introduction," vii-xix.

20. Yawney, "Don't Vex Than Pray," 15–16.

21. Brodber and Green, "Reggae and Cultural Identity."

22. For a brief discussion of Jamaican *I-words* (words in which the vowel "I" replaces the first syllable), such as *I-vine* (divine) and *I-ses* (praises), see Pollard, "Social History of Dread Talk," 33–35.

23. For an economic analysis of harvesting marijuana see Hamid, "Pre-Capitalist Mode of Production."

24. For the classic account of the matricentric Jamaican family structure, see Clarke, *My Mother Who Fathered Me*.

25. See my detailed discussions of the scholarship on the movement in Johnson-Hill, *I-Sight*, 41–68.

26. I have summarized what is a very technical sociological argument in the concluding chapter of Johnson-Hill, *I-Sight*, 307–326.

27. Even though Rastafari is now in its fourth generation, there are no reliable census data that indicate its size or distribution in Jamaica or around the world. One commentator estimated that over half of the youth who reside in Kingston (a city with a population over one million) identified with Rastafari (see Johnson-Hill, *I-Sight*, 3.)

28. The following account of the Anancy tradition draws heavily on the description in Johnson-Hill, *I-Sight*, 327–329.

29. Clarke, "Eternal Gospel," 51.

30. Olson, *Building with Christ*, 14–16.

31. See Nelson, *Disciples of Christ*.

32. Davis, *Church in the New Jamaica*.

33. Following the lead of the Rasta poet Mikey Smith, I have defined the movement as a certain consciousness of oneself (*I-n-I*), one's lifestyle (*livity*) and one's understanding of good (*Ithiopia*) and evil (*Babylon*). See my discussion of this and other definitions in Johnson-Hill, *I-Sight*, 3–9.

34. See Preface, viii, note 3, regarding the translation of *basileia tou theou* as "divine domain."

35. I am indebted to the New Testament scholar, Krister Stendahl, who first enlightened me concerning the centrality of the kingdom in the message of Jesus during my studies at Harvard Divinity School in the early 1970s. Modern scholars are in general agreement on this point. Sullivan, e.g., quotes Reumann as follows: "Ask any hundred New Testament scholars around the world . . . and the vast majority of them—perhaps every single expert—would agree that this message centered in the 'Kingdom of God'" (*Rescuing Jesus*, 7). Feminists and other scholars have argued that the expression "Kin-dom" is less patriarchal and authoritarian than the traditional "Kingdom," and points to a more inclusive, less sexist and more communal understanding of God's domain.

36. See Funk's brief, incisive collection of Jesus sayings on counterintuitive values in *A Credible Jesus*, 87–88.

37. Unless otherwise indicated, all translations of Scripture quoted in the text are taken from Funk, Hoover, and the Jesus Seminar, *Five Gospels*.

38. While Thomas 42 is open to a variety of interpretations, and the Fellows of the Jesus Seminar were evenly divided on its authenticity, I have utilized it as a point of departure because I want to accent Jesus' identity as a follower of John the Baptist, and this passage reflects John's apparently counter-cultural lifestyle. It also serves as a bridge to the concept of the "liminal" self who is in transition from one established place, stage or identity to another place, stage or identity that is yet to materialize.

39. Van Gennep defined the "liminal" as "all the ceremonial patterns which accompany a passage from one situation to another" (*Rites of Passage*, 10). Turner expanded the concept to include persons in movements and larger social processes in which "the past has lost its grip and the future has not yet taken definitive shape" (Turner, "Liminality and Morality"). Such periods are marked by "hitherto unprecedented modes of ordering relations between ideas and people" (Turner and Turner, *Image and Pilgrim*, 2).

40. It should be noted that this is the only time the term "acquitted" or "justified" is used in the gospels with reference to an individual, while it is prominently employed in Paul's letters. Therefore, its inclusion may be more reflective of the early Christian movement than it is of the historical Jesus' utterances. But, since it is a key element in explicating the sense in which the parable points to a stunning reversal, it is legitimate to emphasize the term here. See Funk, Hoover and the Jesus Seminar, *Five Gospels*.

41. The Fellows of the Jesus Seminar viewed this depiction of John with skepticism because of its stereotypical description of a prophet's attire. See Funk and the Jesus Seminar, *Gospel of Jesus*, 90–91.

42. See H. R. Niebuhr's classic discussion of "The Social Gods and the Many Gods" in *Radical Monotheism*, 24–31.

43. For a synopsis of the Seminar's thinking regarding Jesus and an apocalyptic view of history, see the cameo "God's Imperial Rule" in Funk, Hoover, and the Jesus Seminar, *Five Gospels*, 136–137.

44. By re-burying the treasure and buying the field without telling the owner, the person exhibits deception. Perhaps Jesus uses this questionable moral example as a way of suggesting that even God's imperial rule is not exempt from human corruptibility.

45. Since leaven was invariably a symbol of corruption and evil, and three measures (fifty pounds) of flour is a repeated sign of God's presence, Jesus' metaphor is all the more shocking.

46. *Babette's Feast*, a film in which a French chef converts a lottery win into an elaborate celebrative meal for guests, who themselves experience "changes of heart" in the process of eating the meal, is suggestive of these themes.

47. Both the latecomers and the early arrivals are surprised in the parable, and the graciousness shown to the latecomers parallels God's reversal of expectations for the poor. See Funk, Hoover and the Jesus Seminar, *Five Gospels*, 225.

48. Although it would be erroneous to take the passage literally—it evokes comic imagery of a camel being squeezed through a narrow passage—it does resonate with a "context where wealth functioned as an impediment to entering God's domain" (Funk, Hoover and the Jesus Seminar, *Five Gospels*, 223).

49. I am indebted to Karen Baker-Fletcher for her insights regarding the essentially "intercultural" nature of human being. Interview, Perkins School of Theology, September 5, 2006.

50. See Tatum, *Why Are All the Black Kids*, 7f.

CHAPTER SIX

1. Clearly, however, not all U.S. citizens distinguished between the policies of the Nazi regime and the German people.

2. My wife and I worked as Overseas Staff of both the Christian Church (Disciples of Christ) in the United States and Canada and the United Church of Christ, both of whom had merged overseas mission operations in what became known as the Common Global Missions Board.

3. The following brief account of the University of Durban-Westville (UDW), including incidents of conflict and violence during the mid-1990s, represents a distillation of the more detailed account in my book, Johnson-Hill, *Seeds of Transformation*, 8–23.

4. During the apartheid regime, the term "black" was commonly used to designate all persons of color, including Indians and peoples of mixed races. In this chapter, unless otherwise indicated, the term "black" will be used to refer to black South Africans, as distinct from "Indian," "colored" or "white" South Africans.

5. This vision is set forth in a major policy document of the African National Congress, *Reconstruction and Development Programme*.

6. The "lost generation" is the large group of South African youth, many in their late 20s and early 30s, who boycotted schools during the 1980s in protest against the apartheid system. They were particularly resistant to requirements for learning Afrikaans. Many were detained and jailed by police.

7. The interview format, along with a more detailed account of interviewee responses, can be found in my book, Johnson-Hill, *Seeds of Transformation*.

8. Johnson-Hill, *Seeds of Transformation*, 64.

9. Given the seismic shift occurring in southern Africa today, from traditional, communally oriented chiefly orders to modern, contractually oriented pluralistic societies, it is not surprising that students are engaging in creative thinking about where they have come from, who they are, and where they are going. Some of them characterized themselves as

persons in transition. On the one hand, they are rooted in a traditional notion of self, where the individual's identity is grounded in that of the community and nurtured in the immediate family and larger kin group. But due to changing economic patterns in village life, urban drift and modern communications technology, they are also pressing against traditional boundaries, codes and constraints associated with life in their kin groups.

10. The following descriptions draw heavily from my book, Johnson-Hill, *Seeds of Transformation*.

11. Setiloane, *African Theology*, 13–14. For a classic statement of vital force as "the key principle" in Bantu philosophy, see Tempels, *Bantu Philosophy*, 175.

12. Setiloane, *African Theology*, 14.

13. Shutte, "Philosophical Ethics," 30.

14. "*Africanization*" refers to a reflective self-analysis from the vantage point of a "social situatedness" deeply rooted in the African continent. For many of today's black African youth, it functions as a powerful symbol that evokes the interrelated values of relationality, empowerment and alterity described in the text.

15. Jeff Thomas, lecture, "Practical Zulu," University of Natal, Durban, June 2, 1995. While each African linguistic group understands the self in ways that are more or less unique to its own people, there is nevertheless a striking degree of continuity on this subject among different African groups in South Africa, and between South Africans and other Africans in sub-Sahara Africa. For an incisive introduction to African concepts of the person in three different cultural contexts, see Ray, *African Religions*, 132–140. For a detailed account of the concept among the Tallensi, see Fortes, *Religion, Morality and the Person*, 247–286.

16. See Funk, *Credible Jesus*, 72.

17. It should be noted that the marriage relationship in ancient Palestine was a very patriarchal affair that did not necessarily include concepts of "intimacy" and "close relationships" that we moderns typically associate with the institution of marriage. Wife and daughters were the husband's property.

18. I am indebted to Ron Flowers for this translation of "*basileia*."

19. Funk, *Credible Jesus*, 21.

20. For an excellent account of the political context of Palestine in Jesus' time, see Horsley, *Jesus and Empire*. Horsley takes issue with some of the Jesus Seminar's hermeneutical approaches, especially the Seminar's tendency to view Jesus as a wandering cynic philosopher who spoke primarily to individuals in aphorisms; rather than as a religio-political social prophet (perhaps tied more closely to the apocalyptic John the Baptist), who was deeply enmeshed within socio-political networks and who spoke in running narratives to others who were also inextricably linked to socio-political networks. Although both Funk and Horsley sought to take the historical context of Jesus seriously, Horsley not only takes the "political" nature of that context more seriously than Funk, but he has a less "enlightenment-constrained" understanding of how the political is interrelated with the social and the religious. But what is perhaps often lost sight of in this hermeneutical fencing is that both Funk and Horsley agree about the centrality of the poor in the realm of God.

21. Horsley, *Jesus and Empire*, 6.

22. Horsley, *Jesus and Empire*, 12.

23. Horsley, *Jesus and Empire*, 11.

24. Horsley, *Jesus and Empire*, 17.

25. For a recent study of the cruel impact of Roman rule on subject peoples see Mattern, *Rome and the Enemy*.

26. By and large the Fellows of the Jesus Seminar did not believe that Jesus preached an apocalyptic message.

27. Horsley, *Jesus and Empire*, 14.

28. Here the more familiar word, "*mammon*" is translated as "bank account" because *mammon* referred to "a kind of pseudo-god"—"the pull of wealth"—"under whose spell one may readily fall." See Funk, *Credible Jesus*, 28.

29. For an incisive description of toll collectors in ancient Palestine, see Funk, *A Credible Jesus*, 50–51, 54–55.

30. Of course in the parable, the invitation to those in "the streets and the alleys" comes only after the dinner host has been rebuffed by the "guests" who were invited in the first place. The fact that the master later sends his slave out "to force" people to come to his party so the "house will be filled," suggests that the invitation to the poor and the physically challenged is at least as much about saving face as it is an act of altruism.

31. Horsley contends that the temple incident constitutes the dominant plot of Mark's gospel in chap. 5, *Hearing the Whole Story*.

32. Funk, *Credible Jesus*, 59. Funk believed that ". . . the cosmic background of life is apparently neutral," and he also held that the God of Jesus (in contrast to the "God pictured in the Bible" who "is highly partial and often quite vindictive") was impartial or "appears to have no favorites." (59) On this point I both agree and disagree with Funk. While it may well be the case that the God of Jesus was "inclusive" to the extent that this God loved all of humanity (rich *and* poor, Jew *and* Gentile), Jesus' God may also have been "partial" toward the poor and the social/cultural outcast as the primary agents of the salvation of all of humanity. In other words, where God loves everybody—even the rich—the only way the rich can finally be redeemed or "saved" in actual history is through the liberating work of the poor! That, I submit, is why Jesus says that it is easier for a camel to get squeezed through the eye of a needle than for a rich man to enter the divine domain. The liberationist Gutierrez thus speaks of the "one salvation history" in which God works through social movements that are fired by the power of the poor in history. See esp. chap. one in Gutierrez, *Power of the Poor in History*, 3–22.

33. This passage is a "case parody" or an admonition that, because of its exaggerated nature, prompts fresh kinds of reactions in the face of violent coercion. See Funk, Hoover and the Jesus Seminar, *Five Gospels*, 144–45.

34. For an illuminating account of this and other practices in imperial Rome see Wink, *Engaging the Powers*.

35. Like the saying about walking an extra mile, this passage is also a case parody. As such, it would function to prompt listeners to "react differently to events of aggression" (Funk, Hoover and the Jesus Seminar, *Five Gospels*, 144–45). While it is a mistake to read it—as some pacifists do—as a literal call for non-violent responses, the aphorism does call into question the kind of knee jerk resorts to violence that would be associated with the religion of Militarism.

36. As a parody, this passage would serve as a catalyst for imaginative thinking. For example, it might conjure up an image of defendants walking around naked. Elsewhere, Jesus appears to stress the importance of trying to mediate disputes or settle out of court (Luke 12:58–59).

37. Funk, *Credible Jesus*, 61.

38. The parable of the good Samaritan demonstrates that "tribal enemies rather than personal enemies were the focus of Jesus' concern." (Funk, *Credible Jesus*, 62).

39. In the parable, the reader is invited to identify with the man who was beaten and robbed and to see the aid of the hated Samaritan as at once not wanted, not expected and yet also as a surprising act—"the grace of the Samaritan who was scandalously generous" (Funk, *Credible Jesus*, 167–71).

CHAPTER SEVEN

1. A good, though dated, primer is Holland and Henriot, *Social Analysis*.

2. For notes on such "liminal" spaces in modern contexts, see Turner and Turner, *Image and Pilgrim*, 2.

3. Kuhn, *Structure of Scientific Revolutions*, 111–135.

WORKS CONSULTED

Ackerman, Frank, Neva R. Goodwin, Laurie Dougherty and Kevin Gallagher, eds. *The Political Economy of Inequality.* Washington, DC: Island Press, 2000.

African National Congress. *The Reconstruction and Development Programme: A Policy Framework.* Johannesburg: Umanyano Publications, 1994.

Amadio, Nadine. *Pacifica: Myth, Magic and Traditional Wisdom from the South Sea Islands.* Sydney: Angus and Robinson, HarperCollins Publishers, 1993.

Anonymous. *Imperial Hubris: Why the West Is Losing the War on Terror.* Washington, DC: Brassey's, 2004.

Armstrong, Karen. *The Great Transformation: The Beginning of Our Religious Traditions.* New York: Alfred Knopf, 2006.

———. "Suggestions for a Second Axial Age." Paper presented at the spring meeting of the Westar Institute, Santa Rosa, CA, March 1, 2001.

———. *A History of God: The 4000-Year Quest of Judaism, Christianity and Islam.* New York: Alfred Knopf, 1993.

Baker-Fletcher, Karen. Interview by Jack Hill. Tape recording. September 5, 2006. Perkins School of Theology, Dallas.

Barnet, Richard J. and John Cavanagh. *Global Dreams: Imperial Corporations and the New World Order.* New York: Simon and Schuster (Touchstone), 1994.

Barnet, Richard J. and Ronald E. Muller. *Global Reach: The Power of the Multinational Corporations.* New York: Simon and Schuster (Touchstone), 1974.

Barnett, Thomas P. M. *The Pentagon's New Map: War and Peace in the Twenty-First Century.* New York: G. P. Putnam's Sons, 2004.

Barnhill, David and Roger S. Gottlieb, eds. *Deep Ecology and World Religions: New Essays on Sacred Grounds.* Albany: State University of New York Press, 2001.

Barone, Charles A. *Radical Political Economy: A Concise Introduction.* Armonk, NY: M. E. Sharpe, 2004.

Barrera, Albino. *Economic Compulsion and Christian Ethics*. Cambridge: Cambridge University Press, 2005.

———. *God and the Evil of Scarcity: Moral Foundations of Economic Agency*. Notre Dame: University of Notre Dame Press, 2005.

Barton, John. *Ethics and the Old Testament*. Harrisburg, PA: Trinity Press International, 1998.

Baum, Gregory, ed. *Neo-Conservatism: Social and Religious Phenomenon*. Edinburgh: T & T Clark; New York: Seabury Press, 1981.

Bauman, Zygmunt. *Life in Fragments: Essays in Postmodern Morality*. Oxford: Blackwell, 1995.

Beaglehole, Ernst. *Social Change in the South Pacific: Rarotonga and Aitutaki*. New York: Macmillan, 1957.

Bellwood, Peter. *The Polynesians: Prehistory of an Island People*. New York: Thames and Hudson, 1987.

Berger, Peter L. and Thomas Luckmann. "Secularization and Pluralism." *Internationales Jahrbuch fur Religionssoziologie* 2 (1966) 73-86.

Bernstein, Richard. *Beyond Objectivism and Relativism: Science, Hermeneutics, and Practice*. Philadelphia: University of Pennsylvania Press, 1988.

Betsworth, Roger. *Social Ethics: An Examination of American Moral Traditions*. Louisville, KY: Westminster/John Knox Press, 1990.

Bloom, Alan. *The Closing of the American Mind*. New York: Simon and Schuster, 1987.

Boff, Leonardo. *Cry of the Earth, Cry of the Poor*. Trans. Phillip Berryman. Maryknoll: Orbis, 2003.

Bonino, Jose Miguez. *Toward a Christian Political Ethics*. Philadelphia: Fortress Press, 1983.

Borg, Marcus J. *Meeting Jesus Again for the First Time: The Historical Jesus and the Heart of Contemporary Faith*. San Francisco: HarperSanFrancisco, 1994.

Brock, Rita Nakashima. *Journeys by Heart: A Christology of Erotic Power*. New York: Crossroad, 1988.

Brodber, Erna and J. Edward Greene. "Reggae and Cultural Identity in Jamaica." Working Paper on Caribbean Society, Department of Sociology, University of the West Indies, St. Augustine, Trinidad, October 1981.

Brown, Lester, Hal Kane and David Roodman. *Vital Signs, 1994: The Trends That Are Shaping Our Future*. New York: Norton, 1994.

Brubaker, Pamela. *Globalization at What Price?—Economic Change in Daily Life*. Cleveland: Pilgrim Press, 2001.

Brueggemann, Walter. *Living Toward a Vision: Biblical Reflections on Shalom*. 2nd ed. New York: United Church Press, 1982.

Burnett, P. A., ed. *The Penguin Book of Caribbean Verse in English*. Harmondsworth, Middlesex, UK: Penguin, 1986.

Campbell, I. C. *A History of the Pacific Islands.* Christchurch, New Zealand: University of Canterbury Press, 1989.

Cannon, Katie G. *Black Womanist Ethics.* Atlanta: Scholars Press, 1988.

Carnegie, Andrew. "Wealth." *North American Review* 391 (June 1889) 653–664.

Cashmore, Ernest E. *Rastaman: The Rastafarian Movement in England.* 2nd ed. London: George Allen & Unwin, 1983.

Chandrasekaran, Rajiv. *Imperial Life in the Emerald City: Inside Iraq's Green Zone.* New York: Alfred A. Knopf, 2007.

Childs, James M. *Greed: Economics and Ethics in Conflict.* Minneapolis: Fortress Press, 2000.

Clarke, Edith. *My Mother Who Fathered Me: A Study of the Family in Three Selected Communities in Jamaica.* 2nd ed. London: Allen and Unwin, 1966.

Clarke, W. N. J. "The Eternal Gospel: What Christians Believe." Pp. 51–54 in *Christ for Jamaica: A Symposium of Religious Activities Compiled by the Jamaican Christian Council.* Ed. J. A. Crabb. Kingston: The Pioneer Press, 1951.

Clinebell, Howard. *Basic Types of Pastoral Care and Counseling: Resources for the Ministry of Healing and Growth.* Rev. and enl. ed. Nashville: Abingdon Press, 1984.

Cobb, John. *Earthist Challenge to Economism: A Theological Critique of the World Bank.* Hampshire, UK: Palgrave Macmillan Publishers, 1999.

Cole, David, "Let's Right Terrorism, Not the Constitution." Pp. 37–38 in *Rights vs. Public Safety after 9/11: America in an Age of Terrorism.* Ed. Amitai Etzioni and Jason H. Marsh. Rowman and Littlefield Publishers, 2003.

Coll, Steve. *Ghost Wars: The Secret History of the CIA, Afghanistan, and Bin Laden, from the Soviet Invasion to September 10, 2001.* New York: Penguin Press, 2004.

Collins, Chuck and Mary Wright. *The Moral Measure of the Economy.* Maryknoll: Orbis, 2007.

Crook, Roger. *An Introduction to Christian Ethics.* 5th ed. Upper Saddle River, NJ: Prentice-Hall, 2006.

Cupitt, Don. *Life, Life.* Santa Rosa, CA: Polebridge Press, 2003.

Dalton, Frederick John. *The Moral Vision of César Chávez.* Maryknoll: Orbis, 2003.

Davis, J. Merle. *The Church in the New Jamaica: A Study of the Economic and Social Basis of the Evangelical Church in Jamaica.* New York and London: The Academy Press for the International Missionary Council, 1942.

De La Torre, Miguel A. *Doing Christian Ethics from the Margins.* Maryknoll: Orbis, 2004.

Derrida, Jacques. *Margins of Philosophy.* Trans. Alan Bates. Chicago: University of Chicago Press, 1982.

———. *Ecriture et la Difference (Writing and Difference).* Trans. Alan Bates. Chicago: University of Chicago Press, 1978.

Diamond, Larry. *Squandered Victory: The American Occupation and the Bungled Effort to Bring Democracy to Iraq*. New York: New York Times Books, 2005.

Dougherty, Mike. "Genes, Ethics and Religion: A Blueprint for Teaching." Paper presented at a pre-conference workshop of the annual meeting of the American Academy of Religion, San Antonio, Texas, November 19, 2004.

Draut, Tamara and Heather C. McGhee. "Retiring in the Red: The Growth of Debt among Older Americans." Briefing paper, Demos (A Network for Ideas and Action), New York, February 2004.

Draut, Tamara and Javier Silva. "Borrowing to Make Ends Meet: The Growth of Credit Card Debt in the '90s." Briefing paper, Demos (A Network for Ideas and Action), New York, September 2003.

Dussel, Enrique. *Ethics and Community*. Maryknoll: Orbis, 1988.

Dye, Thomas. *Understanding Public Policy*. 9th ed. Upper Saddle River, NJ: Prentice Hall, 1998.

Edwards, Andres R. *The Sustainability Revolution: Portrait of a Paradigm Shift*. Gabriola Island, BC, Canada: New Society Publishers, 2005.

Edwards, Jonathan. "The Latter Day Glory Is Probably to Begin in America." Pp. 55–60 in *God's New Israel*. Ed. Conrad Cherry. Englewood Cliffs, NJ: Prentice-Hall, 1971.

Ellison, Marvin. *Erotic Justice: A Liberating Ethic of Sexuality*. Louisville, KY: Westminster John Knox Press, 1996.

Everest, Larry. *Oil, Power and Empire: Iraq and the U.S. Global Agenda*. Monroe, ME: Common Courage Press, 2004.

Faristzaddi, Millard, ed. *Itations of Jamaica and Rastafari*. Hamburg: Rogner and Bernard, 1982.

Farley, Margaret. *Just Love: A Framework for Christian Ethics*. New York: Continuum, 2006.

Fisher, Mary. *Living Religions*. 7th ed. Upper Saddle River, NJ: Prentice-Hall, 2008.

Fortes, Meyer. *Religion, Morality and the Person*. Cambridge: Cambridge University Press, 1987.

Foucault, Michael. *The Archaeology of Knowledge*. Trans. A. M. Sheridan Smith. London: Tavostock, 1972.

Frankfort, Henri, H. A. Frankfort, John A. Wilson and Thorkild Jacobsen. *Before Philosophy: The Intellectual Adventure of Ancient Man—An Essay on Speculative Thought in the Ancient Near East*. Baltimore, MD: Penguin Books, 1973.

Franklin, Benjamin. *The Autobiography of Benjamin Franklin*. Ed. Peter Conn. Philadelphia, PA: University of Pennsylvania Press, 2005.

Funk, Robert W. "An Enlightened Faith for an Enlightened Age." Keynote address at the spring meeting of the Westar Institute, New York, March 3, 2004.

———. *A Credible Jesus: Fragments of a Vision*. Santa Rosa: Polebridge Press, 2002.

Funk, Robert W., Roy W. Hoover and The Jesus Seminar. *The Five Gospels: The Search for the Authentic Words of Jesus*. Santa Rosa, CA: Polebridge Press, HarperSanFrancisco, 1993.

Funk, Robert W. and The Jesus Seminar. *The Gospel of Jesus According to the Jesus Seminar*. Santa Rosa, CA: Polebridge Press, 1999.

———. *The Acts of Jesus: The Search for the Authentic Deeds of Jesus*. Santa Rosa, CA: Polebridge Press, HarperSanFrancisco, 1998.

Galbraith, John Kenneth. *The Culture of Contentment*. Boston: Houghton Mifflin Co., 1992.

Galbraith, Peter W. *The End of Iraq: How American Incompetence Created a War Without End*. New York: Simon & Schuster, 2006.

Garcia, Ismael. *Dignidad: Ethics Through Hispanic Eyes*. Nashville: Abingdon Press, 1997.

Gardner, Lloyd C. and Marilyn B. Young, eds. *Iraq and the Lessons of Vietnam: Or How Not to Learn from the Past*. New York: The New York Press, 2007.

Geering, Lloyd. *Christianity Without God*. Santa Rosa, CA: Polebridge Press, 2002.

Gill, Robin. *Christian Ethics in Secular Worlds*. Edinburgh: T & T Clark, 1991.

Gillett, Richard W. *The New Globalization: Reclaiming the Lost Ground of our Christian Social Tradition*. Cleveland: Pilgrim Press, 2005.

Gilman, James E. *Fidelity of Heart: An Ethic of Christian Virtue*. Oxford: Oxford University Press, 2001.

Gore, Al. *An Inconvenient Truth: The Planetary Emergency of Global Warming and What We Can Do About It*. New York: Rodale Books, 2006.

Goudzwaard, Bob, Mark Vander Vennen and David Van Heemst. *Hope in Troubled Times: A New Vision for Confronting Global Crises*. Grand Rapids, MI: Baker Academic, 2007.

Griffin, David Ray. *Christian Faith and the Truth Behind 9-11: A Call to Reflection and Action*. Louisville: Westminster John Knox Press, 2006.

———, ed. *Founders of Constructive Postmodern Philosophy*. Albany: State University of New York Press, 1993.

Griffin, David Ray, John B. Cobb Jr., Richard A. Falk and Catherine Keller, eds. *The American Empire and the Commonwealth of God: A Political, Economic and Religious Statement*. Louisville, KY: Westminster John Knox Press, 2006.

Gustafson, James. *Christ and the Moral Life*. Chicago: University of Chicago Press, 1968.

Gutierrez, Gustavo. *The Power of the Poor in History: Selected Writings*. Trans. Robert Barr. Maryknoll: Orbis, 1983.

Habermas, Jürgen. *Theory and Practice*. Trans. John Viertel. Boston: Beacon Press, 1973.

Hamid, Ansley. "A Pre-Capitalist Mode of Production: Ganja and the Rastafarians." Ph.D. diss., Columbia University, 1981.

Hauerwas, Stanley. *A Community of Character: Toward a Constructive Christian Social Ethic.* Notre Dame: University of Notre Dame Press, 1981.

Hauerwas, Stanley and William Willimon. *Resident Aliens.* Nashville: Abingdon, 1989.

Hawken, Paul, Amory Lovins and L. Hunter Lovins. *Natural Capitalism: Creating the Next Industrial Revolution.* New York: Little, Brown and Company, 1999.

Hicks, Douglas A. *Religion in the Workplace: Pluralism, Spirituality and Leadership.* Cambridge: Cambridge University Press, 2003.

Hill, Jack. "The Boy Scout and the Mafia Boss: Is There a Future for Christian Ethics in America?" Pp. 218–241 in *The Future of the Christian Tradition.* Ed. Robert J. Miller. Santa Rosa, CA: Polebridge Press, 2007.

––––––. "Teaching for Transformation: Insights from Fiji, India, South Africa and Jamaica." *Teaching Theology and Religion* 8, no. 4 (October 2005) 218–231.

––––––. "Was Jesus Green? Reflections on the Sayings of Jesus from a Cross-Cultural Perspective." *The Fourth R: An Advocate for Religious Literacy* 15, 5 (September-October 2002) 3–8.

––––––. "Doing Ethics in the Pacific Islands: Interpreting Moral Dimensions of Prose Narrative." *Annual of the Society of Christian Ethics* 21 (2001) 341–360.

––––––. "Global Ethics: What We Can Learn From Christians Overseas." *Christian Ethics Today* 7/4 (2001) 23-25.

––––––. "Putting the Township in the University: Moral Resources from Former Freedom Fighters in South Africa." *Journal of Religious Thought* 56,2/57,1 (2001) 21–42.

Hobsbawm, Eric. *The Age of Extremes: A History of the World, 1914–1991.* New York: Random House, 1994.

Hoehn, Richard A. *Up from Apathy: A Study of Moral Awareness and Social Involvement.* Nashville: Abingdon Press, 1983.

Holland, Joe and Peter Henriot. *Social Analysis: Linking Faith and Justice.* Rev. and enl ed. Washington, DC: Dove Communications and Orbis Books in collaboration with The Center of Concern, 1988.

Holloway, Richard. *How to Read the Bible.* London: W. W. Norton and Company, 2006.

––––––. *Godless Morality: Keeping Religion Out of Ethics.* Edinburgh: Canongate Books, 1999.

Horsley, Richard. *Jesus and Empire: The Kingdom of God and the New World Order.* Minneapolis: Fortress Press, 2003.

––––––. *Hearing the Whole Story: The Politics of Plot in Mark's Gospel.* Louisville, KY: Westminster John Knox, 2001.

Hudson, Winthrop S. *Religion in America.* New York: Macmillan, 1987.

Huntsman, Judith, ed. "Tokelau Tales Told by Manuele Palehau." Working Paper in Anthropology, Archaeology, Linguistics and Maori Studies 58, Department of Anthropology, University of Auckland, New Zealand, 1980.

————. ed. "Ten Tokelau Tales." Working Paper in Anthropology, Archaeology, Linguistics and Maori Studies 47, Department of Anthropology, University of Auckland, New Zealand, 1977.

Huntsman, Judith and Anthony Hooper. *Tokelau: A Historical Ethnography.* Honolulu: University of Hawai'i Press, 1996.

Isikoff, Michael and David Corn. *Hubris: The Inside Story of a Spin, a Scandal and the Selling of the Iraq War.* New York: Crown Press, 2006.

Jacob, C. G. A. *A Second Handful of Popular Maxims Current in Sanskrit Literature.* Bombay: Nirnaya-Sagar Press, 1902.

Janzen, Waldemar. *Old Testament Ethics: A Paradigmatic Approach.* Louisville, KY: Westminster/John Knox Press, 1994.

Jardine, Murray. "Sight, Sound and Epistemology: The Experiential Sources of Ethical Concepts." *Journal of the American Academy of Religion* 64,1 (Spring 1996)1–22.

Jefferson, Thomas. *The Life and Morals of Jesus of Nazareth, Extracted Textually from the Gospels of Matthew, Mark, Luke and John.* New York: Eakins Press, 1968.

Johnson, Chalmers. *The Sorrows of Empire: Militarism, Secrecy and the End of the Republic.* New York: Metropolitan Books, 2004.

Johnson, Luke Timothy. *The Real Jesus: The Misguided Quest for the Historical Jesus and the Truth of the Traditional Gospels.* San Francisco: Harper-Collins, 1996.

Johnson-Hill, Jack [Jack Hill]. *Seeds of Transformation: Discerning the Ethics of a New Generation.* Pietermaritzburg, South Africa: Cluster Publications in association with the Centre for Constructive Theology, 1998.

————. *I-Sight—The World of Rastafari: An Interpretive Sociological Account of Rastafarian Ethics.* American Theological Library Association Monograph Series, 35. Lanham, MD & London: The Scarecrow Press, 1995.

————. "Elements of an Afro-Caribbean Social Ethic: A Disclosure of the World of Rastafari as Liminal Process." Ph.D. diss., Vanderbilt University, 1988.

————. "Unheard Voices: Jamaica's Struggle and the Multinational Media." *Caribbean Quarterly* 27, 2/3 (June-September 1981) 1–20.

Johnson-Hill, Jack [Jack Hill] and Lydia Johnson-Hill [Lydia Johnson]. "The Dolphin Christ." *Horizons* 4, no. 4 (May-June 1991) 14–15.

Kammer, Charles. *Ethics and Liberation: An Introduction.* Maryknoll: Orbis, 1994.

Kanongata'a, Keiti A. "A Pacific Women's Theology of Birthing and Liberation." *Pacific Journal of Theology* 2, no. 7 (1992) 3–11.

Kant, Immanuel. *Critique of Pure Reason.* Trans. Ed. Paul Guyer and Allen Wood. Cambridge: Cambridge University Press, 1998.

Kirch, Patrick. *The Evolution of Polynesian Chiefdoms.* Cambridge: Cambridge University Press, 1984.

Kristol, Irving. *Neo-Conservatism: The Autobiography of an Idea*. Chicago: Ivan R. Dee, Publisher, 1995.

———. *Reflections of a Neoconservative: Looking Back, Looking Ahead*. New York: Basic Books, 1983.

Kuhn, Thomas. *The Structure of Scientific Revolutions*. 2nd ed., enl. Chicago: University of Chicago Press, 1970.

Kuper, Adam. *Changing Jamaica*. Kingston: Kingston Publishers, 1976.

Kurtz, Paul. *In Defense of Secular Humanism*. Buffalo, NY: Prometheus, 1983.

Lasch, Christopher. *The Culture of Narcissism*. New York: W. W. Norton, 1979.

Leaves, Nigel. *The God Problem: Alternatives to Fundamentalism*. Santa Rosa, CA: Polebridge Press, 2006.

Lee, Jung Young. *Marginality: The Key to Multicultural Theology*. Minneapolis: Fortress, 1995.

Lendon, J. E. *Empire of Honor*. Oxford: Oxford University Press, 1997.

Lewis, Bernard. "The Revolt of Islam." *The New Yorker* 77, no. 36 (November 19, 2001) 50-63.

Liechty, Daniel. *Theology in Postliberal Perspective*. London: SCM Press, 1990.

Lind, Michael. *Up from Conservatism: Why the Right is Wrong for America*. New York: Free Press, 1996.

Linnekin, Jocelyn and Lin Poyer, "Introduction." Pp. 1–16 in *Cultural Identity and Ethnicity in the Pacific*. Ed. Jocelyn Linnekin and Lin Poyer. Honolulu: University of Hawai'i Press, 1990.

Long, Steven D. and Nancy Ruth Fox, with Trip York. *Calculated Futures: Theology, Ethics and Economics*. Waco, TX: Baylor University Press, 2007.

Locke, David. *Science as Writing*. New Haven: Yale University Press, 1992.

MacIntyre, Alasdair. *Whose Justice? Which Rationality?* Notre Dame: University of Notre Dame Press, 1988.

———. *After Virtue: A Study in Moral Theory*. Notre Dame: University of Notre Dame Press, 1981.

Malan, Jannie. "Educating Multicultural South Africans for Mutual Understanding and Constructive Interaction." In *Multicultural Conflict Management in Changing Societies*. Ed. Louise Nieuwmeijer and Renee du Toit. Pretoria: Human Sciences Research Council, 1994.

Manley, Michael. *Jamaica: Struggle in the Periphery*. London: Third World Media Limited in association with Writers and Readers Publishing Cooperative Society, 1982.

Margolis, Diane. *The Fabric of Self: A Theory of Ethics and the Emotions*. New Haven: Yale University Press, 1998.

Marx, Karl. *Economic and Philosophical Manuscripts (1844)*. Pp. 279–400 *in Karl Marx: Early Writings*. Trans. Rodney Livingstone and Gregor Benton. New York: Vintage Books, 1975.

Marx, Werner. *Towards a Phenomenological Ethics: Ethos and the Life-World*. Albany: State University of New York Press, 1992.

Mathies, David. "Sati, Understanding and Condemnation: Reflections on the Problem of (Comparative Religious) Ethics." Working paper in author's possession, Fort Worth, Texas, 2004.

Mattern, Susan P. *Rome and the Enemy: Imperial Strategy in the Principate.* Berkeley: University of California Press, 1999.

McAuliffe, Patricia. *Fundamental Ethics: A Liberationist Approach.* Washington, DC: Georgetown University Press, 1993.

McDonough, William and Michael Braungart. *Cradle to Cradle: Rethinking the Way We Make Things.* New York: North Point Press, 2002.

McGuffey, William H. *McGuffey's Fifth Eclectic Reader.* Cincinnati: American Book Co., 1879.

McKeon, Richard, ed. *Introduction to Aristotle.* New York: Modern Library, 1947.

McQuilkin, Robertson. *An Introduction to Biblical Ethics.* Rev. ed. Wheaton, IL: Tyndale House, 1989.

Mead, Margaret. *Growing up in Samoa: A Psychological Study of Primitive Youth for Western Civilization.* New York: Blue Ribbons Book, 1928.

Mead, Sidney. *The Nation with the Soul of a Church.* New York: Harper & Row, 1975.

Meeks, Wayne. *The Origins of Christian Morality: The First Two Centuries.* New Haven: Yale University Press, 1993.

Meyer, Marvin. *The Gospel of Thomas.* San Francisco: HarperSanFrancisco, 1992.

Miller, Perry, ed. *The American Puritans.* Garden City, NY: Double Day, Anchor Books, 1956.

Miller, Robert J. *The Jesus Seminar and Its Critics.* Santa Rosa, CA: Polebridge Press, 1999.

Miller, T. Christian. *Blood Money: Wasted Billions, Lost Lives, and Corporate Greed in Iraq.* New York: Little, Brown and Company, 2006.

Mohr, Richard. *Gay Ideas: Outing and Other Controversies.* Boston: Beacon Press, 1992.

Nelson, Julie. *Economics for Humans.* Chicago: University of Chicago Press, 2006.

Nelson, Robert. *Disciples of Christ in Jamaica: 1858–1958.* St. Louis: The Bethany Press, 1950.

Nettleford, Rex. "Introduction." *In Dread: The Rastafarians of Jamaica,* by Joseph Owens, vii-xix. Kingston, Jamaica: Sangster, 1976.

New English Bible with the Apocrypha: Oxford Study Edition. Ed. Samuel Sandmel, M. Jack Suggs, and Arnold J. Tkacik. New York: Oxford University Press, 1976.

Niebuhr, H Richard. *The Responsible Self: An Essay in Christian Moral Philosophy.* New York: Harper & Row, 1963.

———. *Radical Monotheism and Western Culture.* New York: Harper & Brothers Publishers, 1960.

———. "War as the Judgment of God." *Christian Century* 49 (August 1942) 953–55.

———. *The Kingdom of God in America*. Chicago, New York: Willett, Clark and Co., 1937.

Nussbaum, Martha. *The Fragility of Goodness: Luck and Ethics in Greek Tragedy and Philosophy*. Cambridge: Cambridge University Press, 1986.

Olson, George. *Building with Christ in Jamaica*. Anderson, IN: Missionary Building of the Church of God, 1956.

O'Neill, Nena and George O'Neill. *Open Marriage*. New York: Avon Books, 1972.

Owens, Joseph. *The Rastafarians of Jamaica*. Kingston: Sangster, 1976.

Packer, George. *The Assassin's Gate: America in Iraq*. New York: Farrar, Straus and Giroux, 2005.

Palmer, Parker J. *The Courage to Teach: Exploring the Inner Landscape of a Teacher's Life*. San Francisco: Jossey-Bass Publishers, 1998.

Paris, Peter J. *The Spirituality of the African Peoples: The Search for a Common Moral Discourse*. Minneapolis: Fortress Press, 1995.

Parsons, Susan Frank. *Feminism and Christian Ethics*. Cambridge: Cambridge University Press, 1996.

Pearce, Fred. *When the River Runs Dry: Water—The Defining Crisis of the Twenty-First Century*. Boston: Beacon Press, 2006.

Peters, Rebecca Todd. *In Search of the Good Life: The Ethics of Globalization*. New York: Continuum, 2004.

Pollan, Michael. *The Omnivore's Dilemma: A Natural History of Four Meals*. New York: Penguin Press, 2006.

Pollard, Velma. "The Social History of Dread Talk." *Caribbean Quarterly* 28, 4 (December 1982) 17–40.

Pollitt, Katha. *Reasonable Creatures: Essays on Women and Feminism*. New York: Alfred Knopf, 1994.

Primavesi, Anne. *Making God Laugh: Human Arrogance and Ecological Humility*. Santa Rosa, CA: Polebridge Press, 2004.

Prothero, Stephen. *American Jesus: How the Son of God Became a National Icon*. New York: Farrar, Straus and Giroux, 2003.

Rand, Ayn. *The Virtue of Selfishness*. New York: The New American Library, 1964.

———. *For the New Intellectual: The Philosophy of Ayn Rand*. New York: Random House, 1961.

Rasmussen, Larry. *Earth Community, Earth Ethics*. Maryknoll: Orbis, 1996.

Ravuvu, Asesela. *The Fijian Ethos*. Suva, Fiji: Institute of Pacific Studies, University of the South Pacific, 1987.

Rawls, John. *A Theory of Justice*. Cambridge: Harvard University Press, 1971.

Ray, Benjamin C. *African Religions: Symbol, Ritual and Community*. Englewood

Cliffs: Prentice-Hall, 1976.

Reed, A. W. and Inez Hames. *Myths and Legends of Fiji and Rotuma*. Auckland, New Zealand: Reed Books, 1967.

Rennie, Bryan and Philip Tite, eds. *Religion, Terror and Violence: Religious Studies Perspectives*. New York: Routledge, 2008.

Revering, Alan. "'God Bless America': Patriotism and Political Theology." Paper presented at the annual meeting of the American Academy of Religion, Toronto, November, 2002.

Rich, Arthur. *Business and Economic Ethics: The Ethics of Economic Systems*. Leuven, Belgium: Peeters, 2006.

Ricks, Thomas E. *Fiasco: The American Military Adventure in Iraq*. New York: Penguin Press, 2006.

Riggs, Marcia. *Awake, Arise & Act: A Womanist Call for Black Liberation*. Cleveland: Pilgrim Press, 1994.

Ritzer, George. *The McDonaldization of Society: An Investigation into the Changing Characters of Contemporary Social Life*. Thousand Oaks, CA: Pine Forge Press, 1996.

Roof, Wade C. *Spiritual Marketplace: Baby Boomers and the Remaking of American Religion*. Princeton: Princeton University Press, 1999.

Rorty, Richard. *Achieving Our Country: Leftist Thought in Twentieth-Century America*. Cambridge: Harvard University Press, 1998.

Sanders, Cheryl. *Empowerment Ethics for a Liberated People: A Path to African American Social Transformation*. Minneapolis: Fortress Press, 1995.

Schutz, Alfred and Thomas Luckmann. *The Structures of the Life-World*. Vol. 2. Northwestern University Studies in Phenomenology and Existential Philosophy. Trans. Richard Zaner and David J. Parent. Evanston, IL: Northwestern University Press, 1989

——. *The Structures of the Life-World*. Vol. I. Northwestern University Studies in Phenomenology and Existential Philosophy. Translated by Richard M. Zaner and H. Tristram Engelhardt, Jr. Evanston, IL: Northwestern University Press, 1973.

Setiloane, Gabriel. *African Theology: An Introduction*. Johannesburg: Skotaville, 1986.

Shipler, David K. *The Working Poor: Invisible in America*. New York: Alfred Knopf, 2004.

Shutte, Augustine. "Philosophical Ethics." Pp. 24–35 in *Doing Ethics in Context: South African Perspectives*. Ed. Charles Villa-Vicencio and John W. De Gruchy. Maryknoll: Orbis, 1994.

Sibley, Inez Knibb. *The Baptists of Jamaica: 1793–1965*. Kingston: The Jamaica Baptist Union, 1965.

Sider, Ron. *Rich Christians in an Age of Hunger*. New enl. ed. London: Hodder and Stoughton, 1990.

Smedes, Lewis. *Choices.* New York: Harper Collins, 1991.

————. *Mere Morality.* Grand Rapids: Eerdmans, 1983.

Smil, Vaclav. *Energy at the Crossroads: Global Perspectives and Uncertainties.* Boston: The MIT Press, 2005.

Smith, Mikey. *It A Come: Poems by Michael Smith I, II.* San Francisco: City Lights, 1986.

Spencer, F. Scott. *What Did Jesus Do? Gospel Profiles of Jesus' Personal Conduct.* Harrisburg: Trinity Press International, 2003.

Sperling, John. *The Great Divide: Retro Versus Metro America: An Un-Civil War.* New York: Soft Skull Press, 2004.

Stover, Dale. "Postcolonial Sun Dancing at Wakpamni Lake." *Journal of the American Academy of Religion* 69 (2001) 817–36.

Strauss, David. *Life of Jesus Critically Examined.* Trans. George Eliot. London: G. Allen, 1913.

Strauss, Leo. *The Rebirth of Classical Political Rationalism.* Chicago: University of Chicago Press, 1989.

————. *Natural Right and History.* Chicago: University of Chicago Press, 1953.

Streng, Frederick J., Charles L. Lloyd and Jay T. Allen. *Ways of Being Religious: Readings for a New Approach to Religion.* Englewood Cliffs, NJ: Prentice-Hall, 1973.

Subramani. *South Pacific Literature: From Myth to Fabulation.* Rev. ed. Suva, Fiji: Institute of Pacific Studies, University of the South Pacific, 1992.

Sullivan, Clayton. *Rescuing Jesus from the Christians.* Harrisburg, PA: Trinity Press International, 2002.

Swomley, John. "Nuclear Arms and the American Military Empire." *Christian Ethics Today* 9, no. 4 (October 2003) 25–26.

————. "Ethics of the War on Terrorism." *Christian Ethics Today* 8, no. 4 (October 2002) 6–7.

Tatum, Beverly D. *"Why Are All the Black Kids Sitting Together in the Cafeteria?" and Other Conversations About Race.* New York: Basic Books, 1999.

Taylor, Mark C. *Erring: A Postmodern A/Theology.* Chicago: University of Chicago Press, 1984.

Tempels, Placide. *Bantu Philosophy.* Trans. Colin King. Paris: Présence Africaine, 1959.

Tillich, Paul. *The Shaking of the Foundations.* New York: Charles Scribner's Sons, 1948.

Tinker, Tink. *Spirit and Resistance: A Political Theology and American Indian Liberation.* Minneapolis: Fortress Press, 2004.

Tokelau Dictionary. Apia, Western Samoa: Office of Tokelau Affairs, 1986.

Tracy, David. *The Analogical Imagination: Christian Theology and Cultural Pluralism.* New York: Crossroad, 1981.

————. *Blessed Rage for Order: The New Pluralism in Theology.* New York: Seabury Press, 1975.

Trimiew, Darryl. *Voices of the Silenced: The Responsible Self in a Marginalized Community.* Cleveland: Pilgrim Press, 1993.

Turner, Victor. "Liminality and Morality." Firestone Lecture delivered at the University of Southern California, Los Angeles, 1980.

Turner, Victor and Edith Turner. *Image and Pilgrim in Christian Culture: An Anthropological Perspective.* New York: Columbia University Press, 1978.

Tuverson, Ernest L. *Redeemer Nation.* Chicago: University of Chicago Press, 1968.

Twiss, Sumner B. and Bruce Grelle, eds. *Explorations in Global Ethics: Comparative Religious Ethics and Interreligious Dialogue.* Boulder, CO: Westview Press, 1998.

Unger, Craig. *House of Bush, House of Saud.* New York: Scribner, 2004.

Van Gennep, Arnold. *The Rites of Passage.* Trans. Monika Vizedom and Gabrielle Caffee. Chicago: University of Chicago Press, 1960.

Walzer, Michael. *Spheres of Justice: A Defense of Pluralism and Equality.* New York: Basic Books, 1983.

Weaver, Jace, ed. *Defending Mother Earth: Native American Perspectives on Environmental Justice.* Maryknoll: Orbis, 1996.

Weber, Max. *The Protestant Ethic and the Spirit of Capitalism.* New York: Charles Scribner's Sons, 1958.

Welch, Sharon. *A Feminist Ethic of Risk.* Minneapolis: Fortress Press, 1990.

Wendt, Albert. "Novelists and Historians and the Art of Remembering." In *Class and Culture in the South Pacific.* Eds. Antony Hooper, Steve Britton, Ron Crocombe, Judith Huntsman and Cluny Macpherson. Auckland, New Zealand; Suva, Fiji: Institute of Pacific Studies, University of the South Pacific, 1987.

White, Lynn. "The Historical Roots of Our Ecological Crisis." *Science* 155 (March 1967) 1203–1207.

Wilfred, Felix. *On the Banks of the Ganges: Doing Contextual Theology.* Kashmere Gate, Delhi: Indian Society for Promoting Christian Knowledge, 2002.

Wilkins, Michael J. and J. P. Moreland, eds. *Jesus Under Fire.* Grand Rapids, MI: Zondervan Publishing House, 1995.

Wink, Walter. *Engaging the Powers.* Minneapolis: Fortress Press, 1992.

Winter, Gibson. *Liberating Creation: Religious Social Ethics.* New York: Crossroad, 1981.

Winthrop, John. "A Model of Christian Charity." Pp. 79–84 in *The American Puritans: Their Prose and Poetry.* Ed. Perry Miller. Garden City, NY: Double Day, Anchor Books, 1956.

Wittgenstein, Ludwig. *Philosophical Investigations.* Trans. G. E. M. Anscombe. New York: Macmillan, 1953.

Wolfe, Regina Wentzel and Christine E. Gudorf, eds. *Ethics and World Religions: Cross-Cultural Case Studies.* Maryknoll: Orbis, 1999.

Wong, Orlando [Oku Onuora]. *Echo*. Kingston: Sangster's, 1977.

Woodward, Bob. *The State of Denial*. New York: Simon and Schuster, 2006.

Wright, Lawrence. *The Looming Power: Al-qaeda and the Road to 9-11*. New York: Alfred Knopf, 2006.

Yarri, Donna. *The Ethics of Animal Experimentation: A Critical Analysis and Constructive Christian Proposal*. New York: Oxford University Press, 2005.

———. "The Suspension of Rights of Suspected Terrorists in the Aftermath of 9-11: Exigent Circumstances or Descent into Moral Anarchy?" Paper presented at the annual meeting of the Society of Christian Ethics, Chicago, January 10, 2004.

Yawney, Carol. "Don't Vex Than Pray: The Methodology of Initiation Fifteen Years Later." Paper presented at the Qualitative Research Conference, University of Waterloo, Canada, May 15–17, 1985.

INDEX

absolutist ethics, 18
Afghanistan/Afgans, 2, 9, 120, 128
Africa/Africans, 4, 22, 82–83, 86, 103,
    109–11, 123
African Americans, 25, 36, 125
African National Congress, 103, 108
al-Qaeda, 2–3, 117
alterity (in African ethics), 110–11, 119,
    123
altruism, 33–34, 39, 80, 133
American Empire, 13, 33–34, 96, 117,
    119, 121–23, 127
American Enterprise Institute, 32
Anancy Folk Tradition, 85–88
Anglo-Saxons, 25, 32
Anti-Sweatshop Campaign, 96
apartheid, 80, 105–06, 108, 110–11,
    113–15, 121, 127–28, 132
Aristotle, 15
Asian Americans, 25, 36, 125
Axial Age: first, ix, 44; second, ix–x, 40,
    44

Bloom, Alan, 32
baby boomers, 8, 26, 36–40, 129
Babylon/Babylonians, 81–82, 84, 87,
    89–90, 96, 98, 114, 119, 127–28, 130,
    132
Barnett, Thomas, 33
basileia (dominion or royal power), 112
Bible, 18, 23–24, 29–30, 34–36, 65,
    70–73, 82–83, 88–96, 112–18, 120,
    123, 126, 132
Biblical covenant, 26, 29–32, 34, 37, 40
birds, 50–51, 57–69, 71–72
Black Nationalism, 83
Buddha, 44
Buddhism, 17, 22, 43, 93
Bush, George (Administration of), 2–3,
    5, 8–9, 33, 99–100, 117, 119, 127

Caesar, 112–13, 121, 123
Caribbean, 41, 75, 86, 119
charity, ix, 80, 84, 117, 119, 128–29, 130
chief (Polynesian), 53–54, 56, 66
class (social), 43, 75–98, 111, 121–26,
    130–32
Clinebell, Howard, 16
coconuts, 49, 65
comfort zone, 4, 5, 6, 34, 129
common moral sensibility, 17–18, 20,
    34, 131
commoners, 53–56, 87, 126
communalism/communalists, 25, 29–32,
    38, 46, 83–85, 126, 130
community/communities, 15, 20, 26–27,
    30–31, 40, 43, 45, 56–59, 63–64,
    69–70, 73, 75, 77, 80, 87, 91, 96, 105,
    109, 114, 117, 123, 126, 132, 134
conservatives, xi, 1, 30
Cook Islands, 50–51, 56–59
Crusades, 120

Declaration of Independence, 34
deontological ethics, 23–24
Derrida, Jacques, 38
Disciples of Christ, 43, 75, 80–81, 88, 103
divine domain (Kingdom of God), ix, 29–30, 44, 71–72, 89–90, 93–95, 112–14, 121, 123, 128, 133–34
dogmatist, 16–17
dolphins, 64–69
Dolphin Christ tale, xvi, 65–69, 72

earth, x–xi, 10–14, 40, 45, 53, 55, 66–67, 69, 71–72, 82, 86, 112–13, 128, 134
ecological destruction, x, xii, 10–14, 73, 131, 134
ecological ethics, 45–46, 51, 55, 59, 61, 64, 68–69, 129, 131, 134
economic inequity, xii, 5, 8–10, 13–14, 78–79, 86, 90, 93, 107–09, 120, 131–32
Economism, x–xiii, 6–10, 13, 80, 83, 85–98, 125, 131, 133–34
economy: anxiety about, 6–10, 13, 84, 90; and dimensions of, x, xiii, 1, 3–4, 6, 10, 16, 34–37, 42, 45, 78–79, 83, 89–90, 92, 94–95, 97, 101, 108–09, 111, 114–15, 118–120, 132; and impacts on, x, 1, 9, 34, 54, 89, 107–08, 116, 127, 131, 133
empire, 13, 33–34, 96, 112, 114–16, 121, 123, 126–27
empowerment (in African ethics), 109–11, 114–16, 123
enemy, xi, 99–100, 112, 116–18, 121–22, 134
Enlightenment, ix–x, 23, 26, 34–38, 40, 43–44, 46, 66, 128
environment/eco-system, x, xiii, 6, 10–14, 37, 55, 59, 61, 67–68, 71–73, 134
Essenes, 44
ethic of re-connection, ix–xiii, 45–46, 69, 72, 109, 125–34
Europe/Europeans, xi, 1–5, 9, 20, 22, 32, 44, 83, 87–88, 103
evangelicals, 1, 21
evolution, 35, 66–67

exorcism of demons, ix, 94, 96, 114, 121–22

Fair Trade Movement, 96
feminist tradition, 25, 36–37, 57
Fiji, 50–56, 64–65
fish, 11, 49–50, 56–58, 60–69, 75
foreigners, xii, 31, 33, 42, 44–45, 50, 119, 122, 125, 127, 130
forgiveness, ix, 56–57, 59, 67, 81, 94, 110–11, 117–18, 121–22
Foucault, Michael, 39
Franklin, Benjamin, 34, 51
fundamentalism/fundamentalists, 16, 21, 67, 128–29
Funk, Robert, ix–x, xvi, 112, 117

Galbraith, John Kenneth, x, 35–36
Galilee/Galileans, 70, 113–14, 116–17
Gandhi, Mahatma, 43
ganja (marijuana), 24, 83–84, 86, 88–89, 91, 96, 132
gay rights movement, 25, 37
gender issues, 36–37, 54–55, 57–58, 96–97, 111
Golden Rule, 117
good life, 8–11, 37, 39, 89, 119, 132
grace, 34, 71–72, 94, 99, 101–02, 115, 118, 121–22
Greeks, 91, 114
Gutierrez, Gustavo, 39, 42

Habermas, Jürgen, 38
Hauerwas, Stanley, 30, 43–44
Heritage Foundation, 32
hermeneutics/interpretation, ix, xii, 52, 70–73, 96
Hezbollah, 117, 128
Hicks, Douglas, 43
Hindu moral teaching, 43
Hispanics, 34, 125
Holloway, Richard, 18
Horsley, Charles, 113–14

I-n-I, 81–84, 86–91, 96, 126–28, 132–33
I-Sight, xvi, 83, 89, 132, 134
India, 41, 43, 103, 108, 127

Indians (in South Africa), 103, 106–08, 110

indigenous peoples, xi–xii, 16, 46, 79, 88, 91, 108, 125, 127, 131

interfaith dialogue, 121, 133

Iraq (Iraqis), 2, 3, 5–6, 9, 12–13, 33, 98, 120–21, 123, 128

Islam/ Muslims, 4, 16, 22, 119–20

Israel/Israelites, 4, 29, 32, 114, 120

Ithiopia, 84, 87, 90, 93, 128

Jamaica/Jamaicans, 10, 44, 75–98, 119

Japanese Americans, 4, 121

Jefferson, Thomas, 34

Jesus, ix, xi–xii, 10, 13, 30, 34, 44–45, 65, 69–73, 80, 85, 87–96, 98, 109, 111–17, 121, 123, 125, 127–28, 130–31, 134

Jesus movement (early), xi–xii, 41, 44–45, 47, 80, 85, 89, 91, 112, 115–16, 126, 131–34

Jesus' sayings (tradition), ix, xi–xiii, xvi, 34, 67, 69–73, 85, 87, 90–96, 103, 107, 111–18, 120–21, 123, 126, 128–29, 132–33

Jesus Seminar, ix, xi–xiii, 44, 70, 89, 92

John the Baptist, 92–93

Jones, Jim, 43

Judaism/Jews, 22, 44, 70, 91, 113–14, 116–17

just war, 5

justice, 24, 34, 36–37, 39, 41, 44–46, 62, 77, 82, 84, 86–87, 93, 114, 120, 126–27, 130–31

Kanongata'a, Keiti Ann, 45

Kant, Immanuel, 35

kava/kava bowl, 52–53, 64, 69, 132

Kristol, Irving, 32–33

Kuhn, Thomas, 134

Kurtz, Paul, 36

Kyoto Treaty, 12

land, xii, 11, 31, 36, 55, 67, 82, 84, 86, 91, 113

late modern age, xii, 16–27, 45, 67, 72, 125, 127

Latin America/Latin Americans, 22, 25, 36, 39

Lebanon, 4, 120

Levite, 117–18

liberalism, 25, 34–36

liberals, xi, 34–36, 39–40, 44, 46, 89, 128–30

liberation, 25, 31, 46, 55, 89, 114, 121

liberation theologies, 31, 36, 39, 42

lifestyles, x, xii, 9–13, 19, 38, 41, 47, 80–85, 90, 97, 127, 131–32, 134

life-worlds, 39, 41, 61, 71

liminal space (liminality), 55, 91–92, 94, 132

Lind, Michael, 35

livity, 82–86, 90, 128

lost generation (South African youth), 107

love/compassion: of enemy, ix, 99–123, 126, 133; as erotic passion, 53–56, 68; of neighbor, 30–31, 43, 53, 59–65, 68–72, 84, 87, 93, 110, 115, 118

MacIntyre, Alasdair, 30

Mandela, Nelson, 103, 107

Manifest Destiny, 32, 37

marginalized persons, x–xi, xiii, 19, 27, 29, 31, 34, 42, 50, 62–64, 84, 95–96, 107–09, 111, 114, 121–22, 125–26, 128–30, 134

Margolis, Diane, 22–24, 69

Meeks, Wayne, 45

Melanesia, 50

Mexicans, 121

Micronesia, 50

Middle East, 4, 6, 9, 98, 114, 123

Militarism, x–xiii, 1–3, 5, 9–10, 33–34, 99, 103, 109, 119, 123, 125, 127, 130–34

mission of America, 20, 26, 32–34, 37–38, 40

Missionary Christian tradition, 85, 87–89

modern life/modernity, 3–5, 11, 21–22, 38–39, 68, 82, 85, 109

modernist paradigm/perspective, 3–4, 12, 21–22, 25, 35, 38–39

Native America/Native Americans, 4, 25, 36, 40, 121, 125
natural law, 24, 35, 56
nature, ix–x, 40, 50, 55–56, 58–59, 61–64, 66, 68–69, 71–73, 82, 94
Nazi movement, 43, 99
neo-conservatism/neo-conservatives, 25, 32–34, 39, 44, 46, 121, 126–27, 130
New American Century, 32
New South Africa, 106, 109–111, 123, 128
Niebuhr, H. Richard, 24, 42, 93
non-human animal species, x, xii, 13–14, 61–62, 64, 66, 68–69, 71–72, 87, 128
North America/North Americans, xi–xii, 22, 39, 41, 87, 119, 125

other/otherness, xiii, 16, 26, 31, 39–43, 45, 49–51, 62–63, 67, 78, 82, 96, 110, 116, 118, 122, 128, 130
oppression/oppressed, xi, 31, 36, 42, 96, 110–11, 113–14, 116–17, 121, 127–28, 132
Osama Bin Laden, 2, 128

Pacific/Pacific Islanders, x–xii, xvi, 13, 46, 49–72, 126, 128–29, 132–33
Palestine/Palestinians, 67, 85, 113–14, 120–21, 132–33
Palmer, Parker, 69, 130
peace, 6, 34, 37, 56, 82, 84, 87, 93, 107, 122, 130
peacemaking, 29, 46, 130
personal fulfillment story, 20, 26, 36–40
Pharisees, 44, 91–92
Pilgrims, 29–30, 32, 37–38
politics/political life, x–xi, xiii, 6, 9, 33–38, 40, 42, 54, 80, 84–85, 98–99, 103, 106–09, 111–13, 115, 119, 122, 127, 133
Pollitt, Kate, 36
Polynesia, 45, 50, 55–66
poor people, ix–x, 8, 29–31, 34, 36, 43, 52–53, 78–79, 82–86, 89, 95–96, 114–16, 120–21, 125–26, 132, 134
post-liberal perspective, 25
postmodern context, 38, 40–41, 44–45

postmodernism/postmodernists, ix, 18, 25, 38–41, 46, 129–30
Primavesi, Anne, 66
Prodigal Son parable, 94, 114–15
prohpets , 29, 31, 44, 82–83, 87, 96, 112, 125, 129, 132
poverty, 3, 8, 33, 75, 78, 82, 132, 134

Qur'an, 120

race: black identity, 75–96, 101–02, 106–08, 110, 115; as complex continuum, 75–76, 81–82, 95–96, 98, 103, 106–07, 110, 129–30, 132; and racism, 32, 43, 84, 93, 96, 101–02, 105, 107–09, 111, 120–21; and white identity, 25, 75–78, 83, 87, 97, 101–03, 105–07; 120–21, 130, 132
Rand, Ayn, 36
Rastafarians, xi–xii, xvi, 10, 44, 79–98, 119, 126, 128–29, 131–32, 134
Rawls, John, 25
reconciliation, 6, 51, 55–56, 58, 69, 84, 110–11, 128, 130
relational ethics, 24, 135
relationality (in African ethics), 109–10, 121, 123, 126, 128, 132
relativist, 16–17
rights: equal, 82–84, 93; and human, 16, 33, 35, 37, 44, 49, 57, 100, 127; and unalienable, 32, 35
Roman Empire (imperial order), 112–16, 121

Sadducees, 44
Samaritan parable, 117–18, 127–28, 133–34
Samoa, 49–50, 60
Santa Claus, 51, 83
sea, xii, 49–50, 52, 55–56, 58–59, 61–62, 64–69
secular humanism, 36, 97
secularism, 21–22, 133
self, xii, 16, 22–25, 27, 32, 34, 37, 39, 41, 45, 50, 54, 59, 62–63, 72, 80–86, 88, 90–92, 94, 97, 109, 128
Smedes, Lewis, 30

social ethics, xii–xiii, 13, 15–22, 26, 41–42, 45–46, 51, 125–30

social movements, xi–xii, 41–44, 46–47, 96, 125, 129, 131, 133–34

solidarity with suffering, 30, 39, 42, 46, 59, 82–85, 87, 96, 109, 121, 126, 130, 134

Sothos, 107

South Africa/South Africans, 5–6, 80, 102–05, 107–08, 110–16, 119, 121–22, 126, 128, 132

South African freedom fighters, xi–xii, xvi, 5–6, 44–45, 106–09, 113, 115, 126–27

South Pacific islands, xvi, 45, 49–70, 72

Speciesism, xi–xiii, 65–73, 78, 125, 131, 133–34

storytelling, 17, 19–20, 29–40, 45, 50–72, 110–118, 127–129

Strauss, Leo, 32–33

Syria, 114

Tagimoucia (tears of despair) legend, 52–56, 66–69, 126

Taoist tradition, 43

Tavake (tropical bird) tale, 59–65, 68–69, 72

Taylor, Mark C., 39

Te Ana Takitaki (the cave to which one is led) legend, 56–59, 67–68

techno-consumerist vision, 37–38

teleological ethics, 23–24

Ten Commandments, 23

terrorists, 1, 4–5, 11, 33, 99–100, 117, 120

Tokelau Islands/Tokelauans, 49–51, 59–65

Tracey, David, 38

transformation, x, 16, 21, 43, 55, 59, 64, 67–68, 84, 103, 106, 108, 110, 129

Truth and Reconciliation Commission, 110–11, 121

ukunxulumana (side-by-sidedness), 109

umuntu ngumuntu (a persons is a person through other persons), 110

Vakaturaga (chiefly way), 54–55

Vanuatu, xvi, 50–51, 64–65

Walzer, Michael, 35

war on terror/terrorism, xii, 1–6, 8–10, 12–13, 32, 99–100, 122

weapons of mass destruction, 2–3, 5, 99

Weber, Max, 21

web of life, 65, 109

Westar Institute, ix, xvi

Wilfred, Felix, 41

Wittgenstein, Ludwig, 21

womanist tradition, 25, 31

Xhosas, 107, 109

Zealots, 44

Zulus, 107, 110

ABOUT THE AUTHOR

Jack A. Hill is Associate Professor of Religion (Social Ethics) at Texas Christian University in Fort Worth, Texas, where he lectures on Christian and comparative religious ethics, ecology and world religions. In addition to teaching and writing, Hill has coordinated peace and justice programs and served as an ethics consultant for churches, universities and grass-roots organizations in the U.S., Fiji and South Africa. He is a trained mediator, teaching mentor and former pastor, and frequently mediates conflicts, leads teaching workshops and speaks in churches, while also actively contributing to professional societies. His other books include *Seeds of Transformation: Discerning the Values of the Next Generation*, 1998, and *I-Sight: The World of Rastafari*, 1995.